Trade Unions in the European Union
A Handbook

Trade Unions in the European Union

A Handbook

EDITED BY
WOLFGANG LECHER

TRANSLATED BY
PETE BURGESS

Lawrence & Wishart
LONDON

Lawrence & Wishart Limited
144a Old South Lambeth Road
London sw8 1xx

First published 1994 by Lawrence and Wishart

Translation © Pete Burgess 1994

ISBN 0 85315 766 9

Typeset in Baskerville by Ewan Smith
Printed and bound in Great Britain
by Redwood Books,
Trowbridge

Contents

Translatoror's Preface   vii

PART I   1

The Current State of Trade Unions in the EU Member States   3
WOLFGANG LECHER & REINHARD NAUMANN

Belgium 6   *Denmark* 11   *France* 15   *Germany* 20
Great Britain 32   *Greece* 42   *Republic of Ireland* 49
Italy 56   *Luxembourg* 63   *Netherlands* 69   *Portugal* 75
Spain 82   *The Future: structural change, internationalisation
and the trade union response* 87   *Background statistics* 90

PART II   127

Trade Union Organisation and Employee Representation   129
SIEGFRIED MIELKE, PETER RÜTTERS & KURT P. TUDYKA

Belgium 131   *Denmark* 138   *France* 146   *Germany* 157
Great Britain 172   *Greece* 188   *The Republic of Ireland* 195
Italy 199   *Luxembourg* 208   *Netherlands* 213   *Portugal* 218
Spain 224   *A European model of employee interest representation* 231

PART III   235

The Co-ordinates of Trade Union Policy for Europe   237
FRITZ RATH

1   Europe as a challenge for the trade unions   237
2   The political challenge of European integration – and the
   trade union response   241
3   Trade unions and the economic challenge of the Single
   European Market   243

4 European trade union co-ordination   249
5 The new dimension: European level trade union activity   255

Appendix

1 European trade union organisations   275
2 European industry committees   278
3 Standing committees and working groups in ETUC   281
4 EU powers and trade union influence   282
5 Member confederations in the UNICE   288
6 Agreement on social policy (the 'social chapter')   288
7 Protocol on social policy (the UK 'opt out')   292

Bibliography   293

Translator's Preface

Trade Unions in the European Union first appeared as *Die Gewerkschaften in den 12 EG-Ländern* (Bund Verlag, Cologne, 1991), edited by Wolfgang Däubler and Wolfgang Lecher, as part of a series of handbooks on Europe published by the German Trades Union Confederation, the DGB. This translation is a revised and updated version of the original book. In particular, it reflects the changes in the legislative machinery of the European Union introduced by the Maastricht Treaty. The new arrangements are set out in Part III, and extracts from the Treaty have been included in the Appendix. The chapters on Germany and the United Kingdom were also substantially revised and expanded to meet the needs of the changed readership. The publishers are grateful to Paul Marginson (University of Warwick) for his comments on drafts of the UK chapters. Where more recent data was available, the tables which follow Part I were updated.

PART I

The Current State of Trade Unions in the EU Member States

WOLFGANG LECHER & REINHARD NAUMANN[1]

The Context

Profound structural changes in both the economies and societies of the industrialised nations have been at work since the mid 1970s, with major implications for the trade unions and their relations with employers and the state. By the early 1990s the main contours of these transformations have become clear. We distinguish three main elements of change here. Firstly, there has been *a transformation in the relationship between the economy and the quantity and character of work*. In the highly industrialised countries of the European Union, investment aimed at rationalising existing operations has taken precedence over investment directed at expanding capacity. The main consequences have been mass unemployment, the persistence of an industrial reserve army with a growing share of long-term unemployed, a segmentation of the labour market into 'insiders' in employment and 'outsiders' on the peripheral labour market, and a transformation in the structure of employment away from full-time permanent jobs and towards atypical, precarious forms of employment.

Secondly, there has been *a transformation in the relationship between state social policy and individual provision*. Within the framework of a neo-monetarist supply-side approach, carried out with the tools of monetary policy and combined with widespread deregulation, the state has been weakened and space created in which the operation of private capital has been fostered. The growing individualisation which has accompanied this process is two-edged: depending on the prevailing level of social security, it can on the one hand offer enhanced scope for individual development, while imposing additional limitations on individuals' hopes and prospects on the other.

3

Thirdly, and finally, there has been *a transformation in the relationship between technology and work*. The modernisation of production and administration, based on the new technologies, has gone hand-in-hand with a drive towards greater flexibility in the organisation of work and a decentralisation of decision-making (and collective bargaining). At the same time, the increasingly international links between companies have frequently matured into fully-fledged mergers and acquisitions, with a corresponding concentration of power at the topmost level of multinational undertakings. And it is this aspect which highlights what is probably the most important consequence of the structural transformation experienced by the highly industrialised countries: the internationalisation of their economies and societies into supranational spaces equipped with a corresponding infrastructure of ever more integrated social, legal and employment structures.

Following the demise and break-up of the socialist bloc, three such centres exist, each at different stages of realisation: the USA, Japan, and Europe. In contrast to the USA and Japan, Europe is confronted by the overriding problem of integrating its constituent nation states and creating supranational bodies and instruments. This coincidence of structural economic and social transformation with the 'Europeanisation' of nation states poses enormous problems for the trades unions and the traditional, nationally-rooted patterns of industrial relations. Internationalisation is built in to the logic of the development of 'capital' and takes place through an armoury of tried and tested techniques. In contrast, for 'labour' – and the human beings who actually work for a living – the process of internationalisation is fraught with additional frictions (change of home, colleagues, language, etc.), which are generally and quite correctly perceived not as opportunities but as risks and burdens.

The following overview of the context and practice of trade union activity in the twelve countries of the European Union sets out to outline the current position of the trade union movements in each national setting and to assess the scope and difficulties each has in dealing with structural change and internationalisation. Since the constraints of space forbid any claim to comprehensiveness, our aim is to offer starting points for interpretation based on a consideration of the following main dimensions, some of which may be more important in individual countries:

— trade union structure;
— membership and level of organisation;
— collective bargaining and relationship to the state;
— participation in institutionalised and informal systems;
— governmental attempts at deregulation;

— employer initiatives towards flexibility;
— the political context;
— threats to and scope for trade union development.

The aim is not primarily to offer a complete national picture of the trade union and industrial relations situation – additional information is given in Part II – but rather to elaborate the characteristic features of each country and the problems experienced by their trade union movements, providing an overall context in which the reader may interpret and make use of information gained elsewhere. The order of presentation is alphabetical; in our view, attempts to categorise countries by distinct models (typically, 'Roman-Mediterranean', 'Central European', 'Anglo-Saxon', 'Scandinavian') usually end up suppressing important features through which countries diverge from the formal criteria of such categories. The result is often an overhasty typology rather than an objective and non-partisan framework for analysing complex factual material. This section is complemented by a number of comparative statistical tables on basic economic, social and industrial relations issues.

Note

1. The chapters on Belgium, Germany, France, Great Britain, Italy, the Netherlands and Spain were written by Wolfgang Lecher, and those on Denmark, Greece, Ireland, Luxembourg and Portugal by Reinhard Naumann.

Belgium

Although the position of the trade unions and the overall context of the crisis are very similar in Belgium and the Netherlands, the common features shared by the two countries must be seen against the background of a number of profound differences. Despite the superficial attractions of a supposed 'Benelux core' to the European Union, each merits distinct consideration. What both share is that since the onset of the phase of persistent crisis in the 1970s each has had an above-average level of unemployment, rooted in the rapid decline of traditional branches of industry; and both are dependent on large multinational companies and consequently on decisions which are made on the basis of conditions prevailing in the world market. The two countries are also highly exposed to foreign trade, with imports and exports accounting for between 50 per cent and 60 per cent of overall output. Industrial relations are institutionally formalised with considerable influence exercised by the state in some areas. Both were subject to a highly restrictive social policy during the 1980s.

However, above and beyond these shared experiences, Belgium has a number of unique and distinguishing features of direct relevance for employment matters in general, and trade unionism in particular. Firstly, there are linguistic differences: Belgium is divided into a Flemish- and a French-speaking region, which broadly coincides with a zone of relative economic prosperity and a zone of declining traditional industries. Secondly, there are religious differences: the trade union movement is fundamentally divided between a Christian federation (CSC) and a socialist federation (FGTB), with a third, small, liberal confederation; these differences overlap with, and magnify, the regional and linguistic problems. And thirdly, and despite the persistence of widespread unemployment and industrial decline, Belgium continues to exhibit a high level of trade union membership, with a nominal union density just short of 75 per cent.

One immediate question, therefore, is how has trade unionism been able to maintain such a stable level of organisation despite political fragmentation and the harsh social and employment environment of the past decade. Were the political measures and pressures exerted by recession simply too weak to shake what is evidently a firmly anchored trade union movement, in contrast to the experience of unions in Britain or the Netherlands? Or does the explanation lie in the specific structures and patterns of recruitment of the Belgian trade unions? Some insight may be gleaned from a look at social and economic development during the 1980s and the organising principles and structures of the trade unions.

The coming to power of the Social Christian-Liberal coalition under Prime Minister Wilfried Martens in 1981 marked the beginning of a new era of neo-liberal economic policy whose basic direction matched policy changes implemented elsewhere in the European Community. The main priorities of economic policy became cutting public sector borrowing, promoting private investment and curtailing the social security system. Following the re-election of the coalition in 1985, the Government announced the most severe austerity programme in Belgian history, a programme pursued in its essentials up until the present. (At the time this chapter was completed for the English-language edition, in December 1993, a new austerity and incomes policy had been imposed by the ruling coalition). Public spending has been held down both directly through cuts in civil service employment as well as via reductions in social spending. In contrast, the five-party coalition under Prime Minister Martens which was in power until 1991 cut corporation tax payable by limited liability companies on retained profits from 43 per cent to 39 per cent, with a special low rate of 30 per cent for 'small' profits. At the same time, and despite considerable public criticism, there was no corresponding move to end the tax deductibility of investment costs to ensure at least a semblance of parity of sacrifice between capital and labour. This 'recovery programme' was introduced via emergency legislation in February 1986, which also gave the cabinet the power to intervene directly in collective bargaining. Government powers to intervene in the process of pay determination were also strengthened by a 1989 law to protect competitiveness, under which Belgian economic performance is measured against that of its main competitors using a series of indicators: should the national position worsen, the Government has powers to suspend agreed provisions or intervene in the system of pay indexation. Intervention took place several times during the 1980s, always to the advantage of the employers. For example, in the early 1980s, a system of working-time flexibility was introduced which allowed for cuts in pay to accompany reductions in hours, and there have also been periods of incomes policy, in which pay indexation was suspended.

In contrast to the Netherlands, and in a way more closely resem-

bling developments in the United Kingdom, the Government has therefore intervened directly in industrial relations to the detriment of the
trade unions and the employed workforce, contributing to a worsening
of the overall social climate. In contrast to the UK, however, this did
not lead to a destabilisation of the trade unions, or a dramatic fall in
union membership. There are three main reasons for this.

Firstly, despite their religious divisions, Belgian trade unions have
managed to work together during the bulk of the 1980s, and argue for
realistic alternative programmes for tackling the public sector deficit.
Following an initial cut in real pay of some 6 per cent as a result of the
Government's austerity programme, and the lack of success of strikes
carried out by the union confederations in the early 1980s, often in
isolation from one another, in 1985 the two union centres collaborated
to present an alternative programme which proposed: a fair distribution of the gains from productivity growth, out of which the step-by-
step industry wide introduction of the 35-hour week could be financed,
together with adequate social security for the long-term unemployed
(long-term unemployment accounts for over half of total unemployment,
the highest proportion in the European Community); a redistribution
of the burden of taxation to be achieved through higher value-added
tax on the construction industry, greater efforts to combat tax evasion,
the introduction of a wealth tax of up to 1 per cent on large fortunes,
and strict controls on the export of capital; and a call for cuts in public
spending to be made by lowering the interest rate on public debt and
by making savings on health expenditure through greater stringency on
doctors' fees.

The fact that the savings from these measures were just as great as
those offered by the Government's proposals, which in addition imposed a one-sided burden on the working population, led them to be
seen as both a popular and credible alternative. Such initiatives have
strengthened the position of the unions in Belgian society.

Secondly, Belgian unions have gained in stability through the mutual
connection between high levels of union membership and the existence
of well-established institutional structures of industrial co-operation, consultation and bargaining. Moreover, each of the main union confederations are broadly equal in strength, and neither feels jeopardised by the
other. This structure has ensured that, despite political and religious
differences between the union centres, there has been no marked trend
towards a decentralisation of negotiations and other powers to the
workplace at the expense of more general union concerns.

At industry level, collective bargaining takes place in established joint
committees, consisting of senior officials of trade unions and employers'
organisations relevant to that industry. These bodies, which are chaired
by an independent figure appointed by the Ministry of Labour, bargain

and conclude collective agreements for their sector. Joint committees currently exist in more than eighty branches of industry and embrace virtually all employees' and employers' organisations. In some cases, where a branch has a diverse structure, sub-committees can be established by delegation, and committees may also be set up at national level. A horizontally structured or highly diversified concern might, therefore, be covered by several negotiating committees, especially given the strict separation between negotiating committees for blue-collar and white-collar employees. Of the total of eighty sectoral committees, only fourteen cover both categories, compared with fifty exclusively for blue-collar workers and sixteen solely for white-collar employees. Each individual union is represented in proportion to its national strength and importance within the specific industry.

In addition to these crucial branch level collective bargaining organisations, which are responsible for setting the basic framework of agreements, the period since the early 1970s has also seen a growth in the importance of the National Labour Council (*Conseil National de Travail*), first established in 1952. The Council is composed of twenty-four representatives, twelve from the recognised trades unions and twelve from the three central employers' confederations which embrace the spectrum from agriculture, the craft sector, and industry, to the banks. It is chaired by an independent economic and social policy expert appointed by the Ministry of Labour. All members are confirmed in office by royal decree – that is, in effect, by law. The Council's original function was to the advise the government and legislature on social issues by issuing opinions on policy proposals, an activity not only conferring considerable public prestige but also securing a major influence for the Council in the shaping of Belgium's pioneering social legislation. Since 1968, the Council's functions have been widened by law to embrace the competence to bargain and conclude collective agreements, both at national level and for those industries where no joint committee exists. Of these, the more important is the conclusion of national agreements covering broad issues such as the level of the guaranteed minimum wage, and the volume and type of information which must be disclosed to works councils.

Despite the substantial potential for state intervention in bargaining, this firmly institutionalised machinery has remained intact, and has provided the trade unions with a powerful lever for shaping terms and conditions of employment in the broadest sense, and for warding off those tendencies towards fragmentation, via the decentralisation of bargaining to workplace level, seen in many other European countries.

Finally, and thirdly, a good deal of the relative stability of Belgian industrial relations, and in particular the high level of union organisation, lies in the privileges enjoyed by Belgian trade unions and their members. Numerous branch level agreements have been concluded with employers' associations providing for premium pay rates for trade unions, termed a 'social allowance' which typically cover union contributions but may be higher. In some industries, other financial benefits, 'supplementary social allowances', including additional unemployment benefits, have also been reserved for trade union members. Moreover, the state pays a contribution to the main union confederations for civil servants, irrespective of whether they are members or not of a trade union. Finally, the payment of unemployment benefit also takes place through the trade unions.

A study carried out by the main Belgian employers' association in 1986 found that the financing of trade union premiums and the training of shop stewards cost Belgian companies some Bf 4.3 billion (£85m) per year. In a number of branches these payments are directly tied to the maintenance of peaceful industrial relations by unions. Companies justify payments by the importance they ascribe to strong and representative trade unions and the training of lay union officials. For their part, the trade unions feel that because of the role that the unions play in improving the working conditions of all employees, these financial benefits are legitimately confined to their own members.

To summarise, despite state intervention in collective bargaining and a worsening of the overall economic and social situation for working people, trade union strength has proved remarkably resilient. This is primarily attributable to the high degree of formalisation of industrial relations, pragmatic co-operation between the different union confederations and, not least, the exclusive services which unions provide for their members. Belgium therefore represents a model of relative stability of formal union strength, even when accompanied by a clear deterioration in the material situation of the working population.

Denmark

Compared with trade unionism elsewhere in the European Union, the Danish trade union movement has been able to withstand the crisis of the 1980s and safeguard gains put in jeopardy elsewhere. There has, for example, been no large-scale deregulation of industrial relations and the extensive coverage of the Danish workforce by collective agreements has remained intact. This is closely related to the fact that the traditionally high level of trade union organisation, at around 80 per cent of the workforce, has not only been maintained under adverse conditions, austerity policies and mass unemployment, but has actually increased. Representatives of the main trade union confederation, the LO (*Landsorganisation i Danmark*), which organises 1.4 million workers out of a total labour force of 2.7 million, regard this as a success for the 'Scandinavian model' of employer-union co-operation – a model which they vigorously advocate within the European Trade Union Confederation (ETUC).

The substance of this 'model' has two major components:(a)'Realistic' co-operation between trade unions and employers in representing the interests of their members, with explicit recognition of the pressures exerted by international competition on national industry, in which the emphasis is less on regulation than on collective bargaining and a 'culture of co-operation'; (b) political activity directed at advancing 'economic democracy'.

Following the failed attempt to bring about economic democracy in the 1970s by means of legal reform, in collaboration with the then ruling Social Democratic Party (the LO is closely bound to the Social Democrats), the LO moved to advocacy of a simple form of profit-sharing in which 10 per cent of corporate profits were to be invested at company level in a form of employee investment fund. This much more modest aim, compared with the 1970s proposals, was, however, pushed down the agenda by other demands. In the first place, the LO concentrated its efforts on extending employee codetermination in the field of new technology, and in 1986 succeeded in negotiating a national agreement with the main employers' association (the DA), widely seen as one of the most advanced agreements of its type in Europe. Inaddition, in 1987 the LO succeeded in winning a 37-hour week, to be introduced over a four-year period, while maintaining and slightly increasing pay.

Nevertheless, this generally positive balance from the 1980s does have its debit side. Most notably, Danish trade union influence over broader social issues sharply declined following the end of the long period of Social Democratic government in 1982. As yet, it is too early to say whether the re-election of the Social Democrats to lead a coalition in the 1993 general election will enable them to regain the long-term initiative. The 1980s were characterised by a sustained period of austerity policies and the reorganisation of both the welfare state and the Danish economy under the successive conservative-led coalitions of Poul Schlüter – a programme characterised by the German daily, the *Frankfurter Allgemeine Zeitung*, as the 'slow but steady return to health of the Danish economy' (15 November 1989).The fact that the Social Democrats remained the largest single party in the Danish Parliament was not translatable into politically effective opposition to this trend.

The efforts of the Schlüter government were primarily directed at restructuring public finances through cuts in social spending and an 'incomes policy' which led to direct state intervention in collective bargaining and curbs on free negotiations. Immediately on taking office in 1982, the Schlüter Government abolished the index-linking of pay in collective agreements and imposed a five-month pay pause. Following on from this, and up to 1985, pay growth was limited to 4 per cent annually against average consumer price inflation of around 10 per cent. Despite trade union opposition, there was broad popular support for the policy of shifting the burden of adjustment to the economic crisis onto the employed labour force and the Schlüter Government emerged stronger from the 1985 election, bolstering the coalition's position in a conflict which followed shortly afterwards. When the LO called a nationwide strike in support of working time cuts and pay increases two months after the election – the first such strike for twelve years, involving 300,000 workers either on strike or locked out, the Government immediately passed a law imposing compulsory arbitration and requiring a cessation of all strike action after only a week. This was followed by the imposition of a pay 'edict' limiting increases to 1.25–2.0 per cent in 1987. Although this prompted the biggest mass protests in recent Danish history, the law could not be defeated. Any increases above these prescribed levels, achieved in some areas, were won by negotiations at the level of individual unions rather than across-the-board.

Similar state intervention under the Social Democrats had followed the outbreak of the world economic crisis in 1973 – albeit with the distinction that this was rooted in a policy of crisis management agreed with the trade unions and in which efforts were made not to impose a one-sided burden on workers. Squeezed between the need to correct the balance of payments deficit and public indebtedness on the one hand, and the justifiable demands of its political constituency on the other, in 1982 the Social Democrat-led minority Government under ex-LO General Secretary Anker Jörgensen capitulated in the face of massive economic problems and left the field to those conservative forces eager to implement the type of restructuring already in evidence in the UK. The failure of the programme of economic democratisation pursued in the 1970s laid bare the weaknesses of the trade unions' and Social Democrats' aspirations to re-shape social and work relationships. This failure, and the subsequent conservative ascendancy, of necessity reduced union power in areas such as housing, taxation, pension and training policy, and led to a growing distance between the unions and the Social Democratic Party, paralleled by a strengthening of the left both in the form of the Socialist Peoples' Party and within the unions.

In addition to its focus on working hours and the introduction of new technology, the LO primarily responded to this new situation by actively preparing for the Single European Market. This has involved several dimensions. For instance, the LO has been seeking to reshape the structure of the trade unions by moving towards a form of industrial unionism: as yet, the divergent interests of skilled workers and unskilled and semi-skilled workers continue to pose obstacles to the completion of this process (see the chapter on Denmark in Part II for a more detailed discussion of union structures and bargaining arrangements). The first step has been the formation of trade union 'cartels' which bring together unions organised along varying principles (principally craft and general) for national branch bargaining. Union rationalisation has also been pursued for some time through a policy of mergers, with the number of unions affiliated to the LO falling from sixty-five in 1966 to twenty-nine by 1990. In addition to these efforts to create the preconditions for a rationalisation and unification of the European labour movement at national level, the LO has also sought to move the national employers' associations to conclude an agreement on the regulation of industrial relations in the single market – paralleling the 'Scandinavian model' practised domestically. As yet, the employers have not been prepared to engage in such discussions. These initiatives are located in the LO's wide-ranging work on a cross-border campaign to secure the 'social dimension' to the Single Market.

The Danish trade unions have survived the 1980s in remarkably good shape as far as their basic structure is concerned, partly due to an active policy to retain and support the unemployed, and both government and employers continue to regard them as an important component of the national political and social culture. Nevertheless, the refusal of employers to negotiate over an extension of the 'Scandinavian model' within the Single Market is one indicator that this model may now be at risk within the wider European 'economic space'.

France

Of all the member-states in the European Union, none is perhaps more under the spell of modern technology than France. Despite the enduring paternalistic style of French management, the concept of 'modernisation' has bewitched employers, the state and trade unions alike and served as a central theme in the shaping of industrial relations. Beginning with the Left Government of socialists and communists, continuing with the conservative-liberal coalition interlude under Chirac, and sustained under the Socialist Government since its election in 1988, it has provided a thread running through the 1980s. There is, however, an important difference between 'progressive' and 'conservative' understandings of modernisation. Whereas for conservative forces, policy was rooted in the formula 'new technology plus growth = crisis management', left approaches to modernisation policy have favoured a dual strategy of fostering social as well as technical modernisation, at least in theory. However, such efforts have had to struggle under a major handicap: French trade unions, potentially a key actor in the implementation of a policy of social modernisation, have been caught up in a struggle for survival since the onset of the economic crisis in the mid 1970s. In their present condition, they would be barely able to bear the weight of such a task.

The structure of French trade unions is marked by political, and to a lesser degree, religious fragmentation, combined with the recent re-emergence of vigorous syndicalist currents. The militant class-struggle approach of the CGT and CFDT was tempered in the wake of the economic crisis, with a shift during the 1980s towards more moderate trade unions such as the FO, CGC and CFTC (see Section 2, below). The informal alliance between the communist CGT and socialist CFDT also foundered, mainly as a result of the sudden demise of the Communist Party, and the defensive return of the CGT to traditional positions, but also because of the CFDT's sometimes ill-thought-out pursuit of modernisation. Moreover, at the moment when each of these two organisations began to witness a decline in the influence of ideological positions – in the CGT's case its assertion of uncompromising class struggle and for the CFDT the cause of workers' self-management – and sought to move towards policies grounded in conventional collective bargaining and the pursuit of consensus, the French trade union movement was plunged into a membership crisis.

Currently, only some 10 per cent of the workforce is organised in the six national trade union confederations. Whereas union density is at 10–15 per cent in the public secor, it is probably in the region of 6 per cent in the large and medium sized companies in the private sector. Trade union activity is virtually non-existent in very small firms. The CGT, in particular, has suffered heavily with a loss of over 50 per cent of its membership since the early 1980s. It now accounts for roughly one million of the total of 2.3 million unionised workers in France. The number of days lost in strikes fell from five million to 1.3 million over the course of the 1980s, with some increase towards the end of the decade as a result mostly of autonomous action undertaken by workers in the public sector, principally on the railways and in the health service.

This major recession in the fortunes of trade unions in France, especially at industry and national confederation level, has had two notable consequences. Firstly, there has been a trend towards greater decentralisation of bargaining to plant/company level, a tendency fostered by the patriarchal management style seen in many small and medium-sized companies. The diminishing influence of industry level agreements has boosted the role and significance of company agreements, with employers able to enjoy greater scope for flexibility, partly due to the complicated arrangements for employee representation at company level. Secondly, there has been a revival in the role of the state, despite attempts to shift the responsibility for pursuing the social dimension of modernisation onto employers and unions through the promotion of collective bargaining in the 1982 'Auroux laws' (see Part 2 below).

This can be seen in the Government programme, the national employment plan, devised by the Rocard administration at the end of 1989, and mirrored in a number of subsequent policy developments. The programme provided for tax incentives, lower employer social security contributions and measures to discourage overtime working with the aim of stimulating job creation. Jobs plans announced in the autumn of 1991, and by the incoming Conservatives in 1993, have built on this approach, by providing for further exemptions from social insurance contributions. Even under the Conservative coalition, elected in the spring of 1993, the initiative on working time cuts as a means of preserving employment has been taken by the government.

Unemployment persisted at 9–10 per cent throughout the 1980s. By 1993, registered unemployment stood at 11.7 per cent of the labour force. The fastest growing, and politically most challenging, section of the unemployed are young people suffering long-term unemployment. The Government believes that small and medium-sized companies will play a key role in job creation, as well as paving the way to industrial modernisation through the introduction of new technology. Incentives have been targeted at this type of enterprise in the expectation that they have the flexibility to respond appropriately. The main approach has been to encourage employers to recruit by reducing statutory social security contributions. For example, small firms hiring their first employee are exempt from all social security charges for that employee for 24 months. The 1989 programme also provided for tax cuts for companies which take on extra staff for weekend work. In order to curb overtime, any hours worked above an annual individual quota of 130 are to be paid at double time, rather than time-and-a-half as previously, for example. Subsidies for integrating school leavers and the young unemployed into work have also been raised and special measures introduced for the long-term unemployed. Companies taking on a long-term unemployed person benefit from state subsidies and temporary exemptions from social security charges.

This 1989 plan, as well as subsequent developments, typify the modernisation strategies initiated and promoted by the state during the 1980s. On the one hand, investment incentives for companies have been increased, for example by cutting taxation on re-invested profits; on the other, the Government has been seeking means to respond to the continuing difficulties of both unemployed and employed, and compensate, at least to some degree, for the consequences of modernisation and rationalisation. Given the past failure of traditional policies of conflict and industrial militancy, the trade unions have been forced to pursue their industrial and economic objectives through collective bargaining. However, a comprehensive and democratically rooted system of collective bargaining, comparable with the German pattern, has not been successfully installed in France. The development of collective bargaining has been seriously retarded by state intervention, lack of co-ordination between the various bargaining levels (national, industry, firm), and not least by the attachment to the strategy of the political strike, characteristic of the left wing of the union movement over recent decades. In the face of all this, not even the annual obligation to bargain (although not to agree) at sectoral level mandated by the 1982 Auroux laws has been able to produce any wholly satisfactory results.

In contrast, company level bargaining has been steadily increasing in importance in recent years and has become one of the focal points of French industrial relations. Although formally signed by workplace level trade union sections, in practice the substance of collective agreements is very much influenced by works committees, which have no formal trade union status. In addition to the problems caused at company level by this tri-polar structure of works committees, staff representatives and trade union sections, workplace level bargaining is also hedged around by a number of limitations.

Firstly, the low level of membership of French trade unions makes it difficult for them to resort to industrial action in a disciplined way to achieve bargaining objectives at company level which are consonant with those of the organisation as a whole. Secondly, the high degree of autonomy developed by local trade union organisations has isolated the workplace level from the influence of nationally negotiated provisions and policies, inasmuch as these can be devised and implemented at all under present circumstances. Thirdly, the ideological divisions which characterise the French trade union movement, and the correspondingly high profile given to political concerns by members and officials, hinders co-operation both on immediate bargaining issues (for example, unions may compete to conclude the most innovative company agreement), and on strategic goals (for example, technical and social modernisation vs. traditional nationalisation).

Fourthly, the potentially conflictual nature of a system of industrial relations rooted in extensive individual but limited collective rights continues to obstruct efforts to strengthen national union structures through more effective integration of local and workplace-based organisations. Unco-ordinated, local agreements, fostered by legislation to encourage local bargaining, predominate. Moreover, despite the decline in individual preparedness to take industrial action, the system continues to be conducive to forms of industrial militancy which the trade unions cannot readily adopt and extend to their wider memberships. Despite their traditionally strong grassroots orientation, and a continuing willingness by members to take action at local level, French trade unions are only able to exercise the core tasks of a truly independent union movement in a limited sense – that is, to bargain collectively at both central and local levels, and to make a free choice of bargaining objectives.

As a consequence, the scope for trade union industrial participation is very limited indeed when compared to other countries. This is due primarily to the weakness and fragmentation of the unions, the overriding centralism of the French state, and the indifference or refusal of employers, particularly in small and medium-sized companies, to see collaboration with trade unions and employees as a positive contribution to what is otherwise fêted as the 'new corporate culture'.

Since the onset of the economic crisis of the mid 1970s, the political context in which the unions operate has been marked by a massive shift towards decentralisation, irrespective of which political party has been in power. Atypical employment has increased (fixed term contracts, subcontracting and temporary work with minimal social security cover). In 1985 one of the last acts of the Left Government was to initiate discussions on the subject of flexible working. The CGT and parts of the CFDT and FO (though resistance within the CFDT was slight) were fiercely opposed to the terms of a flexibility agreement which the Government was hoping to conclude with the main employers' organisation, the CNPF. However, in the spring of 1986 the Government passed a law aimed at overturning the notion of the 'normal working day'. The law, in force since 1987, encouraged the practice of adapting working time to economic (rather than simply technical) exigencies. Weekly working time may be averaged out on an annual basis, with local implementation through workplace agreements which the trade unions, because of their organisational weakness, are generally unable to negotiate. Following the interim conservative Government, which undertook further deregulation measures, such as relaxing the law on redundancy, this policy has been continued by the post-1988 socialist administrations (of Rocard, Cresson, Bérégovoy). Further proposals to increase flexibility on working hours in conjunction with working time cuts were announced by the incoming Conservative coalition in the summer of 1993.

The aim has been to forge a 'coalition of the centre' able to initiate a process of modernisation of capital in order to bolster French prospects within a more integrated Europe. However, there are grounds for fearing that given the difficult internal and external circumstances within which the trade unions operate, this process will entail a further weakening of free collective bargaining and workplace democracy, possibly putting in jeopardy the very existence of trade unionism in France.

Germany

The German trade union movement is currently facing a formidable set of challenges, the most urgent of which are posed by the process of unification and its economic and social consequences, made all the more severe by the economic downturn which began in mid 1992. In addition to the massive increase in unemployment in the regions making up the former German Democratic Republic, the contraction of economic activity in western Germany in 1992/93 was joined by a corporate shake-out in the face of new European and worldwide competition. The rise in unemployment east and west not only fostered social tensions, manifested in an enlarged share of the vote for right-wing parties, but also led to a crisis in the financing of the unemployment benefit system. At the same time, the collapse of the former Soviet Union, and the political and economic transition in Eastern and Central Europe, triggered a new wave of migration into Germany by asylum-seekers, those fleeing the wars in the former Yugoslavia and elsewhere, and ethnic Germans previously resident throughout the countries of the former Communist bloc who automatically enjoy German citizenship. In all, an estimated 1.1 million individuals are thought to have entered Germany in 1992, fuelling political debates over labour market regulation, and over German policies on asylum and nationality.

The political context for trade union activity during the 1980s was initially set by the coming-to-power of a Christian Democrat-led (i.e., Conservative) coalition in 1982, following the decision (in the wake of the 1981–82 recession) by the liberal Free Democratic Party to leave the Social Democrat-led coalition, which had been in power through the 1970s. Within this new coalition, which won the Federal elections in December 1990 following unification, the Free Democratic Party (FDP) consistently pushed for greater deregulation, although with varying degrees of success. Traditionally, the Economics Ministry has been run by an FDP minister, whereas the department of Employment and Social Affairs has been the responsibility of the Christian Democrats (CDU) who, in contrast to British conservatism, have a 'social wing' with active union links. Nevertheless, the 1980s and early 1990s have seen moves towards greater labour market deregulation and the selling-off of Federal government holdings in industry.

Real wages fell or stagnated in the early 1980s, under the impact of high unemployment. There was also a union emphasis on negotiating cuts in working hours, with some degree of trade-off for pay increases. However, at least in the private sector, settlements picked up from the mid 1980s, aided by a revival in German exports as other EC countries re-equipped in the run-up to the Single Market and culminating in the immediate post-unification boom which ended half-way through 1992. Nevertheless, employee incomes as a percentage of total national income fell from 70 per cent in 1981 to 62 per cent by 1990 as profits growth outstripped wage settlements. The 1992–93 recession further depressed settlements, in some cases pushing them below inflation, and putting pressure on real incomes.

The financing of unification, the costs of which were seriously underestimated by the Government in its effort to present an optimistic picture prior to the 1990 elections, has triggered a new phase of spending cuts on social measures, including levels of unemployment benefit, income support and parental benefit. The exceptional cost of unification, combined with the general recessionary climate, has created a tougher environment for trade unions and has placed strain on the German structure of industrial relations.

The outstanding feature of the German system of *collective bargaining* is the separation between the trade unions on the one hand, and elected workplace representative bodies, 'works councils', on the other (see also the section on Germany in Part II below). This institutional separation corresponds to a distinction between collective bargaining proper, typically conducted at industry level by trade unions, and the conclusion of individual works agreements by works councils. Each type of agreement is regulated by different statutory provisions, and reflects the differing concerns and exigencies operating at each level. Industry (or, more rarely, company) collective agreements (*Tarifvertrag*), regulated by the Collective Agreements Act, are legally binding and take precedence over works agreements (*Betriebsvereinbarung*), whose scope is laid down in the 1972 Works Constitution Act (the law on workplace employee participation). However, a collective agreement may devolve powers to workplace level on some issues, such as the detailed implementation of agreed working time provisions. Of central importance is the fact that, whereas unions enjoy the right to strike in order to back up their negotiating position (to prevent 'collective bargaining becoming collective begging' to quote one Labour Court judge), works councils are legally required to refrain from industrial action and enjoined to promote 'industrial peace' at the workplace.

Within this dual structure of representation, the dominant elements are a commitment to free collective bargaining on the one hand, combined with legally anchored rights of participation and codetermination on the other. The existence of statutory rights of codetermination – according to which, should employees choose to set up a works council, it must be recognised and dealt with by the employer – also indicates the high degree to which industrial relations are regulated by law in Germany (so-called 'juridification'). However, the law merely sets out a framework: how unions, works councils, employers and the state behave and interact in any specific context, and the extent to which rights are enforced and asserted, depends on many circumstances. These might include the prevailing political climate, informal attempts at intervention by the state in collective disputes, the strengths and weaknesses of the respective parties during negotiations, the importance and influence of statutory codetermination rights at the various levels of the workplace, the nature of the establishment, the character of the company, the overall state of the economy, and more recently the influence of the European community.

Free collective bargaining in Germany is rooted in Article 9 of the founding constitution of the Federal Republic, the 'Basic Law'. This guarantees 'the right to form associations to safeguard and improve working and economic conditions ... to everyone, and all trades, occupations and professions'. This is the only collective right laid down in the Basic Law and provides the legal basis for freedom of association. Under the Collective Agreements Act, individual employers as well as employers' associations may sign collective agreements with trade unions. In the main, collective bargaining within this legal framework is not carried out by central union confederations or national employer organisations but by individual unions, which within the *Deutscher Gewerkschaftsbund* (DGB) union confederations are organised along industry lines, and industry level employer associations. Company level collective bargaining only covers some 6 per cent of the workforce.

The state has no formal right to intervene in collective bargaining and, in contrast to many other EC countries, there was no attempt at a formal incomes policy during the 1980s. There is no system of official compulsory arbitration, although this does not rule out the possibility that the government might seek to exert indirect influence through the media, or by putting public pressure on negotiations. The 1991-92 and 1993 pay rounds in both eastern and western Germany saw an unprecedented degree of activity and comment by the Government. In the case of eastern Germany, the Government used its direct financial control over companies still in the ownership of the state holding company, the *Treuhand*, to play a major role in the decision by the employers to refuse to implement an agreed pay increase. In addition to ministerial exhortations, the opinions and recommendations of the Council of

Economic Advisers (*Sachverständigenrat*), and the comments and monetary policy of the Bundesbank, also shape the climate and conduct of collective bargaining.

As elsewhere in the European Union, the primary focus of collective bargaining is on pay, working conditions and working time. These are primarily settled by negotiation between employers and unions, with statutory provision playing only a minor or background role. For example, although legislation on working time dating from 1938 provides for a 48 hour normal working week, in practice the actual average, collectively agreed, working week is around 37.5 hours and still falling. (Reform of the 1938 'Working Time Ordinance' is, in fact, expected in 1994.) The freedom of collective bargaining from formal state interference is mirrored in the political independence of the German trade unions. The fundamental principle of non-party political organisation underlying the largest union centre, the German trade union confederation (the *Deutscher Gewerkschaftsbund*), rules out the type of party influence on trade union policies – and thus collective bargaining – seen in countries with a politically divided trade union movement. In fact, the opposite situation prevails: the political parties are assessed by the unions and measured in terms of their commitment to employee interests. At election times, for example, this typically takes place through the issuing by the unions of guidance notes known as 'electoral touchstones'. Although formally not aligned to any specific party, however, German unions are far from non-political. Historically, the unions have always been close to the Social Democratic Party (SPD), but the relationship between the unions and the SPD is not entirely untroubled. Differences between trade union and SPD positions on major issues often emerge, which are then debated and resolved in public. In recent years, for example, there have been differences over the forms, extent and financing of cuts in working time. As the governing party in many local and regional authorities, the SPD also sits *opposite* union negotiators as a public employer. During 1993, for example, state governments in some SPD controlled *Länder* have proposed increases in weekly hours for established civil servants (*Beamte*) in local government service.

The most important instrument possessed by the trade unions within the framework of free collective bargaining, for exerting pressure to conclude collective agreements, is the right to strike – even if, and perhaps precisely because, resort to it is infrequent. Employers in Germany also have a corresponding right to lock employees out – a right put to active use on occcasions, and often in contravention of the legal axiom of 'proportionality'. This principle, developed via case law in the courts, requires that industrial action should not be disproportional to the action's aim or the action taken by the opposing side. The trade union view is that the right to lock out enjoyed by German employers violates what ought to be a basic parity of strength between the two parties in bargaining. As buyers, sellers and users of labour, employers already have an inbuilt advantage over employees, who are in a dependent situation – an asymmetry, the unions argue, which is exaggerated by the employers' right to lock out. Union efforts to limit or ban the lock-out have been an enduring theme in German industrial relations.

The basic pattern of collective bargaining can be illustrated by turning to some basic figures on the German system. At present, some 30,000 currently valid collective agreements cover an estimated 90 per cent of employees in west Germany. The main subjects covered include working conditions in the broadest sense: wages and salaries, financial benefits (holiday bonus, insurance, employer-financed savings schemes, etc.), working time, and skills and training (which have received greater emphasis recently). The duration of agreements is specified in the agreement itself, and there is an obligation not to resort to industrial action during the lifetime of the agreement and for a period – usually four weeks – after it has expired. Both signatory parties must be members of organisations deemed competent to sign collective agreements. Criteria for competence have been developed by the courts, based on the constitutional clause providing for freedom of association. For example, a trade union must be genuinely independent of employers, meet certain minimum standards of internal democracy, aim to conclude collective agreements and abide by them, and have the power to represent a viable opposition to the employer by wielding effective industrial action, if necessary, in pursuit of its economic demands. Any agreement signed by an organisation which does not meet these criteria will be invalid and unenforceable.

Should a union wish to strike following the expiry of the agreement's 'peace clause', then a 75 per cent majority of union members in a secret ballot is required; a vote of 25 per cent of members is sufficient to end a dispute. Works agreements concluded between company managements and works councils can improve on the provisions of an industry collective agreement, although there are some limitations on the areas which may be regulated by this type of local agreement. The capacity to conclude workplace agreements is an important component of works councils' overall role and rights, and is characteristic of the close link between collective bargaining and workplace bargaining.

Properly speaking, the right to conduct collective bargaining ought to be numbered among the range of instruments available to trade unions for the exercise of codetermination (*Mitbestimmung*). By convention, however, the meaning of 'codetermination' has been restricted to a specific set of rights and obligations granted under the 1972 Works Constitution Act, and, within that, more narrowly to situations in which works councils can block a management initiative or insist on concluding a works agreement (see below). Nevertheless, German trade unions have always continued to advocate a broader notion of codetermination as the achievement of a system of representation, based on elected representatives, through which union perspectives on economic and social matters can be argued for and implemented, independently of the state and political parties. The struggle for codetermination is, therefore, a struggle for the extension of trade union rights. Present-day institutions for codetermination, in this broader sense, embrace a number of different levels and forms, with a range of possibilities for influence and participation. The *levels* include:

— The individual job. Although this remains a relatively weakly developed area, efforts have been made to place greater emphasis on it, especially since the introduction of new technology and associated new skills has made it into a focal point of both conflicts and opportunities. Trade unions have been involved in a number of initiatives dealing with multi-skilling and teamwork: the metalworkers' union IG Metall, for example, has developed a programme for collective bargaining over the coming decade, known as *Tarifreform 2000*, which includes issues such as job definition and control, and skill-based pay.
— The workplace, that is, the plant or establishment (*Betrieb*). This is the level at which works councils, and their associated rights, presently operate. Although rooted in the individual establishment (a factory, a shop, one unit in multi-plant company), works councils may be constituted, via delegation, to represent employee interests at company and, within a conglomerate, at combine level.
— The level of the company or enterprise. German law provides for employee representation on the supervisory boards of companies meeting certain size and other formal criteria. All German public companies and limited liability companies above a certain size have two boards: a supervisory board (*Aufsichtsrat*), which oversees the general affairs of the company, and a management board (*Vorstand*), which is responsible for the day-to-day running of the company. The supervisory board sets overall policy, monitors the general running of the business, and appoints the management board and/or managing directors. The number of employee representatives varies according to company size (for details, see the chapter on employee representation in Part II, below).
— The economy as a whole. There are no rights of codetermination at this level and, as yet, nothing has come of trade union demands for national and industrial councils within the framework of an overall structural policy. The increasingly important process of regional co-

ordination within the framework of European regional economic development also currently takes place without any form of trade union influence.

The *forms* of codetermination include:

— Systems of representation, including works councils and supervisory boards, with functions often exercised by the same individuals.
— Collective agreements, which, as noted above, represent an equally important form of effective codetermination.
— Arrangements between managements and works councils on the involvement of employee representatives in problem-solving at workplace level. The lack of formality of such agreements and the absence of any binding legal commitment, however, means that such arrangements are constantly at risk of being withdrawn. This currently applies, for example, in the field of the introduction of new technology, for which no enforceable rights of codetermination are granted under works council legislation.

Finally, there are also a number of possibilities through which influence can be exerted via formal codetermination machinery. These include:

— Veto rights and rights of initiative, especially under works council legislation, on such issues as personnel matters and working time. For example, works councils can refuse an employer's request to introduce overtime working.
— Rights of control, especially those exercised by supervisory boards. This has recently been the subject of considerable discussion as trade union and employee members of supervisory boards do not, in practice, enjoy the same access to information as the shareholders' side, making it more difficult to exercise their formal rights.
— The more frequently and more intensively used consultation rights which works councils have, principally on financial and business matters.
— Finally, works councils and supervisory boards have extensive rights to information disclosure on both business and employment questions.

In general, the strongest legally guaranteed rights are in the areas of personnel and workplace social provision. These include questions of appointment, regrading, and transfer together with working time arrangements (though not the length of the working week, which is set by industry collective agreement), health and safety, and the 'principles of remuneration' (but not minimum pay levels, which are also set by industry collective agreement). By contrast, enforceable rights on financial and business matters at company level, and on broader economic issues beyond this, are comparatively weak.

How has this unique system of industrial relations, with its dual system of industry-based collective bargaining by trade unions and workplace-based statutory codetermination, fared over the past decade or so?

At first sight, German trade unions appear to be in a fairly strong position, compared with circumstances in some other EU countries. The level of union density is around 40 per cent, with 35 per cent of the workforce in unions affiliated to the principal union centre, the DGB. There is also broad public support for the social role of trade unions: for example, according to a public opinion poll carried out in the autumn of 1987, around half the population and more than half the employed workforce in Germany (the then West German part) regarded trade unions as 'indispensable'.

Membership of DGB unions dipped by some 125,000 between 1980 and 1987, around 1.5 per cent of the total of 7.8 million members, but recovered to end the decade with a slightly increased membership of 7.9 million. Unification, which involved the dismantling of the former GDR union centre and the merger of individual industrial unions with their western equivalents, initially brought a surge of new members. By the end of 1992, the total membership of DGB-affiliated unions was 11.8 million. However, economic collapse in eastern Germany has taken its toll, and a substantial proportion of the new membership, especially in manufacturing industry, has been lost. Of those remaining, many are on short time or in job schemes, and pay only minimal contributions.

Compared with the dramatic losses suffered by trade unions in France and Great Britain, the maintenance of German union membership in the west represents a high degree of stability. However, lurking behind this relative stability, the present membership structure does harbour a number of serious difficulties for union organisation and representativeness. Although white-collar workers now account for more than 50 per cent of the labour force, they make up only 23 per cent of trade union members. Similarly, women account for only 24 per cent of DGB members in western Germany, but make up 40 per cent of the workforce. The situation is even more grim as far young people's participation in trade unions is concerned. Only 13 per cent of young workers are in trade unions, and the number of young members in DGB-affiliated unions has been falling for several years. In addition, the share of union membership accounted for by part-timers, the unemployed and pensioners has been steadily growing – with problematic effects on trade union finances.

The financial consequences of these structural changes in the membership have been exacerbated by the long-running problems associated with co-operative ventures sponsored by the trade unions (the so-called *Gemeinwirtschaft*), and in particular by the crisis and crash of the *Neue Heimat* housing organisation in the mid 1980s, the effects of which are still felt in the movement. What is often overlooked, both in Germany and abroad, is the fact that trade unionism in Germany is faced with a dual structural weakness. First, the level of union density in small establishments with less than thirty employees, in which around half of all employees work, is below 10 per cent; and second, the goods-producing sector in Germany is currently much larger than in other EU countries, mirroring the high level of export-dependency in the German economy. Given the shift to a more service-based economy seen throughout the developed world, some contraction of manufacturing industry is almost inevitable and, with it, a loss of potential and actual trade union members – a process dramatically illustrated, albeit under unique circumstances, in east Germany since 1990.

Besides the internal problems of union organisation, over the course of the 1980s the trade unions were faced with a number of additional challenges in the shape of government efforts at deregulation in areas such as support for students in higher education, the protection of young workers, the provision of unemployment benefit for workers laid off as a result of industrial action, and measures to encourage fixed-term contracts. In some respects, these efforts have intensifed in the first years of the new decade. An official Commission on Deregulation, established by the Conservative-led coalition in the mid 1980s to examine 'obstacles to the operation of markets' reported in 1991: it proposed a number of measures to weaken the legal status of collective agreements. Although by and large rejected by both sides of industry, the Commission's proposals indicated the extent to which established institutions have been placed in question by the rationale of economic liberalism. There is a continuing debate about the balance between industry and company level bargaining, with the central employer's organisation (the BDA) and ministers arguing for greater scope for terms and conditions to be set at workplace level (where unions have no formal bargaining rights under industry bargaining), with industry agreements providing only a minimal floor.

The effects of this trend in employment and labour market policies, together with the changes sought directly via collective bargaining by the employers, have become crystallised in the concept of 'flexibility', a term which has come to dominate social and economic debate since the mid 1980s. Working time in particular, but also broader conditions of employment, social benefits and social insurance, labour law and the works council system itself have become targets for arguments about 'adjustment' to changed economic and political circumstances. This has led to demands for greater flexibility in employment law, such as easing the law on temporary employment, through which a move away from the notion of permanent full-time employment as the norm is being engineered.

The trade union response to the Government's deregulatory measures and philosophy, which were immediately incorporated into the employers' bargaining agenda, has been a dual one. In the first place, they have sought to retain jobs for full-time employees by negotiating cuts in working time. After a six-week strike in the metalworking industry in 1984, successive bargaining rounds have lowered average weekly hours across a range of industries with the 35-hour week agreed for all employees in the metalworking and printing industries from 1995. And second, they have attempted to counterpose employer concepts of working time flexibility with a strategy designed to meet employees' needs for greater flexibility in their working hours. This notion of individual preference, centred on the notion of employees' 'time sovereignty', is intended to yield, for example, guaranteed time off for training, more leisure time when employees want to take it, easier and more flexible transitions to retirement, and a more balanced relationship between the development of working time and advances in productivity. The collective bargaining rounds of the next few years will show the extent to which the trade unions are capable of linking cuts in working time with individual wishes for control and flexibility over working and non-working hours, and of embodying such arrangements in binding collective agreements.

The overall situation, then, of the German trade union movement at the start of the 1990s can be outlined under the following main headings: unification, collective bargaining, the separation of parties and trade unions, and the dual system of employee representation.

Unification has brought the trade unions shaped in the former West German economic and social context new members, new responsibilities and enormous challenges. The financing of unification, especially during a period of recession, has been characterised both by increases in direct and indirect taxation, as well as a restrictive monetary policy – putting pressure on households' disposable incomes. Whereas workers in eastern Germany are being confronted by unprecedented economic insecurity, much of which can only be alleviated in the short term by financial transfers from the west, union members in western Germany are being forced to accept pay settlements at or below inflation and higher taxes.

The transposition of the west German system of industry bargaining to the new regions of the former GDR has drawn the trade unions into an economically complex and politically delicate series of negotiations and conflicts. For reasons of social harmony and fairness, unions have pressed for a fairly rapid pace of pay harmonisation between east and west, at least on minimum rates. Moreover, the unions have pointed to the need to retain skilled workers in eastern Germany, and argued that the threat to the existence of industrial jobs in the east is less connected with levels of pay than with a nexus of macroeconomic and structural factors: the breakdown of the entire East and Central European market, the traditional destination of former East German exports, outmoded equipment and products, the flooding of eastern Germany with western consumer goods, often at cut-throat prices, and difficulties in gaining access to markets in the West. During 1991, agreements were concluded between unions and employers' associations providing for convergence on industry minima by 1995, with revision clauses allowing a re-opening of negotiations in the light of developments. Overtaken by the pace of economic collapse in the east, the employers have since sought either to negotiate delays in implementing agreements or, as in the metalworking industry, to renege on agreed pay increases following unsuccessful attempts at conciliation. In 1993, following industrial action in the metalworking industry a new agreement was reached under which the timetable for pay convergence will be extended, with the option of exemption from scheduled pay increases for enterprises under exceptional hardship. Concerns about sustaining the structure of bargaining in the east have also fed back into the employers' agenda for loosening existing arrangements in the west.

Despite these concerns, *collective bargaining*, understood as the free negotiation of working conditions in the broadest sense between employers' organisations and trade unions has proved to be productive, progressive and flexible. To date, trade unions have managed to retain sufficient organisational strength to use collective bargaining as an effective instrument against excessive deregulation. However, this too is under pressure: for example, the Government has issued proposals under which a number of existing statutory and agreed regulations would be set aside in order to provide employers with a financial cushion to pay for a new scheme of care for the elderly and disabled. Whether this intervention into freely agreed arrangements is compatible with constitutional rights is a matter likely to be tested in the courts.

The *principle of separation of parties and trade unions* as different pillars of the labour movement remains firmly anchored. Union movements divided on political grounds have experienced major problems in winning social recognition compared with independent non-party union centres. An over-intimate relationship between parties and trade unions evidently damages both organisations – a phenomenon witnessed in many EU countries.

The *dual system of employee representation* through trade unions (collective bargaining, backed up by the right to strike) and works councils (workplace agreements, and the obligation to maintain industrial peace) has proved to be effective both as a system of representation and in terms of economic efficiency. However, there are latent problems related to the issue of the autonomy of works councils, and their scope for pursuing localised and special interests, especially when placed under economic pressure. This issue has now emerged as an acute difficulty for the unions (and, in fact, for employers' organisations) in eastern Germany, where local managements and works councils have sought to be exempted from the wage rates specified in industry agreements. Moreover, this question could also take on greater significance in the longer term should hopes for enhanced codetermination at workplace level come to fruition. But the system does provide a relatively flexible mechanism for resolving problems and a relatively high capacity for achieving compromises, as each of the two components of the respective systems derives its legitimacy from different roots.

The existing system of statutory codetermination is primarily concerned with the individual establishment and the firm. Given the greater need for employee codetermination at the immediate workplace, on issues such as technical and organisational innovation, and the need to develop regional and structural policies at European level, there is both scope and some imperative for the extension of codetermination to these, as yet, untackled fields of activity. Meeting the need and aspirations for individual and collective codetermination, and thus contributing to industrial peace and social harmony, requires a structure of employee, works council, and trade union influence at all these levels.

Looking to the future, complex and highly industrialised societies, such as Germany, still have to grasp the full implications of the fact that their systems of industrial relations, with their associated impact on employee motivation, represent a central, productive social force – no less important than the customary technical and economic components of productivity. The crucial issue for the trade unions in the short and medium term is whether they can link the related issues of economic efficiency and social progress in a form which benefits working people. In view of German economic strength within the European Union, how these issues are resolved within Germany will also have a major impact on the rest of Europe. At the moment, the employers have accumulated years of experience in wielding the 'soft technologies' of quality circles, user-involvement, corporate culture, and other new management methods. The trade unions still have much ground to make up.

Great Britain

The deregulation of employment in Great Britain during the 1980s not only represented a direct response to the economic crisis of the 1970s, in which industrial relations were seen to have played a major role, but was also one component of ideologically-motivated efforts to purge both labour and product markets of their institutional 'imperfections' in order to lay the foundations for a British economic revival built on free market principles.

Following the election of the Conservative government under Margaret Thatcher in 1979, policy on industrial relations was marked by a re-regulation of trade unions, especially in the fields of industrial action and internal union organisation, extending far beyond Conservative efforts in the period 1970–74, the pursuit of flexibility in labour markets, in part through an easing of statutory regulations in areas such as dismissals, and massive privatisation and restructuring of the economy. Measures introduced during the 1974–79 Labour Government to encourage trade union recognition and the effective extension of collective agreements were repealed. The extent to which the entire legislative strategy towards trade unions was pre-planned by the Conservatives in opposition remains controversial. Much of the legislation was framed in response to specific developments, most notably the 1978–79 period of industrial strife during the latter part of the Labour Government's incomes policy (the 'Winter of Discontent'). However, the piecemeal approach – six acts were passed on unions and industrial action between 1980 and 1993 – ensured that no one measure was seen as posing a massive and illegitimate challenge. Non-compliance, which had destroyed previous Conservative attempts to regulate union conduct via statute in 1971, was insignificant as a force in holding back the advance of the law. And although use of the new legal possibilities by employers has been fairly infrequent, the implied or explicit threat of recourse to the law has, arguably, been effective in numerous instances. Moreover, the organisational and personal consequences of losing in the courts have been sufficiently serious both to ensure widespread compliance and make unions much more cautious about initiating industrial action. At the same time, the reforms in procedures imposed on unions have served to legitimate them as institutions and strengthen their hand in certain situations. The statutory conciliation and arbitration service ACAS commented in its 1987 report that a large majority in a ballot for strike action over a pay claim was a negotiating tactic which 'some employers have found difficult to counter'.

The main areas of legislative intervention between 1980 and 1993 were:

— Closed shop: progressively restricted and finally effectively rendered illegal in 1990.
— Industrial action: the scope for lawful industrial action reduced through tightened definition of a 'trade dispute'. Employers enabled to obtain damages from unions for 'secondary industrial action', such as boycotts ('blacking') and picketing of employers not directly involved in a dispute and political strikes or other forms of action not undertaken in pursuit of a trade dispute. Official strikes must be preceded by a ballot – which from 1993 must be conducted by post. In 1990 unions were made liable for unofficial action by their members unless they take steps to repudiate it. Official strikers can be dismissed provided the employer dismisses all those on strike: selective re-engagement is possible after three months. In theory, unofficial strikers can be selectively dismissed.
— Union organisation: union executive committees and senior union officials must be elected by secret ballot. From 1993 arrangements for direct deduction of union dues ('check-off') must ensure that individual consent is given in writing at least every three years – a move likely to hit union finances.
— Political funds: British unions maintain 'political funds' which can be used to make contributions to political parties, provide financial support for individual candidates for political office (typically sponsorship of Members of Parliament), and run general campaigns. The fund is financed by individual members who agree to pay a political levy. Originally subject to statutory control in 1913, the funds were subject to tighter regulation under the 1984 Trade Union Act which widened the scope of political objects on which expenditure must be met from a political fund, and introduced a mandatory review by postal ballot on the maintenance of the fund every ten years. When the legislation was introduced the Government hoped that the declining support for the Labour Party amongst trade unionists, revealed in the 1983 General Election, would translate into a rejection of the maintenance of political funds. In fact, the need to conduct ballots galvanised many union bureacracies into consulting and com-

municating with their memberships. By stressing the importance of unions having the right to campaign on social and political issues, where necessary independently of the Labour Party, union leaderships were able to win overwhelming support for the continuation of political funds in a series of ballots in 1985–86 which marked a turning point following a succession of political and industrial defeats for the trade union movement.

This legal approach to changing the relationship between labour and production took place against an economic background characterised by persistently high unemployment and a sharp contraction of manufacturing industry. Pressure has also been exerted on union organisation in the public sector through privatisation in the form of the flotation of public enterprises on the Stock Market, the reduction in the state's holding in nationalised concerns, the introduction of compulsory competitive tendering (CCT) and 'market testing' into the provision of public services, and the fragmentation of structures of public administration through the creation of agencies and 'quangos'.

In contrast to the spectrum of protective, mitigating and delaying measures in place in other countries, the Thatcher Government adopted a rigorous commitment to the 'creative destruction' unleashed by the free operation of the market – accepting that this implied the rapid demise of entire industrial sectors. During the mid 1980s in particular, the Government took the view that manufacturing did not warrant particular support, that the future lay in the creation of a service-based economy, and that the UK's status as a major oil producer anyway meant that manufacturing would have to give ground. Employment in the automotive industry fell from 472,000 in 1979 to 222,000 by 1990. The textile and clothing industry contracted from 800,000 employees in 1979 to 414,000 by 1991. In contrast, employment in finance and business services rose from 1,622,000 in 1979 to 2,700,000 by 1991. Employment in industry fell from 39 per cent of the labour force in 1979 to 29 per cent by 1990 – slightly below the EU average of 31 per cent but well below the German figure of 40 per cent. The fall was especially rapid in the early 1980s as a result of the recession and high value of the Pound sterling induced by the government's monetarist policies. One consequence of this relatively rapid pace of de-industrialisation has been the emergence of a chronic trade deficit, despite North Sea oil, with the first ever deficit in manufactured goods in UK history in 1986.

One major element in the Government's strategy has been to promote the UK as an attractive location for foreign direct investment. Indeed, the desire to attract foreign investment has also been cited by the UK government as one reason for opposing EU social measures and for negotiating an 'opt out' on the social provisions and new procedures agreed under the Treaty of Maastricht. Japanese direct investment in manufacturing, although not large in absolute terms, has had a major influence in such areas as relations with suppliers, industrial relations, and quality management. Industries such as consumer electronics and the car industry have been, and are being, transformed by the direct and exemplary effect of Japanese producers. The UK has received an estimated 40 per cent of total Japanese manufacturing investment in the EU, much of which was searching for a location prior to the completion of the Single European Market. By 1992, for example, there were 195 Japanese manufacturing enterprises operating in the UK compared with 128 in France and 111 in Germany. The rising share of foreign employers (especially US and Japanese) in total private manufacturing has also accelerated the trend towards single-employer arrangements (both in unionised and non-unionised plants) for setting pay and conditions (see below): in general, non-UK owned businesses have been less willing to join British employers' associations and more keen to implant, suitably adapted, their own managerial approaches.

This economic approach and context has also been accompanied by a political strategy aimed at weakening and excluding intermediate organisations combined with populist attempts to establish a direct, if ultimately fictitious, relationship between Government and people. For the trades unions, with the churches the most important intermediate social organisation, this meant an effort to exclude them as much as possible from national political life and to individualise, and with that to depoliticise, the relations between union members and union organisations. The formal exclusion of trade unions from national bodies (some of which were themselves dissolved) and the drying up of informal links has been one of the most decisive political changes of the 1980s. Moreover, British trade unions were particularly vulnerable to such a strategy. Although trade unions were politically active as participants in national institutions and tripartite arrangements during the 1960s and 1970s, a period of growing union membership, problems of internal organisation, discipline and democracy were exposed and exacerbated by the developing crisis of the late 1970s.

The trade union structure continues to be characterised by a large number of diverse organisations, still engaged in a process of consolidation and evolution, with the predominant union type a form of conglomerate of once craft and/or general unions. Although a process of mergers and amalgamation has reduced the degree of fragmentation of the British union movement (the Trades Union Congress now embraces some 70 unions, accounting for 80 per cent of total trade union membership), this rationalisation has run in parallel with a dramatic fall in membership and union density. TUC membership has dropped from over 12,000,000 members in 1979 to around 7,780,000 by 1992. Union density has fallen from approaching 55 per cent to just over 35 per cent by the early 1990s.

The reduction in trade union power which these developments have implied can also be read off in the statistics for industrial action. During the 1970s, there were on average 2,500 stoppages a year with 7-10,000,000 days lost through industrial action, involving c. 1,000,000 workers a year. This peaked in 1979 with a total of 29,500,000 days lost in strikes involving 4,600,000 workers. By 1992, the number of days lost had fallen to 528,000, with 148,000 workers involved.

The weakening in trade union power has also been reflected in changes in the system of collective bargaining. This has affected both the overall incidence of collective bargaining and the level at which bargaining takes place. Firstly, there has been a substantial decline in the proportion of the workforce covered by collective bargaining. According to the 1990 Workplace Industrial Relations Survey (WIRS), some 54 per cent of the workforce in establishments with 25 or more employees were covered by collective bargaining compared with 71 per cent in 1984. (Allowing for the much lower incidence of collective bargaining in small workplaces, the actual coverage of the whole workforce by collective bargaining was probably below 40 per cent in 1990). Coverage for non-manual employees and in private services is generally substantially below that for manual employees in manufacturing and in the public sector.

Recognition of trade unions by employers for the negotiation of pay and conditions has also undergone a substantial decline since the early 1980s. In 1984, the Workplace Industrial Relations Survey found that 66 per cent of establishments recognised trade unions: by 1990, the figure had fallen to 53 per cent. Decline was registered in private manufacturing (65 per cent to 44 per cent), in private services (44 per cent to 36 per cent) and in the public sector (99 per cent to 87 per cent). Within private manufacturing, the decline in recognition was especially marked in the engineering industry, and in printing and publishing. Excluding these two branches, recognition remained broadly constant in manufacturing industry – lending weight to the view that, despite the major changes in the political context of trade unionism and the elimination of many once-unionised jobs in manufacturing, there are major elements of continuity in industrial relations at workplace level.

The decline in union membership, trade union recognition and coverage by collective bargaining reflects the restructuring of the economy as well as changes in personnel policies away from support for or toleration of trade union organisation and towards greater individualisation. During the first half of the 1980s, changes in the composition of the workforce – associated with an abrupt fall in manufacturing employment (see below) – were probably the dominant feature. In the mid to late 1980s, changing management techniques and approaches may have had an additional important effect. These might also offer some explanation as to why trade unions have not been able to organise successfully in new areas of employment growth. The recession, which has wiped out a further tranche of jobs in manufacturing since 1990, has led to a further phase of serious membership losses.

None the less, collective bargaining remains the predominant form of pay setting for some groups of employees. For example, according to the 1990 WIRS survey, some 70 per cent of manual employees in manufacturing still have their pay and conditions set collectively (albeit a fall from the 79 per cent recorded in 1984). And those typically fairly well-unionised plants in manufacturing which have survived the two recessions continue to exhibit a high degree of continuity in industrial relations arrangements.

Secondly, there has been a steady decline in industry level bargaining towards either single-employer bargaining (and in many instances to workplace or business unit level) or, as noted above, to unilateral decision by the employer. The overall pattern of bargaining has been shaped not only by decisions made to change existing arrangements, but also by the pay-setting mechanisms established on new sites. The practices of foreign-owned companies, which tend not to join employers' associations, may have been especially influential during the 1980s in bolstering single-employer bargaining. Up until the late 1970s, the setting of pay and conditions by collective bargaining took place in many industries through a two-tier structure, with often very broad framework provisions at industry level filled out at company or workplace level. Company and workplace bargaining had developed in particular during the 1960s, in response both to the growing influence of shopfloor representatives (shop stewards) and the desire of companies to gain greater control over the setting of pay and conditions. During the 1980s and early 1990s there has been a progressive abandonment of industry level bargaining by the employers in both the private, and increasingly the public (and once public) sectors. By 1990, multi-employer bargaining was the main basis for pay increases for only 19 per cent of manual employees in private manufacturing and for only 6 per cent of non-manual employees.

Both these changes – the declining coverage of collective bargaining and the growing importance of single-employer bargaining – have accompanied and reflected a diminishing role for employers' associations. Historically weak in comparison with many of their Mainland European counterparts, the fall off in industry level bargaining in the 1980s has removed an important source of direct and practical influence. In response, some employer organisations, such as the Engineering Employers Federation (EEF) have shifted towards a more consultative and lobbying role, whilst others have wound themselves up altogether.

Attempts to develop a response to the changing legal, bargaining and economic environment created enormous strains within the union movement during the 1980s. The broad offensive mounted both by government and capital led to a polarisation in the trade union movement between sections forced onto the defensive (mining, printing, textiles, steel) and groups more able to benefit to some degree from the shifts in the pattern of activity (electronics, chemicals and pharmaceuticals). As well as differences in bargaining approaches, tensions also emerged over how readily unions should adapt to the new legislation on trade unions. Some unions argued for, and accepted, the use of state funds to support postal ballots, despite official TUC opposition. These tensions culminated in 1988 in the exclusion from the TUC of the electricians and plumbers union EETPU. The context was the union's strategy for recruitment and sole recognition based on offering employers agreements which included elements new to British union and industrial relations traditions (such as 'final offer' or 'pendulum arbitration', and 'no-strike' clauses). However, the immediate cause of the EETPU's expulsion was its refusal to abide by a TUC ruling on spheres of influence for union recruitment, reflecting conflicts between unions, many of which had been compelled to move beyond their traditional occupational and industrial spheres during the 1980s.

An acceleration of mergers, including the readmission of the EETPU to the TUC after merger with the engineers' union AEU, may have mitigated this aspect of the crisis within the trade union movement. Moreover, despite their public prominence, the new practices introduced so controversially during the 1980s have not been widely adopted by employers.

The impact on trade union and individual employee rights of deregulation, decentralisation and the Conservative government's employment legislation has offered a striking demonstration of the vulnerability created by the absence of legally enforceable rights, in particular rights of employee representation. And ironically, the British example also illustrates that informally or only weakly secured rights can be swiftly overwhelmed by a programme of targeted statutory incursion.

The underlying aims of the Conservative government's trade union legislation must also be seen in the context of other policies on labour market flexibility and the privatisation and restructuring of the public and private sectors. In contrast to the government's eagerness to legislate to curtail informal trade union rights, the lack of regulation on issues such as forms of atypical employment – so controversial in some other EU member-states – has not been seen as problematic. For example, in contrast to many other member-states, fixed-term contracts do not require a material reason. Temporary work via agencies is not regulated as far as employment contracts are concerned: there are, for example, no limits on the length of time for which temporary workers can be employed. Although part-time work in the United Kingdom accounts for a much higher proportion of the labour force than the EU average (25 per cent compared with 13 per cent), the lack of new provisions in the field of temporary working has meant that its share of total employment did not, in fact, change markedly during the 1980s: according to European Commission sources in 1991, temporary employees accounted for about 7 per cent of all posts, virtually unchanged since 1983, compared with 10 per cent in France (up from 3 per cent in 1983) and 30 per cent in Spain (up from 16 per cent in 1983). This lack of growth of fixed-duration contracts in Britain may be attributable to the relative ease with which permanent contracts can be terminated. Dismissal protection was further weakened during the 1980s by the extension of the minimum qualifying period for bringing a complaint of unfair dismissal from 1 to 2 years in legislation introduced in 1985.

The weakening of individual rights in areas such as dismissal, combined with the overall climate of industrial relations has meant that individual employment law problems have grown in number. However, the decline in trade union representation has meant that these are now increasingly being taken by individual employees to be resolved by other sources of advice. For example, the National Association of Citizens' Advice Bureaux dealt with 850,000 employment related problems in 1991-92, an increase of 10 per cent on the previous year.

The third thrust of deregulation has taken the form of the reprivatisation of social provision. The Government's thinking is crystallised in the weakening of the state earnings related pension (SERPS) and the encouragement, through tax incentives, of private pension provision. In addition to weaknesses in regulation, the emerging system is likely to exacerbate the growing income inequalities seen in the UK during the 1980s. The large-scale sale of social housing at discount prices to tenants was also an important practical and ideological step towards individual versus social provision. Although initially popular with many tenants, rising unemployment in the recession since 1990 has exposed the fragility of private ownership of housing for lower income groups unable to pay back home loans. The UK has the highest rate of private home ownership in the European Union but also amongst the highest rates of homelessness and housing problems.

One of the first acts of the government was also the abolition of the earnings-related element of unemployment benefit. To a greater extent than in other European Union countries, the unemployment associated with economic restructuring has been a potent source of impoverishment in Britain.

Complementary to all these developments have been the various stages of privatisation of once state-owned industries – with two main motives, often difficult to disentangle. On the one hand, the privatisation programme represented a major step in the implementation of the government's free market agenda, added to which was an opportunity of mounting an attack on trade union strength in the public sector. The fostering of 'popular capitalism' through the encouragement of small-scale share ownership in some privatisations was also intended both to win short-term popularity (by being underpriced on first sale to the public via individual application, shares often jumped in value when traded on the stock market) and encourage public interest in the workings of the market. On the other hand, privatisation represented a key contribution to the public finances at a time when the government was pursuing a strategy of cutting direct taxes. Privatisation proceeds between 1980 and 1991 totalled some £40 billion. As well as privatising state-owned enterprises in manufacturing industry, often preceded by and entailing savage rationalisation, as in the case of British Steel, the government also moved to privatise public utilities such as telecommunications, gas, electricity and water. (For their part, the privatised enterprises have become active international companies in their respective fields). However, doubts about the scale of the privatisation programme have grown, especially as the difficulties in the energy market have become apparent. Plans to privatise British Rail have encountered open opposition from within the Conservative camp.

The contours of trade union policy for the 1990s are now beginning to emerge in the wake of the fourth successive victory of the Conservative Party at the 1992 General Election. Issues such as training, including more effective training of union representatives, and participation in European initiatives are expected to be given a higher profile. (The TUC opened its own European office in Brussels in November 1993.) And, as noted in Part II below, observation of the comparative security offered by statutory systems of employee representation elsewhere in Europe, has led to a willingness to explore alternatives to collective bargaining as a means of asserting employee interests.

The divisions which racked the movement in the mid 1980s have generally given way to a greater degree of acceptance of the new status quo. Manufacturing industry, for example, has seen widespread changes in working practices implemented through programmes negotiated with trade union representatives. Traditional barriers between trades and trades unions have been diluted through greater individual flexibility and the trend to single-table bargaining. And although excluded from national political influence and constrained by the raft of legislation during the 1980s, trade unions have clung onto important positions at workplace level. The public image of trade unions is also now much more positive than in the early 1980s. However, turning this into a successful drive for more members is unlikely to succeed in the face of employer hostility or lack of encouragement for collective bargaining without statutory support.

The Labour Party, should it regain power in the late 1990s, would be unlikely to reverse the bulk of the Conservative legislation, and is currently seeking to establish greater formal separation from the trade union movement. At the same time, it has committed itself to restoring and strengthening a number of individual employment rights, including rights to protection against unfair dismissal.

Greece

At first glance, the Greek trade union movement would appear to represent one of the most enduring traditions of organisational unity and continuity in Europe. The General Confederation of Greek Labour (GSEE) has been able to sustain its position as the sole representative of the interests of Greek workers ever since its foundation in 1918. (The only qualification is the existence of a separate confederation for civil servants, ADEDY.) However, this initial impression is misleading. In reality, the history of GSEE has been marked by persistent interference and misuse by the state, combined with severe internal political fragmentation, the consequences of which have continued to dog the Greek trade union movement to the present day. Although 1990 saw a major overhaul of bargaining arrangements, in which the state − in theory − has intended to withdraw from intervention in collective negotiations, this has been paralleled by a stringent incomes policy in the public sector, and a tightening of the law on industrial action.

At the root of many of the problems of Greek trade unionism lies the fact that, in contrast to developments in Spain and Portugal, the transition from dictatorship to democracy which took place in Greece in the mid 1970s was not accompanied by a fresh start in the trade union movement. Instead, the renewal of Greek trade unionism, following years of exploitation by the state and widespread political and criminal corruption, has proved to be a very protracted affair. The initial failure to sweep away the undemocratic statutes and electoral rules of the many regional craft unions meant that their leaderships, which in many cases had collaborated with the dictatorship, were able to cling onto power during the late 1970s. At the same time, those organisations which had been dissolved or restructured under the dictatorship (1967–74), representing the democratic tradition within Greek trade unionism, were excluded from involvement in many of the industry-wide and local trade union centres and federations, as well as in the decision making bodies of GSEE itself. It was not until the electoral victory of the Panhellenic Socialist Movement (PASOK) in 1981 that these democratic forces, consisting of socialist, communist and (smaller) euro-communist tendencies, were finally able to topple the GSEE leadership, a group made up of supporters of the Conservative Government which had come to power in 1975 together with various right-wing extremists.

The tradition of 'state syndicalism', in which the state controlled and partly financed the unions through a network of corporatist relationships, also continued to exhibit a remarkable resilience in the immediate wake of the transition from dictatorship. Although the 1975 Constitution contained clear provisions on the rights of association, the right to strike and free collective bargaining, in practice the system of compulsory arbitration, dating from the 1930s, and state control of trade union finance continued for several more years (see below). Attempts by the GSEE leadership to wrest some autonomy from the state consisted of little more than pronouncements which bore no practical fruit. For example, they unhesitatingly joined the tripartite Council for Employment and Social Policy (SKOP), formed in 1975, and acceded to the 1976 strike law which outlawed spontaneous political and sympathy action, legalised lock-outs, and banned strikes following compulsory arbitration. Further limitations on the right to strike were imposed in 1977 through a law which allowed the government to intervene directly in strikes and in certain cases to end them through a form of compulsory conscription of the workforce.

Resistance to this policy was, of necessity, either confined to oppositional trade union bodies or developed at workplace level in autonomous factory unions; and inevitably, protest soon came up against the limits of legality. Sustained by those workplace trade union organisations and workers' commissions, and co-ordinated by opposition currents within the trade union movement, and despite political differences which hampered more enduring co-operation, a major wave of strikes swept through Greece in the years following the end of the dictatorship, peaking at over 20,000,000 days lost through industrial action in 1980. The main focus was large companies in manufacturing industry. The strikes were aimed at raising real wages, which had been forcibly lowered during the dictatorship, cutting working hours, and improving working conditions. A large number of disputes were also triggered by conflicts between trade unions' grassroots and the GSEE leadership, as well as by state intervention in collective bargaining. The pressure exerted by this strike wave led both to increases in pay (of around 9 per cent for the period 1976–78), with a steady reduction in working time from 45 to 40 hours a week (finally reached around 1981–83) and longer holidays. GSEE was obliged to take up some of the demands raised by the strikers, such as an automatic link between pay and inflation, and in 1979 withdrew from tripartite discussions in order to avoid losing face. However, no fundamental changes in the confederation's structure took place until the change of government in 1981, a transformation heralded by cuts in real pay in 1979–80 as a result of economic recession, and by an intensification of strike action.

PASOK's victory in the 1981 parliamentary elections, in which it won an absolute majority, led to a number of important measures intended to realise free collective bargaining and promote internal trade union democracy. However, the intrinsic weaknesses of the Greek trade union movement, trapped in its corporatist past and unable to push for fundamental change in employment and collective bargaining legislation in its own right, meant that the positive changes which began to take place were largely dependent on the shifting power relations within PASOK and the Government. In 1982, in keeping with the demands of the 1979–80 strike movement, PASOK introduced a system of automatic pay indexation and a legally guaranteed four week annual holiday. 1982 – that is, eight years after the end of the dictatorship – also saw the creation of the preconditions for a fundamental renewal of the trade union system with a law (law 1264/1982) on 'the democratisation of the trade union movement and the securing of employee trade union freedoms'. In the meantime, the old leadership of GSEE had been deposed from its position by the Athens Court on application from opposition trade unionists who accused them of falsifying the last congress (1981) and rejected their claims to representativeness. The Court appointed a management board which had the task of calling a new congress within 18 months. Thanks to the new provisions of the 1982 law on trade union freedoms, this provided the opportunity for the first democratic election of union delegates. Those organisations previously excluded from the internal decision-making processes of the confederation could also participate in the elections which took place in 1983. Denied any prospect of success under the new arrangements, the old GSEE leadership decided not to contest the elections to the Board of Directors which, as a consequence, was now composed exclusively of representatives of what were formerly opposition tendencies. Twenty-six belonged to the Socialist Tendency (PASKE), seventeen to the Communist list (ESAK/S) and two to the Euro-Communists (AEM).

A further provision of the new trade union law set out to dissolve the funds through which the trade unions received direct finance from the state: unions could determine their own membership contributions or collect them through a check-off system with the co-operation of the employers. However, the lack of any agreement on a check-off system between GSEE and the central employers' confederation, SEB, delayed progress in this area. Unions were also caught in the dilemma that raising contributions could have led to a loss of members, and were often reluctant to reduce their dependence on the state. For its part, the state in the 1980s (under PASOK administration) was willing to continue provide money, and it was only with the advent of the Conservative Government in 1990 that legislation finally removed the basis of state funding (law 1915/1990 which came into force from 1 January 1992), putting Greek trade unions into serious financial straits. On the other hand, the withdrawal of state funding may accelerate independence from the state by eliminating the so-called 'paper trade unionism', which had been sustained by the fund, and whose most important function was to ensure that the old GSEE leadership secured the necessary majorities at union congresses.

The 1982 law also loosened the strict limits on the right to strike and improved dismissal protection for trade union activists. Lock-outs and the hiring of strike breakers during an industrial dispute were banned, and the possibility of sympathy action left open (see below, on the 1990 law which gave employers rights to dismiss strikers under certain circumstances). In all the 1982 law represented an attempt to bring Greek trade union legislation closer to European norms, though not advancing beyond them. Although the 1982 law created the basis for workplace union activity, such as some union facilities, it did not include provisions for workplace employee representation, such as works councils or shop stewards' committes. Legislation on works councils was passed in 1988. These have limited powers, are essentially consultative, and are not permitted to bargain or otherwise displace trade unions at workplace level (see Part II). Moreover, trade union concern about the implications of works councils has, to date, held back their development.

Although the election of the PASOK Government and the 1982 law created the foundations for a renewal of the trade unions, major problems of internal organisation as well as external political and economic difficulties have continued to confront the movement. The capacity of GSEE to tackle its internal problems, and undertake a thoroughgoing structural reform and democratisation, has been massively handicapped by the high level of political and organisational fragmentation of the movement. There are some 4,000 individual unions (of which about 2,500 are active), and over 200 middle-level federations (of which 100 are national craft unions and 100 local 'labour centres'). (Further aspects of the structure of the union movement are dealt with in the chapter on Greece in Part II, below.)

One initiative towards dealing with the system of craft unions and moving to branch and industry unions was the structure of workplace unions which developed after 1974 in well-organised large plants. The trade union tendency closest to the PASOK, PASKE, promoted their spread and was heavily involved in setting up a workplace union confederation, OBES, in 1979. However the high proportion of small and very small establishments in Greek industry meant that workplace unions were unable to develop a broad enough base to serve as the foundation for a restructuring of the trade union structure as a whole. OBES also met with determined opposition from the employers as well from critics within the trade union movement. At the same time, some successes in merging occupational unions into branch federations raised their bargaining capabilities to such an extent that even PASKE gave these preference over workplace unions in its restructuring plans. The completion of this process, however, remains a distant prospect given the serious differences of opinion between the various tendencies in GSEE on this subject. Nevertheless, there are forces both within GSEE and among employers who favour a shift from occupational to industry bargaining.

The delays and contradictions in the establishment of a truly autonomous, and cohesive trade union movement, as well as the limits on free collective bargaining (including compulsory state arbitration which remained in force until 1990 – see below), were dramatically revealed when PASOK effected a radical change of course in its economic and social policy following its second electoral victory in 1985. In the first half of the 1980s PASOK's policies of pay indexation, raising minimum wages and pensions, expanded public investment and infrastructural expenditure on health, as well as extensive nationalisation, had met with the complete support of the ruling socialist majority within GSEE. This had increasingly come to serve as shield for Government policy within the trade union movement, and forfeited the authority and independence to mount an effective opposition to PASOK's austerity policy. Its behaviour towards Government policy remained contradictory. Under the growing pressure of the grassroots membership, the increasingly strong Communist tendencies (the orthodox ESAK, and the Euro-Communist AEM) and a breakaway socialist group, official PASKE representatives resorted to a policy of internal factional struggle, once again demonstrating the lack of any real trade union autonomy and democracy.

The two-year pay pause imposed by the PASOK Government in 1985 led to substantial losses in real wages. It was renewed in 1987, with pay increases of up to 4.1 per cent allowed, compared with inflation of 20 per cent, unchecked by largely ineffective price controls. The involvement of the International Monetary Fund in the new policy was also evident in the range of measures used to tackle state indebtedness and economic stagnation: import restrictions, devaluation and a plan to restructure the state economic sector, with closures and mass dismissals. As early as 1985 trade union resistance began in the form of a wave of strikes throughout large towns.

It was not until January 1987 that GSEE found the strength to organise a widely supported 24-hour general strike against the Government's incomes policy. The Civil Service union ADEDY and the local

Association of Athens Trade Unions, which had taken a leading role in resistance to the austerity policy, managed to win a 20 per cent pay increase in a one-week strike (compared with inflation then at 22 per cent). At the end of 1987 GSEE and over half of the approximately 100 local trade union confederations called a further one-day general strike. In 1988 a further concession was successfully wrung from the Government through major industrial disputes when it agreed not to cut the automatic adjustment of wages to inflation and also concluded a national collective agreement providing for pay increases of around 10 per cent.

Greek trade unions, then, underwent an extraordinarily contradictory development during the 1980s. In the first half important progress was made on the way to autonomy and internal union democracy. The level of trade union organisation rose to an estimated 20 per cent with the main focus in the public sector and in large concerns in the manufacturing industries. The economic crisis which erupted in the mid 1980s and the consequent change in government policy, swiftly put these achievements at risk. GSEE was almost totally paralysed at times by internal political struggles and threatened to fall apart. Nevertheless, signs of an accommodation between the political factions, a broadening bargaining agenda, and a desire across all political parties and on the part of employers to modernise the industrial relations system did ultimately establish some pre-conditions for more effective and independent union activity.

Greece's continuing economic difficulties, many of which are rooted in the large state and semi-state sector and growing public indebtedness, while fostering greater 'realism' in private sector bargaining, have created scope for massive conflicts in the public sector. The election of a Conservative Government in spring 1990 opened the way to widespread privatisation, not only of many of the manufacturing and commercial concerns taken into public ownership, but also of basic services, such as the Athens buses. Pressure to curb public spending and reduce the national debt, in particular from outside institutions such as the EC, which have been providing considerable financial assistance, has also led to a severe incomes policy for public employees, provoking serious industrial action during 1992.

At the same time, law 1915/1990 clawed back some of the union gains on industrial action made in 1982, and gave rights to employers to dismiss workers who obstruct non-strikers, occupy premises or ignore court rulings. This law also finally brought to an end the arrangements under which unions received state funding.

Developments since 1990 have opened up new opportunities for the trade union movement as well as posing new hazards. In the field of collective bargaining, the most important change was made by law

1876/1990 and by the agreement reached in the private sector in 1991. The 1990 legislation has been heralded as a watershed in collective bargaining in that it finally exorcised the spectre of compulsory state arbitration and shifted the onus onto the negotiating parties to find solutions. Under the law, which became fully operative from 1 January 1992, company level bargaining will be legally recognised and fostered by granting the status of full collective agreements to bargaining outcomes in the workplace. In addition, the law establishes new conciliation, mediation and arbitration machinery to be managed and financed independently by the unions and employers. It is hoped that this will foster a maturing of industrial relations and foster a pragmatic approach to bargaining by shifting greater responsibility onto the two sides of industry, and by creating scope for the autonomous resolution of disputes.

The 1991 national private sector settlement between GSEE and the three main employers organisations (SEB, EESE and GSEBEE) also appeared to mark a new phase in bargaining: not only was agreement reached in a comparatively constructive atmosphere, but the bargaining agenda was also widened to include issues such as training and social security as well as pay. Although barely maintaining pay in real terms, the agreement, which was for two years, included an automatic trigger to raise pay in the event that inflation exceeded forecasts, and gave an additional increase from January 1992.

Republic of Ireland

Despite rapid economic growth since the late 1950s, much of which has been based on large-scale foreign direct investment in manufacturing industry, the structural origins behind Ireland's continuing underdevelopment have not been overcome. This has created a particular set of challenges for the Irish trade union movement. Whilst a large, relatively modern exporting sector – employing more than a third of the manufacturing workforce – has been established, largely due to massive state subsidies, productivity levels and incomes in national industry and agriculture have persistently lagged behind the European Community average, despite some modest convergence in the late 1980s. The industrialisation of the Irish Republic, with the creation of a technically advanced manufacturing sector, has also not brought with it any solution to the chronic problems of mass unemployment and underemployment. The 1980s saw a renewed wave of emigration, stemmed only by the onset of recession in the early 1990s which dampened employment prospects in the USA and elsewhere in Western Europe.

The fundamental problems of Ireland's lack of industrial development have also not been addressed. Rather, there has been a process of modernisation which has primarily consisted of a dramatic increase in the economy's exposure to foreign trade. Economic development, and with it the framework for social development, has become enormously vulnerable to the readiness of foreign companies to invest in Ireland and the fluctuations in the markets for Irish exports. This vulnerability was highlighted in 1993 by the decision of Digital Equipment to close down its manufacturing facility in Galway and shift production to Scotland, with a loss of 780 jobs in Ireland. At the same time, the high technology export sector itself needs to be supplied with large-scale imports of capital goods and semi-finished products. Repatriation of profits by foreign-owned companies, attracted by tax concessions, has meant that the Republic of Ireland's gross domestic product (that is, the output produced within its borders) now exceeds gross national product, the incomes actually accruing to Irish residents, by a substantial margin.

The significance of these developments for the Irish workforce in general, and the trade union movement in particular, can be seen by tracing developments from the 1970s through to the early 1990s. During the 1970s, which saw sustained levels of growth worldwide despite the recession in mid-decade, and a continuation of Keynesian policies, employment in Ireland rose by 14.1 per cent, with a sizeable drop in the rate of unemployment to 7.9 per cent by 1979. Much of this was attributable to an expansion of the public sector, where 64,000 jobs were added – a 50 per cent rise in public sector employment and a major increase when compared to total employment in industry and services of around 750,000. By contrast, the highly subsidised and capital-intensive export-oriented sector made a comparatively small contribution to employment growth with an expansion of 14.5 per cent over the period.

Given these relatively favourable conditions, the trade unions, the overwhelming majority of which are affiliated to the sole national confederation, the Irish Congress of Trade Unions (ICTU), were able to secure above average pay awards and improvements in welfare benefits. Pay bargaining, which had been decentralised for most of the 1960s, was subject to a series of efforts at greater centralisation, with attempts to make pay policy one component in a broader, state-led development strategy. In 1970, after threatening to introduce a statutory prices and incomes policy, the Government induced the ICTU and the employers' organisation, the then FUE (see below), to conclude a 'national wage agreement' to take effect from January 1971. This was informally linked to an official prices policy which went some way to meeting trade union demands. During the 1970s, a succession of such agreements were concluded, and after 1975 took on a fully tripartite character with the state linking pay deals to measures to regulate prices, tax and employment policy, and improvements in statutory benefits for workers.

By the late 1970s this model of tripartite bargaining, in which the ICTU participated in the 'national interest' of a stable social and industrial climate as the basis for faster economic development, was running into increasing difficulties. The worldwide recession halted the growth of exports, and the Irish state, which had previously played such an important role in employment growth through the public sector, ran into a serious financial crisis. The weakness of the Irish economy, and its particular susceptibility to fluctuations in world trade, forced the government to switch from the expansionist policies of the 1970s to a strategy of austerity and economic stringency, a policy reversal much more dramatic in Ireland than in the more highly developed EC countries. The national wage agreements of the 1970s ultimately foundered on both employer resistance to prescribed norms and discontent among some unions, representing skilled and specialist workers, that a central policy was inhibiting their capacity to win larger increases. The national wage agreements were supplanted in 1979 and 1980 by a National Wage Understanding, which in turn succumbed to employer determination to localise bargaining and the government's failure to meet its side of the tripartite bargain in areas such as employment and welfare provision. Moreover, the new coalition Government, led by Fine Gael, which held power between 1982 and 1987, was not interested in pursuing a formal agreement with the unions.

As with their counterparts elsewhere in Europe, the economic upheavals and restructuring of the 1970s and 1980s pushed the Irish trade union movement into a serious crisis. In contrast to Great Britain, where ideological factors played a major role, the change in the industrial climate in Ireland was primarily the result of immediate economic pressures. The comparative political weakness of the Irish labour movement, which does not have the equivalent of the direct relationship between British unions and the Labour Party, has led to the real power base of the Irish movement being very directly tied to its capacity to organise and mobilise in the workplace. This power was put under severe pressure by rising unemployment during the 1980s, up from 7.9 per cent in 1979 to almost 20 per cent from the mid 1980s (and into the 1990s). Increased union organisation at the end of the 1970s boosted union density to a peak of 55 per cent in 1979. However, this was followed by a marked drop in 1981, when membership levels suffered their biggest decline ever. Between 1980 and 1984 membership dropped from 525,000 to 500,000, down to 45 per cent of the workforce. The decentralisation of collective bargaining between 1982 and 1987, combined with rising unemployment and a tougher response from the employers, resulted in a sharp fall in industrial action. 'Regaining managerial control' became a central theme in public discussion, and a number of private sector employers began to devise and import strategies for bypassing and weakening the unions. Subsidiaries of foreign-owned multinationals, notably in the electronics industry, were particularly active in the development of new methods of human resource management, the implementation of which was made easier by the fact that much of the newly settled industry was located in greenfield sites away from traditional industrial areas. Public sector companies, which still employed around a tenth of the workforce despite government spending cuts, tried to discipline unions by demanding 'realism', pleading the desperate state of government finances; this demand then served as the driving force behind lower settlements and cuts in real pay.

Given this balance of policial and social power, it was inevitable that, in addition to the burden carried by the unemployed, it was the workforce which bore the brunt of the economic crisis. Real pay fell in the early 1980s, and did not regain 1979 levels until 1986. In the meantime, taxation rose to such an extent that net incomes in 1986 were some 10 per cent below their 1979 levels. There was also a widening of differentials between categories of employee in the private sector. Atypical working (such as part-time work and fixed-term contracts), which is not covered by statutory dismissal protection, became more widespread. The trend towards low pay and less job security, particularly prevalent in sectors with low union organisation such as commerce, food and drink and clerical work, was especially marked for women and workers in their first job, and signalled a major setback to the ICTU's campaign against low pay. Highly unionised sectors, such as manufacturing industry, banking and insurance, suffered as a result of the restructuring of employment, posing serious problems of trade union membership recruitment and retention.

ICTU unions undertook a number of policy reviews in the early 1980s. In 1981 the largest individual union, the ITGWU (Irish Transport and General Workers' Union – since 1990 merged to form SIPTU) initiated a discussion on union strategies on new technology. Its aim was to shift unions from a purely defensive stance and it proposed a national agreement with employers to cover information disclosure, the conclusion of company level agreements, job security, professional qualifications, protection against dismissal and cuts in working time. Although this approach did not meet with success, other union demands on new technology, such as a campaign for state action on training, were met to some degree. (Advertising Ireland's highly skilled workforce and low wage costs are at the heart of government efforts to attract foreign investment to Ireland.)

A debate on the equality of women in employment, also initiated by the ITGWU, resulted in a series of action programmes being agreed at the 1982 ICTU annual congress. Model anti-discrimination clauses for inclusion in company agreements on pay, promotion and sexual harassment at the workplace were drawn up and a training programme for female members of the trade union executive was developed. Although accounting for perhaps around a third of trade union membership (but maybe as low as a tenth according to some estimates), roughly in proportion to their numbers in the workforce, women were greatly under-represented at senior levels in the movement. Another important reason why female employment issues emerged as a focal point in union deliberations was the particularly severe impact of the crisis on women workers, who were especially exposed to cuts in pay levels, widening differentials, diminished job security and the deregulation of the labour market. Not only were women over-represented in traditional low-wage industries, such as textiles, clothing and leather, leading to average weekly pay of barely 60 per cent of male levels, but were also caught up in the wave of change which hit the service sector. The anti-discrimination laws introduced in 1974 and 1977, corresponding to EC Directives, would have been ineffective without complementary trade union efforts to secure collectively agreed and statutory protection for part-timers and those on fixed term contracts of less than twelve months. According to the ICTU, around 8 per cent of the workforce was employed on a part-time basis in 1986, the overwhelming majority of them women. Most were employed for less than eighteen hours a week so that they would not be covered by the general statutory protection enjoyed by employees under Irish law. They therefore had no right to: a written contract of employment; protection against, or notice of, dismissal; paid holiday or maternity leave. Social security protection was restricted to general medical care and protection in the case of industrial accidents. The ICTU mainly wanted to see parity of hourly rates with full-time employees, daily sick pay, pension cover, paid holiday and inclusion in company training programmes for these employees.

These efforts to overcome the new difficulties facing trade union policy were hampered by a widespread failure to maintain workers' real incomes. In 1984, in an effort to regain the initiative, the ICTU's annual congress approved a programme entitled 'Facing the Employment Crisis' which proposed a number of measures for tackling the general social and economic crisis in Ireland well before the political parties had come up with any proposals. The ICTU called for negotiations between the government and the ICTU on a medium-term Programme for National Recovery (PNR) to embrace economic policy, tax reform instead of tax cuts, stabilisation of foreign trade, maintenance of the social security system, the development and strategic use of the public finance sector, and an active employment policy.

The Government of the time, a Fine Gael-Labour Party coalition, was unwilling to take up the ICTU's offer and continued the policy of austerity embarked upon in 1982. The government hoped to solve the problem of unemployment by providing incentives to small firms and expanding public building projects. In 1987 the coalition was brought down by the refusal of the Labour Party to endorse further cuts in spending on health and education. Although output recovered strongly in 1987 (up 5 per cent compared with a drop of 1 per cent in 1986) and the balance of trade was out of the red, unemployment rose to a disastrous 18.6 per cent of the labour force.

Immediately on taking office in 1987, the minority Fianna Fail Government under Charles Haughey cut back recruitment and froze pay in the public sector. Then, in October 1987, the government, the trade unions and the main employers' organisations agreed a three-year Programme for National Recovery which, at least in theory, came close to many union aspirations. Under the PNR, the Government accepted responsibility for implementing economic and financial policies not only aimed at stringency in the conduct of public finances but also at curbing inflation and keeping interest rates down, lowering taxation levels for employees (and hence widening the tax base), and giving priority to national industries in employment matters (while still taking care to meet the needs of foreign investors). In return, unions and employers agreed to keep wage increases down to a maximum of 2-3 per cent from 1988-90 with special provisions for the low paid. Although the pay guidelines were not binding, compliance was overwhelming: over 90 per cent of companies implemented the agreed terms. Under a provision in the PNR, negotiations between employers and unions on a cut in the working week from forty to thirty-nine hours by 1990 began in 1988, and hours cuts in many industries and firms were implemented during 1989–90. This was a breakthrough as employers had until then steadfastly refused to negotiate on this matter.

New legislation on industrial relations was also introduced under the PNR providing new procedures for conciliation and the resolution of industrial disputes, mandatory strike ballots, and the banning of *ex parte* injunctions by employers to stop industrial action. The new arrangements were broadly welcomed by the ICTU.

Although the PNR did encounter criticism and the expression of reservations from within the union movement, especially in the year after the agreement began, rapid economic growth and a fall in inflation over the period 1987–90 helped win support for further efforts at a tripartite settlement to follow it. The employers had strongly supported the plan, but were eager to obtain greater flexibility on the implementation of pay guidelines. Moreover, Irish trade unionists recognised that the alternative to an accommodation with the Government might be the exclusion of the unions from the broad range of economic and industrial policy, as seen in the UK.

The Programme for Economic and Social Progress (PESP), agreed and ratified by the ICTU and the employers' organisation (FIE) in the early part of 1991, not only contained provisions on pay, but also – like its predecessor – a number of aims and commitments on taxation, job creation, protecting social welfare spending, and various items of employment protection legislation. Under the pay clause of the three-year programme (1991/92/93), pay increases were to range from 4 per cent in the first year to 3.75 per cent in the third, slightly ahead of expected inflation; minimum cash increases provided some additional protection for the lower paid. In addition, and in response to criticisms that the PNR was excessively rigid, some scope weas included for extra locally negotiated increases of approximately 3 per cent from the second year of the PESP. According to the newly formed employer's organisation IBEC, around 65 per cent of firms had made use of the scope for local bargaining, with extra increases paid in exchange for changes in work practices.

On jobs, the government and employers made a commitment to create 20,000 jobs a year in manufacturing and 'international services', together with schemes, some of which are subsidised by the EC, for improved local training opportunities.

The two phases of incomes policy have brought a period of relative stability in Irish industrial relations, with most disputes in recent years confined to the public sector. Despite some difficulties in negotiating a successor to PESP, there remains a widespread conviction in the ICTU that, given the unstable economic context within which the Irish economy has to operate, a national consensus on economic objectives offers many benefits. ICTU has advocated active intervention by the state, at both national and Community level, to bring about the social dimension of integration and real parity of economic development. As yet, it still remains uncertain how, and whether, this is to be achieved. In the first place, the aid available (until 1993) from the EC's Structural Fund under the tripartite programmes does not appear to be sufficiently large to effect any real structural change. Secondly, the Irish trade union movement has not yet either convincingly asserted its position within the framework of industrial relations or undergone a thoroughgoing restructuring. The traditional pattern of general unions, organising across industries, co-existing with craft unions still prevails. Rationalisation has taken place in the form of a series of union mergers, rather than, for example, the establishment of industrial unions. At the same time, the onset of recession and the incorporation of the unions into tripartite programmes have weakened union bargaining power and diminished the scope for independent criticism of government policy. This raises the question of how the ICTU will carry out the task it set itself of acting as the main guarantor that the social dimension of European integration is taken account of, and that its concerns will play a role in the continuing restructuring of the Irish economy.

Italy

The postwar course of Italian trade union history has been marked by three major breaks. Each has left a legacy which continues to shape the state of the movement in the early 1990s. Shortly after the Second World War the single non-party trade union confederation established in 1944 broke up into three individual, ideologically defined confederations. The largest, the CGIL (*Confederazione Generale Italiana del Lavoro*) retained the name of the original single confederation, but came under the control of the Communist Party, even though around a third of the membership has continued to be more broadly socialist. In 1990 the CGIL had around 5 million members, of which just over 45 per cent were retired or unemployed. The Catholic CSIL (*Confederazione Italiana dei Sindacati Lavoratori*) currently has around 3.3 million members, of which approximately 40 per cent are retired or unemployed. The social democratic UIL (*Unione Italiana del Lavoro*), closely aligned with the Italian Socialist Party (PSI), has some 1.4 million members, of which 80 per cent are in employment.

In practice, these political divisions have been much more significant at national and central level than in everyday union activity at the workplace. Italian trade unions provide a classical example of local pragmatic co-operation on specific issues combined with publicly aired differences over broader questions of policy and ideology. Indeed, the collapse of the Socialist Party and fragmentation of Christian Democracy may serve to strengthen local-level co-operation. Union density, excluding the large numbers of retired and unemployed members, fell from around 50 per cent at the beginning of the 1980s to just under 40 per cent by 1990. There were marked declines in the level of union organisation in the service sector, a less pronounced drop in manufacturing and agriculture (traditionally highly unionised), and a maintenance of organisation in the public sector, where grassroots unions operating on a sectional basis (the *Comitati di Base* or *Cobas* for short) have sprung up parallel to and challenging the existing confederations. Following the break-up of the old party system in 1993, new trade unions

56

aligned with the Northern League and extreme right have emerged, and are challenging for representational rights.

The second break took place at the end of the 1960s, following a decade in which union influence on Italian society had steadily declined. Following a phase of explosive labour disputes (the 'Hot Autumn' of 1969), there was a period of swift and intense social development which took the form of the securing of basic trade union rights in the 1970 Workers' Statute, a growing identification by employees with their newly created grassroots workplace organisations (also the most basic unit of trade union organisation), and a radical questioning of traditional views of work, with demands for greater humanisation of the production process and improved conditions, especially for the less skilled.

This phase of developing Italian trade union power ended in 1980 in the third break, which took place in the context of a broader social and economic crisis, an increasing drive for workplace flexibility and an erosion of customary ideas of employee solidarity. The most significant single event in this period was the defeat of a strike by the engineering unions, and especially the local organisation, at Fiat, the country's largest private employer. One of the most decisive moments in what proved to be a historic setback was the decision by middle managers, technicians and supervisors to demonstrate against what they saw as a politically motivated strike, and to argue for a more differentiated and less egalitarian pay and employment policy. This public display of disunity and divergent interests led to a re-opening of the old ideological divides between the union confederations, the abandonment of initiatives towards a unified structure of trade union representation at the workplace (exemplified in the integrated engineering union, the FLN) and a ceding of power by local level union organisations to the centre which has persisted until today.

Following the collapse of the tripartite accords between the union confederations, the employers (*Confindustria*) and the Christian Democrat/Socialist coalition over government proposals to curb the operation of the system of pay indexation (the *scala mobile*) in 1984–85, co-operation between the three union confederations also broke down. The Italian trade union movement subsequently entered a phase of crisis characterised by substantial workforce reductions, especially of manual workers, and a restructuring of production by employers into a network of small and medium-sized firms and units, with insecure and informal employment, combined with a small number of giant establishments. The traditional basis of union power at the workplace, the 'mass worker' who had been the driving force behind the union revival of the late 1960s, was increasingly displaced by traditionally weakly organised groups such as white-collar workers, technical specialists, and women.

Scope for trade union activity was constrained not only by factors within the system of industrial relations, but also by the broader context of Italian society. Relations between the trade union confederations dipped to a low point following the referendum over changes to the *scala mobile* in 1984, which the Communist Party (PCI) called for – but then lost. Practical co-operation has continued, both in bargaining at industry and company level, and in continued dialogue with government on such issues as continuing reform of pay indexation (finally abolished in 1992), changes in legislation on collective dismissals (to incorporate EC law and modify substantially the operation of the special lay-off fund, the *Cassa Integrazione*), and individual employment protection. Whereas some of the measures have extended employee rights, for example by offering access to dismissal protection legislation in small firms, others have signified union acquiescence in employer and government efforts to curb labour cost growth and rein back public spending (see below). The unions have also been confronted with a new range of tasks at workplace level, in particular the need to influence the rapid transformations in both technology and work organisation, and the impact of new skills. At central level, the government's desire to pursue cuts in public spending and a thorough reform of industrial relations have created new pressures on union leaderships vis-à-vis their own rank and file – a factor compounded for the CGIL by the reformation of the Communist Party leading to a breakaway faction joined by some industrial militants (see below).

Alongside this, and often overlaying the conflict between capital and labour, has been the issue of core versus peripheral workforces, and the co-existence of a generally highly-regulated labour market with a huge informal, unprotected sector. Within the broader social and economic context, the North-South divide, deregulation, the pursuit of flexibility, poorly administered and often inadequate state benefits combined with extremely high state indebtedness, high unemployment and high inflation have all posed a problematic new context for trade union activity, and demanded more finely tuned responses. All these pressures have been intensified by the contents of the Maastricht Treaty, whose criteria for economic convergence as a prelude to European Monetary Union have led the Government to introduce drastic savings in public spending and to abandon pay indexation. In July 1993, the central employer's association *Confindustria*, the three trade union confederations and the government agreed a new structure for collective bargaining to replace the arrangements which had accompanied the pay indexation system abolished in July 1992. Under the new system, industry level bargaining will take place every four years, instead of the previous triennial pattern, where general conditions of employment are involved. However, pay bargaining will take place every two years, and will be conducted in the light of projected inflation as well as the general economic situation in the branch concerned. Industry agreements will also define the scope for company level bargaining which – it is intended – will be tied to the achievement of objectives agreed at company/workplace level (such as productivity, quality) as well as ability to pay. In order to accelerate the pace of industry level negotiations, temporary interim payments, equal to 30 per cent of the projected inflation rate, will be made to employees if no new agreement is signed within three months following the expiry of a pay agreement.

The July 1993 pact also confirms the March 1991 inter-union agreement on workplace employee representation, established to strengthen the position of the main federations and confer greater legitimacy on workplace representatives (see below).

A pattern is emerging in Italy of division into three very differing regions, measured in terms of economic performance and living standards: a highly industrialised North with large-scale manufacturing and 'sunrise' industries; an aspirant central region of small and medium-sized firms engaged in textiles, electrical engineering and supply industries to large companies, with a rapidly expanding informal economy characterised by precarious forms of employment; and thirdly, the traditionally underdeveloped South still dominated by the structures of small-scale agriculture and plagued by persistently high unemployment. These three zones, which differ profoundly in terms of both economic organisation and the patterns of everyday life, require the trade unions to develop varying, and to some degree contradictory, approaches to organisation and to tackling social problems: in the North, a combination of traditional industrial unionism combined with fresh approaches to the recruitment of emerging groups of highly skilled white-collar workers; in the centre, a strengthening of decentralised workplace organisation and an engagement with newly flexibilised and precarious forms of employment; and in the South, measures to combat political apathy, the Mafia and unemployment, conceived more as social rather than classically trade union tasks. Combining all three is evidently a task which can never be performed wholly successfully, and moreover is one which imposes great strains on the unions' organisational resources.

As noted above, high state indebtedness in tandem with generally poor state benefits have created further challenges for Italian trade unions. The underlying cause of this, at first sight astonishing, paradox is primarily massive tax evasion by industrial capital, property owners and businesses; employees, by contrast, cannot evade the net and are highly taxed. At present, over 70 per cent of total tax revenue and obligatory social insurance contributions is raised from the dependent workforce. This enduring injustice, the target of repeated criticism in

Italy, has in fact proved to be a source of some prestige for the trade unions who have been able to present themselves as representatives of fair taxation and social justice – a status which has certainly contributed to their ability to remain well in line with average levels of union organisation in the European Union.

However, the union position is problematic in many spheres of the public sector, such as schools, the health service and public transport. Although public employees are often markedly underpaid, they also frequently enjoy lifetime job security. Given average national unemployment of just over 10.5 per cent and youth unemployment approaching 40 per cent, this has led, at the very least, to an ambivalent public attitude towards their calls for better pay and conditions, an ambivalence shared by the established trade unions in the face of public concern. In recent years, the lack of clear union support for some demands raised by public sector workers has, in turn, prompted a growth in grassroots activism, especially in schools, involving the formation of *Cobas* to bypass the existing unions. Under the threat of strike action, they have been able to enter into negotiations with the public authorities and win improvements. Together with the growth of so-called autonomous organisations, primarily of highly skilled employees and the self-employed, which are independent of the trade unions, this organisational competition has become a serious threat to the established power and status of the main confederations. The danger is heightened by the fact that the introduction of new technology has often involved the application of 'soft management' techniques and the encouragement of corporate cultures focused on the notion of the self-motivating 'responsible' skilled worker. These developments have been accompanied by a growing individualisation which the unions have not yet been able to respond to in a way which holds out the hope of securing their organisational strength in the longer term. Such trends also parallel the contrast between the highly organised undertakings within the public sector (the state holding companies ENI and IRI), which are now in serious structural crisis, and the flourishing sphere of new, small and medium-sized firms with their often precarious forms of employment and extremely low level of trade union organisation.

Given the multiplicity of problems confronting the trade unions in what is rapidly becoming an increasingly unfavourable social and economic context, the Italian movement can certainly expect a difficult period in the 1990s. Measured against the 'ordered' and comparatively stable structures of some north European, social democratic trade union movements, which have weathered the crisis reasonably intact, the situation in Italy is both complex and fluid. On balance, the risks and difficulties confronting trade unionism appear to be greater than the scope for positive developments. However, there are a number of possible openings through which the unions might be able to regain some control over events, for themselves and the members they represent, in order to consolidate their position as an influential, rather than a marginal, force in Italian society. These opportunities are rooted in four fundamental trends.

— The threat to the three official trade union confederations from the emergence of new conflicts of interest in the service and public sectors (the so-called 'tertiarisation of conflict'), as a result of the decentralised strikes organised by the *Cobas* and autonomous groups, has been taken very seriously. In 1990, it led to an unprecedented readiness on the part of the established unions to accept legal regulation of the right to strike in essential services, and to participate constructively in the drafting of the statute (Law 146/1990). The law provides for the maintenance of minimum services in areas deemed essential 'to guarantee basic human rights to life, health, liberty, security, welfare, education and freedom of communication', the vast bulk of which are provided by the public sector. The level of service can be precisely defined by collective agreement, with an obligation on named individuals to report for work if necessary. This practice of 'requisitioning' employees (*la precettazione*) has in fact been in existence since the 1930s. Unions must give ten days' notice of strike action to the employers, and these in turn must give five days' warning to the public. Infringements of the law can include fines and suspension, but not dismissal. As in Great Britain, some degree of legalisation of industrial relations is no longer regarded purely and simply as an attack on individual autonomy but as a means of offering collective protection against deregulation in situations of economic crisis.

— A step in a similar direction can be seen in the willingness of the union confederations to put their workplace representative structures on a more formal basis, and with that, finally lay to rest the myth of factory councils (which has failed to correspond to reality since the 1984 Fiat strike at the latest). A major step was made with the agreement between the confederations in spring 1991 to change electoral procedures for workplace representatives, and introduce a greater degree of discipline in the conduct of these bodies and their relationship with official union organisations. One of the main aims of the agreement has been to give greater legitimacy to workplace bodies, through regular elections and voting rights for non-unionists, together with minimum levels of support for candidates, in order to forestall complaints by sectional groups that agreements negotiated at workplace level are invalid.

— The rapid expansion of very small-scale plants, often suppliers within the informal economy, in the north east and central region of Italy has created an urgent need for regulation on issues such as dismissal protection, safety, pay in accordance with agreed minima, and working time. Legislation passed on 1 May 1990 marked an important step forward in dismissal protection in small firms. Further trade union successes in this sphere could open up a potential membership of several million members, as yet almost wholly untapped and unrepresented.

— The collapse of communism in Eastern European has accelerated the pace of political transformation, already long since underway, within the Italian left. In 1991, as alluded to above, the Italian Communist Party (PCI) renamed itself the Party of the Democratic Left (PDS), in a further step towards distancing the organisation from its ideological roots. The move triggered a split in the Party, with a leftist group constituting itself as Communist Refoundation (*Rifondazione Comunista*), and attracting former PCI members and CGIL militants. Nevertheless, the way traditional ideologies within the CGIL have been played down has been seen as an important step in boosting the public standing of the union, undermined in the past by the political motivation behind the Fiat strike and *scala mobile* referendum. Viewed against this background, the need for multi-party government coalitions – often judged to be a factor contributing to instability in Italy – and the consequent need for compromise could have a positive influence on efforts to reunite the three confederations, reflecting hopes for trade union collaboration which have never been entirely abandoned. Such purposes might also be promoted by further political realignments in the wake of the rise of the Northern Leagues, the corruption scandals which have shaken the Socialist Party, and the discontent within the loose factional alliance which makes up Christian Democracy. As elsewhere in Europe, how the mixture of socialist, social democratic and Christian democratic influences in the Italian trade union movement develop in future will depend crucially on developments in Eastern Europe on the one hand, and the progress of the social dimension in the EU's single market programme on the other.

Luxembourg

The outbreak of the crisis in the steel industry in the mid 1970s, and the problems of industrial restructuring, rationalisation and cuts in capacity which followed, confronted the trade union movement in Luxembourg with the task of countering the urgent and unavoidable pressures for change with a cohesive and comprehensive stragegy of their own. Not only was it necessary for such a strategy to respond to the economic and social issues raised by the process of restructuring: it also had to indicate how trade union policy positions could be practically realised. From the outset, the so-called 'Luxembourg model' of crisis resolution which developed in response to these challenges, and which was characterised by institutionalised negotiations between trade unions, management at corporate and national level and the government, bore the imprint of the unique features of Luxembourg's economy. Of the total of 150,000 wage and salary earners in the country in 1975, some 29,000 (that is, around a fifth) were employed in the iron and steel industry which accounted for 41 per cent of national industrial output, 61 per cent of exports and was almost wholly owned by the ARBED company. Resolving and surmounting the steel crisis in such a small country, in which this one industry played such a dominant role, inevitably entailed a much greater degree of change in the pattern of social and economic life than in the larger neighbouring economies of Belgium, France and Germany. The significance of EC steel policy, within broader moves towards European integration, was also commensurately greater.

One crucial precondition for union successes in the struggle over measures to cushion the impact of economic restructuring was the progress achieved in the latter part of the 1970s in tackling the movement's own internal divisions. Two main lines of division run through the trade union movement in Luxembourg: one is political, and the other is by employee category. In the 1970s, there was a political division between the social democratic oriented, majority movement, grouped around the Luxembourg Workers' Union (LAV) and the Luxembourg

Christian Trade Union Federation (LCGB). In sociological terms, there was also the traditional separation between manual trade unions and independent white-collar associations. In the late 1970s, however, an internal crisis prompted the leadership of the independent Union of Private Sector Staff Employees (FEP) to accept the long-standing offer of the LAV to establish a unitary trade union centre.

The founding of the 'Independent Trade Union Confederation of Luxembourg' (OGB-L) in 1979 represented a decisive step towards overcoming the traditional occupational divisions of the trade union movement in Luxembourg. The proposal made by the FEP to LAV was for the establishment of a unitary non-political trade union confederation bringing together the Bank and Insurance Workers Union (ALEBA) and the Artisans Union (NHV). However, apart from the LAV, none of these organisations was ultimately willing to disband itself in the context of the planned merger. The FEP and ALEBA were divided on the issue, and only some sections of their membership and leadership joined the OGB-L. After a short initial involvement the LCGB withdrew entirely from the project.

Although the foundation of the OGB-L did not succeed in establishing a wholly unified trade union movement, it did create a representative organisation able to assume leadership, if not entirely undisputed, in subsequent conflicts over the form and substance of economic restructuring. Given the rapid growth in the share of employment accounted for by the service sector (up from 47 per cent in 1974 to 68 per cent in 1991), the broader social and economic base represented by the OGB-L has acquired an importance beyond the internal question of securing greater union cohesiveness in collective bargaining.

However, the distance which the trade union movement in Luxembourg still has to travel to achieve unity is revealed by the relative size of its various contending organisations. The level of union density in 1990 stood at 66 per cent of the employed workforce, with around 100,000 members in all. Of these, some 35,000 were members of the OGB-L, with a further 8,000 employees in the transport, civil service and white-collar union FNCTTFEL, and 1,000 members in the print and media industry union FLTL, both of which co-operate with OGB-L. The LCGB has 21,000 members, with the remaining union membership scattered over around half a dozen independent white collar and occupational unions. The largest of these is the public sector white-collar union, the CGFP, with 15,000 members: the CGFP has usually opposed the positions advanced by the OGB-L in tripartite negotiations.

The history of the 'Tripartite' (*Comité de Co-ordination Tripartite* – CCT), established to tackle the economic crisis of the 1970s, has its origins in a large-scale campaign initiated by the LAV in the mid 1970s for the establishment of an 'action committee' of the government, trade unions and employers. One of the high points of this mobilisation was a large demonstration in 1976, involving all the trade unions in Luxembourg, to demand the setting up of such a tripartite body. The CCT was subsequently established by statute in 1977. Its initial task was the joint formulation of a national strategy for the structural adjustment of the economy to the new situation on the world market, at the core of which lay the restructuring of the steel industry. In 1979, the CCT established a separate steel committee in which the OGB-L took on the leadership role for the union side from the outset.

From its inception, therefore, the policies pursued by the OGB-L involved linking the traditional tasks of representing its members with a much broader engagement in economic restructuring. The chief aim of the OGB-L was to win income and employment guarantees in the steel sector. This took the form of two main demands, which the trade unions were able to win in exchange for a commitment to maintain industrial peace in the steel industry: these were i) a slowdown in the pace of redundancies and ii) government financial support for severance schemes. Specifically, the agreement provided for an extensive, state-supported, investment programme by ARBED. 16,500 jobs were to be guaranteed in the steel industry, and a further 7,500 jobs created to offset those lost by rationalisation.

At the level of the economy as a whole, the OGB-L's view was that manufacturing industry had to diversify, both to create fresh employment and to avoid a new dependency on a limited range of service industries, which were expanding rapidly. The unions also opposed attempts by the steel employers to shrink the industry by closing important areas of production (or relocating them to France and Belgium), leaving only a rump no longer able to engage in a broad range of manufacturing processes. The change of government to a Liberal/ Conservative coalition in 1979, and the withdrawal of the LCGB from the steel committee in the same year, seriously undermined the pursuit of this objective. The OGB-L was obliged to expend a good deal of energy simply persuading the incoming Government to negotiate over the gathering financial crisis at ARBED, and agreeing measures to tackle the consequences of the massive downturn in the fortunes of the steel industry during the recession of 1980.

In an additional agreement, signed and passed as a law in 1981, the 1979 accord was renewed, but ARBED's financial problems were left essentially unresolved. The company's management sought to impose wage cuts and after a further collapse in the steel market in 1982/83, the acute financial crisis at ARBED compelled the union side (represented by the OGB-L and LCGB) to accept an average pay cut of 6 per cent during 1983 and 1984. For the OGB-L a reappraisal of its involvement in the steel committee now became inevitable. In the course of this debate, it emerged that plant closures which had been unilaterally decided by the employers and a faster pace of job loss had meant that, instead of the 16,500 jobs which were to be retained in the steel industry under the agreement, only 12,500 had in fact been kept. Moreover, only one third of the intended 7,500 replacement jobs had been created. Although this employment gap of 9,000 jobs was very considerable, the OGB-L trade unions concluded that their involvement in tripartite and other company level discussions (for example, in the form of an 'employment pool' organised with an 'Anti-crisis Department' at ARBED) had been successful in preventing an even more devastating employment catastrophe.

From the standpoint of the OGB-L, one reason for the failure of its efforts in some areas, besides the policies of the Government which had wanted to cut steel jobs to 8,500, was the European Community's policy on steel. The OGB-L considered that ARBED's management, with the secret complicity of the Government, had exploited the restrictive conditions imposed by the European Commission for the restructuring of the Luxembourg steel industry in order to exclude the Tripartite Committee, and with it the trade union side, from key decisions and to cut capacity beyond the scale ageed in the tripartite meetings. Although the unions tried to forestall this strategy through a number of direct approaches to the European Commission, they failed to win their demands. This experience, coupled with the policy of relocating production to France and Belgium pursued by both the Government and ARBED, led the OGB-L to step up its efforts at co-operation with unions in those countries. One early opportunity for cross-border solidarity was offered by the Belgian–Luxembourg steel pact of 1984, which involved the closure of a plant in Liège. The strike which followed at the Liège plant was supported by the workers at ARBED through a refusal to make up for any production shortfalls by working overtime. In response, the steel workers in Liège took part in a protest demonstration against a plant closure in Luxembourg.

Limited in its scope for shaping events within the various tripartite organisations (see Part II, below), the OGB-L shifted its emphasis to representing the immediate interests of its members. In addition to mobilising against plant closures, in which it drew support from local authorities in affected regions, it also campaigned against the Government's austerity policy and the weakening, and finally the abandonment in 1982, of the automatic link between pay and prices. The high point of this campaign was a 40,000-strong demonstration and a 24-hour national strike, called jointly by the OGB-L and all other trade unions in Luxembourg. In 1986, the Government, which had recently been re-elected, resumed pay indexation.

In the meantime ARBED had completed a drastic slimming down, in which more than half of the workforce had been cut, and in 1986, the company's financial position had stabilised. Through the 1980s, a major shift in employment had thus taken place towards the services, led in particular by an expansion in the banking sector. By 1989 it employed 15,500 staff of which 40 per cent were border workers. Despite some successes in attracting a number of new manufacturing plants (including flat glass production and aluminium manufacture), economic growth was becoming highly imbalanced in a process which the OGB-L viewed as potentially dangerous for both economic development and employment.

Within the Tripartite Committee, which had been revived in the meantime, the OGB-L initiated negotiations on an employment programme and achieved the preparation of an assessment of Luxembourg's status in the emerging Single Market, with particular emphasis on the 'social dimension'. However, the easing of economic conditions in the late 1980s reduced the significance of this body within the work of OGB-L trade unions compared with the earlier period of acute economic crisis. Nevertheless, Luxembourg's exposure to the downturn beginning in 1991 could once again put pressure both on bargaining and the machinery of consensus.

From the mid 1980s, the OGB-L began to redirect its attention to issues more immediately related to its members' interests. For example, it renewed its efforts to harmonise employment and social legislation for workers, salaried employees and civil servants and for improvements in the system of automatic pay indexation to help the low paid. Within collective bargaining, the confederation also sought to bolster its claim to representativeness. Its bargaining agenda included, first and foremost, a simplification of the pay system, and secondly, qualitative demands (in particular, on the introduction of new technology). Working time reductions were regarded as a central strategy to combat unemployment (at 1.5 per cent low by comparison with other EC member states) without agreement as to any one model (daily, weekly, annual or lifetime). Broader economic demands, such as reversing deindustrialisation and implementating modernisation and diversification, were still raised but took a back seat compared with the relatively successful pursuit of social policy aims such as pension reform, introduction of a guaranteed minimum income, and improvements to the health service. Finally, in order to counter the growing flexibility of employment, there was a demand for legal regulation of part-time work, and a complete ban on agency employment.

The OGB-L's 1989 congress, which marked the tenth anniversary of the organisation, reaffirmed the confederation's aspiration to establish a single trade union movement and set new directions for the future.

Although the OGB-L remained committed to future participation in tripartite negotiations, it indicated its determination to resist further cuts in social provision. This was highlighted in April 1992, when both the OGB-L and the LCGB called a national day of action in protest against proposed changes to the system of sickness insurence. For the unions which made up the OGB-L, the Tripartite was primarily a means for averting the most dramatic consequences of the crisis in the steel industry and was seen as having fulfilled its principal aim through the extensive, and largely successful, restructuring of the national economy. It was not seen as an institution for permanent social partnership for which other institutions exist (see Part II). Union support for European integration was likewise conditional on the maintenance of levels of social provision. The OGB-L's determination to back these claims by action was illustrated by its mobilisation for a general strike in support of pension reform, a 35-hour week and a number of other demands in the area of social, health and environment policy.

Netherlands

The profound changes of the 1980s hit the Netherlands especially hard in a number of respects. The participation rate – that is, the ratio of the potential working population (aged fifteen to sixty-five years) to those actually in gainful employment – is now the lowest in Europe. Compared to the highly industrialised countries of the western Europe, the goods producing sector in the Netherlands is proportionally the smallest in Europe (at 20 per cent) and its loss of industrial jobs in the 1980s, together with Great Britain, the greatest. The fall in the level of trade union organisation was correspondingly dramatic: union density fell from 37.4 per cent in 1975 to around 26 per cent by 1988 – again, with Great Britain, the most rapid fall in the EC. But, this swift decline in trade union influence is not in any way attributable to deliberate anti-union measures by the government. On the contrary, Dutch corporatism has not been *formally* abandoned by any of the social partners.

However, and this may well be one of the most important conclusions to be drawn from the Dutch experience, the tripartite corporatist institutions established in the immediate post-war period, such as the Labour Foundation or the Social and Economic Council (see too Part II) have proved utterly unequal to the task of managing the crisis with the traditional tools of welfare state Keynesianism. That is, the neo-liberal economic policies pursued by the centre-right governments of the 1980s have succeeded in improving the environment for private economic activity, withdrawing the state from the management of the economy, imposing public finance stringency and presiding over levels of unemployment which hovered at around 12 per cent in the first half of the 1980s without impinging on the basic institutions of Dutch corporatism. Whether the grand coalition of the Christian Democrats and the Labour Party with Finance Minister Wim Kok (formerly General Secretary of the largest Dutch trade union centre, FNV) proves able or willing to undertake any fundamental change in this situation is highly questionable. Rather, the policies pursued by the coalition appear to have triggered conflict within the Labour Party (PvdA), and between it and the union movement, under the pressures for austerity of the early 1990s. The Netherlands is confronted by a set of circumstances, some the product of its own history, others obviously caused by global trends, which have served to foster de-industrialisation – a trend exacerbated by the process of European integration.

— The country's comparatively late industrialisation was not completed until the 1950s and even at its peak only absorbed around a third of the employed workforce.
— Its agricultural sector remains large in comparison with other north and central European countries.
— The industrial sector is primarily concerned with commerce and transport, mass manufacturing with high capital intensity and a high energy content, and a relatively low rate of innovation.
— The Netherlands operates an extremely open economy, which is therefore vulnerable to external developments, and in which exports and imports account for around 50 per cent of domestic product. Given the rapidly developing Single Market, it is virtually inconceivable that the Netherlands could pursue an autonomous economic policy, even to a minor degree.
— Finally, one major reason for the high degree of dependency of the state on decisions made by private capital is the domination of the Dutch economy and labour market by large multinational concerns (Shell, Philips, Akzo, Unilever). During the 1980s, Dutch multinationals employed over half the labour force working in the goods producing sector. And they determine the fate of many small firms too. The industrial weight of the multinational concerns is heightened still further by the modest size of the Netherlands's own manufacturing sector compared with other countries in northern and central Europe.

The effects of restructuring on the labour market and social security system, and therefore on the position of the trade unions in Dutch society, are illustrated by the following key trends. Despite the economic upswing in the late 1980s, average annual growth of only about 1.5 per cent between 1977 and 1988, with virtually stagnant consumption (a 0.8 per cent rise each year in the period 1980–89) did not prove sufficient to bring any lasting expansion of employment. Unemployment has continued to persist at a high level, remaining between 10-11 per cent throughout the 1980s until 1987, falling to a low of some 6 per cent in 1991, before rising again as the economic slowdown began to bite. The rapid increase in part-time work in the Netherlands has not been sufficient to compensate for the disappearance of full-time jobs. (Two-fifths of all part-time workers, primarily women in the service sector, work less than fifteen hours a week and under Dutch law, at present, and enjoy little or no social or employment protection). However, in 1992 minimum wage legislation was extended to cover employees working for less than one-third of normal weekly hours, who had previously been excluded from coverage, to enable them to receive pro rata payment.

The state of the Dutch social security system is also problematic, and has become the focus of political debate and disagreement between the government and trade unions in recent years. Between 1970 and 1985 the number of Dutch people who were dependent on transfer incomes doubled from 1.6 to 3.2 million. As a result, the share of Dutch gross domestic product devoted to such transfers rose from 15 per cent to 23 per cent. Public sector borrowing hovered at 5–6 per cent of GNP throughout the 1980s, well above the average figure for other north European states. According to the Organisation for Economic Co-operation and Development (OECD), the appropriate remedy was the application of the neo-Liberal policies pursued elsewhere in the 1980s, most notably in the UK. Measures recommended include lowering the statutory minimum wage as a proportion of agreed industry minima, introducing limits on social housing, and tax cuts at the expense of education and the health services.

One of the most prominent areas of disagreement has been the Government's aim of reducing entitlement to statutory disability benefit, provided under the Disability Insurance Act (*Wet op de Arbeidsongeschiktheid*). Originally introduced in 1967, when it was expected that some 150,000 people would claim the benefit annually, by 1992 around 940,000 claimants, 14 per cent of the labour force, were claimants under the scheme. The annual cost has been put at 4 per cent of GNP. Benefits, which range up to 70 per cent of previous salary in the event of complete inability to work, are available once entitlement to sick pay expires after one year. Few claimants return to the labour force, and the scheme has been used as a means of effecting redundancies by employers. In March 1992 the Government introduced limits on the operation of the scheme, amid controversy – especially within the Dutch Labour Party, a member of the governing coalition.

These unfavourable economic and social developments – unemployment, crisis in public spending, the sidestepping of organisations designed to maintain industrial and social peace – have created major challenges for the Dutch trade union movement. As already noted, there was a rapid fall in the level of trade union organisation to around 26 per cent by 1991 (broadly the same the level seen just after the First World War). The largest confederation, the FNV (*Federatie Nederlandse Vakbeweging*), alone has lost a third of its members in recent years, predominantly in its industrial affiliate union, *Industriebond*. At the same

time, the level of trade union organisation among young people fell
from 31 per cent to 19 per cent in the case of men, and from 13 per
cent to 7 per cent for women. The political and occupational divisions
between the trade union centres have further weakened the movement's
political influence: in addition to the FNV (created out of a merger of
the Socialist and the Catholic confederations in 1975), which organises
around 60 per cent of all trade union members, there is an overwhelmingly Protestant oriented Christian Federation (the CNV, *Christelijk
Nationaal Vakverbond*) with around 20 per cent, and the white-collar union
MHP, with around 7 per cent (or around 14 per cent of white-collar
employees). The ACV, a federation primarily organising in the public
sector, was founded in 1990 but has not yet been granted recognition
to participate in national bodies. In all, some 1.5 million employees are
organised in over 200 individual unions, with a substantial number of
industrial and occupational unions within each centre and at various
levels. The 13 per cent of union members in 'independent' unions are
mostly concentrated in public services, such as the military, schools and
hospitals.

In addition to this traditional union fragmentation – itself a product
of the past, fundamentally corporatist (or 'pillared'), constitution of
Dutch society – the trade unions are also now confronted with a series
of problems, many of which are all too familiar from other European
countries.

— The skilled workers who formed the classic backbone of the trade
  union movement are now a minority of union membership. Only
  within the FNV do they still constitute a majority.
— The FNV and CNV have not yet succeeded in satisfactorily organising the growing number of white-collar workers in industry, commerce, transport and banking.
— Around a half of the organised labour force now works in the public
  sector. The CNV is very evidently dominated by public sector unions, although it has not developed any specific services to respond
  to this fact.
— The growing number of female employees continues to be seriously
  under-represented in the trade unions. In contrast, the organised
  membership is getting older and the number of older workers and
  pensioners in the organisation is growing disproportionately. For
  example, the share of members not in employment in the FNV's
  industrial unions rose from 15 per cent to over 25 per cent between
  1980 and 1985.

These structural weaknesses naturally cannot help but hinder Dutch
trade unions in performing not only the task of representing their
memberships but also their broader social role. It is becoming increas-

ingly difficult to cover all employees through collective agreements, and the character of collective bargaining has also changed with greater decentralisation, although industry bargaining still predominates. Union bargaining is generally still more oriented to the needs of male workers rather than women, blue-collar workers rather than white-collar, and those in manufacturing rather than those in services. In all, around 70–75 per cent of the workforce are covered by collective agreements. Those outside the scope of collective bargaining include women in irregular employment or working only few hours, and middle and senior management. The waning strength of the central union confederations, expressed in a fall in the number of full-time officials of around one fifth in the case of the FNV and one third at its *Industriebond* affiliate, is associated with a number of other difficulties with far-reaching consequences for the status of Dutch trade unions both in the industrial sphere and society more generally.

Firstly, workplace or company agreements have grown in importance compared with industry level or central agreements. (Company-only agreements now cover around 13 per cent of the workforce.) The fact that collective bargaining in the Netherlands takes place exclusively at one level means that any increase in workplace agreements will automatically displace central agreements or agreements at other levels. This fact has also encouraged firms seeking to negotiate supplementary provisions at workplace level to bargain with works councils – a development with serious ramifications for the trade unions (see below). Secondly, the trade unions have been unable to resist the drive for flexibility at workplace level. Around a third to a half of all Dutch employees are now estimated to be in some form of 'atypical' employment. For example, part-time work accounts for one-third of all employment. Thirdly, as already noted, the traditional central corporatist consultative institutions have gradually lost influence without this in any way representing an explicit or official policy. The pressing reality of the crisis has simply rendered Dutch industrial corporatism superfluous. Fourthly, the trade unions have not been able to mobilise their members to resist cuts in real wages and a redistribtion of income to capital: the share of income going to capital in the business sector rose from 29.6 per cent in the period 1975–79 to over 40 per cent in the period 1989–91. Cuts have also been made in areas of social provision such as unemployment benefit.

During the 1980s the average length of a strike fell from five to three and a half days, and, with only twenty-six days lost per 1000 employees per year, the Netherlands trailed only Germany between 1977 and 1986 as the least strike prone country in the European Community. This is all the more remarkable given that the declining significance of central corporatist institutions, with their focus on maintaining industrial peace, might have suggested some slackening of the constraints on industrial action. Fifthly, and finally, given this background of fragmentation, decentralisation and declining union militancy, the establishment of works councils via legislation passed in 1979, with rights to information, consultation and participation, weakened rather than strengthened the position of trade unions at workplace level – increasingly the most important level for the conduct of industrial relations. Although a substantial proportion (around 70 per cent) of works council members are union members, there is a noticeable move towards workplace level autonomy. Set in the context of the weaknesses of the trade union movement and the interest of company managements in fostering new forms of workplace co-operation, this represents a very serious development for the existing pattern and nature of union organisation.

All these forces could combine to turn the Netherlands into a, from a trade union point of view, undesirable role model for industrial relations in developed market economies with established systems of workplace employee representation. On the one hand, secure, well-supported and essentially co-operative works councils (or their equivalent) will represent that core of the workforce which stands to gain from economic and business rationalisation; on the other, weakened trade unions will be left to try to organise and represent the losers in this process, the marginalised one-third of society pushed into low-paid, insecure or no employment.

Portugal

Of the trade union movements in the three EC member states (Spain, Portugal and Greece) which were established after the end of the dictatorships in the mid to late 1970s, the Portuguese movement not only went furthest in its pursuit of social and political change but also, initially at least, enjoyed the greatest successes. Intersindical, the trade union confederation which emerged during the latter period of the Salazar/Caetano dictatorship (and renamed the CGTP-IN in 1977) played a vital role in winning double-digit percentage increases in real pay in 1974–75 and in securing major advances in social policy and employment legislation. This embraced, for example, extensive rights to take industrial action, including political strikes, and a ban on employer lock-outs, protection against dismissals, agrarian reform, and the nationalisation of domestic banks and large-scale undertakings.

Intersindical also initially secured a legal monopoly of trade union representation under 1975 legislation – a step reversed in law in the 1976 Portuguese constitution, and later through challenges from rival unions (see below). However, measured against their aims, the Portuguese trade unions, and principally the majority communist current in Intersindical, together with the left parties and sections of the Armed Forces Movement, suffered a historic defeat: the struggle to move the process of democratisation on to a socialist revolution was brought to a halt in the so-called Hot Summer of 1975 by a broad coalition of political and social forces headed by the current President of Portugal and head of the Socialist Party (PS), Mario Soares.

This defeat was decisive in opening the way to parliamentary democracy and the consolidation of a mixed economy. Intersindical, which saw itself as a 'class trade union', was unwilling to accept the transformation in the political environment. It continued to mount a dogged struggle against the dismantling of the 'achievements of the revolution' which it regarded as the starting-point for any future advance towards socialism. However, it could prevent neither the marginalisation of the nationalised sector as an instrument of economic management, nor the

75

progressive abandonment of agrarian reform. Moreover, in agreement with the International Monetary Fund (IMF), the alternating governments of Socialists (PS), Liberals (PSD) and Conservatives (CDS), pursued an economic course which placed the burden of resolving the serious economic and financial predicament of the country wholly on the dependent labour force. This crisis management ranged from particular measures, such as state-ordained pay limits leading to cuts in real pay, to the withdrawal of key elements of protection from dismissal and the effective abandonment of any legal protection for employees in plants where managements defined the business situation as 'difficult'. The consequence was a wave of mass redundancies, in which activists from trade unions and workers' commissions were especially hard-hit. Combined with the return of hundreds of thousands of Portuguese from the former colonies, it led to an increase in official unemployment from 6 per cent in 1976 to 9 per cent by 1981.

At the same time as it was beset by these external difficulties, exacerbated by government attempts to break union resistance by direct intervention into union affairs, Intersindical was racked by an internal crisis whose origins lay in the 'hot phase' of the 1975 revolution. Forces within the white-collar trade unions, in particular, had already refused to back Intersindical's line during some decisive episodes of the revolution. Under the pressure of the post 1975 economic crisis, these organisations considered that they could more effectively defend the real wage gains of the 1974–75 period through co-operation with the government rather than an uncompromising strategy of confrontation. The white-collar opposition to the majority communist current in Intersindical also had deep roots in the fact that Intersindical's approach to social policy and collective bargaining had always been aimed at the needs of workers in industry and agriculture (campaigning for a national minimum wage and literacy). The interests of white-collar workers had been insufficiently integrated into a broader and more sustainable strategy for representing the labour force as a whole.

Intersindical suffered the consequences of this approach when its democratic legitimacy was openly questioned by a number of white-collar unions, led by the bank workers, who argued for the right to form different political tendencies within the confederation. Numerous representatives of manual workers' trade unions from the Catholic tradition, who had found a political home on the left wing of the Socialist Party, also argued for a thoroughgoing transformation of Intersindical's structures and policies. For its part, Intersindical's leadership responded to the approaching danger of fragmentation with a vigorous campaign for trade union unity. In January 1977 it organised a 'Congress of All Trade Unions' supported by almost all blue-collar unions and around half of the white-collar unions. With the participation of the Catholic/socialist elements already noted, together with various smaller political currents, the communist majority succeeded in welding together a functioning alliance committed to class-based trade unionism. Intersindical refounded itself as the General Confederation of Portuguese Workers (CGTP-IN): the organisational structure was democratised, and agreement was reached on an action programme to resist attacks on the social achievements of the revolution. Although this established the preconditions for maintaining a single trade union movement, the decision to split the confederation had already effectively been taken elsewhere.

First, the 1977 congress had not been attended by representatives of those trade unions which believed in 'social partnership', once it had become clear during preparations for the congress that they would not be able to muster a majority. Second, and in the meantime, the Socialist Party decided to establish a rival confederation in alliance with the neo-liberal Social Democratic Party (PSD) and its trade union wing. The UGT (*União General dos Trabalhadores Portugueses* – General Workers Union of Portugal) was constituted in October 1978 by socialist and social democratic trade unions under the auspices of their respective parent organisations, triggering serious protest from the Socialist Party's union wing which had voted to remain actively involved in the CGTP-IN. As a consequence, the founding members of the UGT were reduced to a small group of the larger white-collar unions and a few small blue-collar unions. The UGT's main public stance consisted in its claim to be the sole representative of democratic trade unionism, understood primarily as loyalty to the parliamentary system and prevailing social order, and demonstrated by its marked willingness to co-operate with both government and employers. Initial support for the new organisation from the major West European trade union confederations and social democratic parties provided crucial intellectual and material help in the UGT's development. As well as borrowing many elements of policy from the German confederation, the DGB, the UGT also sought to emulate the German pattern through the establishment of industrial unions to overcome the traditional fragmentation of the Portuguese craft and occupational unions.

These two trade union confederations became vehicles for the implementation of radically opposed projects for the development of Portuguese society. For its part, the CGTP-IN initiated a major wave of strikes and protests against the demolition of the achievements of the revolution, the imposition of the costs of the growing economic crisis on the workforce, and for the maintenance of statutory employment rights. It therefore continued to pursue its aim of changing government policy towards the structural problems of the Portuguese economy to one which emphasised the nationalised sector and agrarian co-operatives. Despite considerable success in mobilisation, which reached its high point in a 24-hour general strike in 1982, the CGTP-IN was unable to exercise any lasting influence over government policy. The strike movement became more sporadic, and its political resolution weakened under the ever more dramatic consequences of the government's austerity policy. By the time of its fifth congress in 1986, the CGTP-IN finally had to concede that its previous strategy had led to a deadend. All too belatedly, the confederation acknowledged the 'realities' which the end of the revolutionary process had created. This primarily meant a recognition that the balance of social and political forces in the country precluded a transition to socialism, and that Portugal's integration into the European Community (which it joined in 1986) and the process of technological modernisation raised a host of new questions – questions addressed by the UGT from the outset.

One of the new realities facing the CGTP-IN was the existence of the UGT itself. Although denied any claim to legitimacy by the older confederation, the UGT had emerged as a serious rival by establishing its own blue-collar unions and mounting competition across the whole spectrum of trade union activity. The UGT opposed the CGTP-IN's strike movement on the grounds that it did not share its objectives and was committed to social partnership. Instead, the UGT attempted to begin negotiations with the government and employers' organisations on a 'modernisation agreement': this was intended to offer a strategy for the necessary restructuring of the Portuguese economy with the priority of minimising the inevitable social costs.

The UGT's tactics for collective bargaining usually consisted in submitting lower claims than the CGTP-IN, enabling it to conclude agreements with the employers without having to mobilise its members for industrial action. Such pay agreements, concluded by unions which often organised only a minority of the workforce, were then declared valid for all occupational groups by the Ministry of Labour through a legal provision stemming from the dictatorship. This approach increasingly derailed the collective bargaining strategy of the CGTP-IN. Not only was the UGT thus able to undermine the CGTP-IN's negotiating position, but it could also portray itself as the more competent negotiator for both workers and employers.

When the PS/PSD coalition established a tripartite Permanent Council for Social Concertation in 1983, the UGT's immediate acceptance of membership enabled it to score a public relations success for its policy of social dialogue, contrasting itself with the CGTP-IN whose underlying reservations about, and protest at, the Government's 'anti-worker policy' held it back from participation. It was not until 1987, following its fifth congress and the landslide election victory of the neoliberal politician Calvaco de Silva, that the CGTP-IN took up the place reserved for it on the Council.

However, the UGT's successes in representing employee interests and consolidating its own position in Portuguese society are more modest than this superficial record might suggest. For example, the UGT has never managed to exercise the influence it would have wished on national policy, or to win the implementation of its proposals for economic and social reform. Its attempts to establish industrial trade unions collapsed under the need to retain and attract existing occupational unions in the face of competition from the CGTP-IN. These same factors also led to the failure of the CGTP-IN to merge its individual unions into larger associations; eventually, it abandoned its initial aim and decided to pursue the more modest goal of linking craft unions by closer, industry level co-operation.

The fact that the rise of the UGT coincided with a general weakening of the Portuguese trade union movement – a weakening actively promoted by the UGT as far as its rival the CGTP was concerned – was illustrated during the 1980s in the evolving pattern of wages and working conditions. Real wages fell substantially, by 6 per cent in 1983 and by as much as 11 per cent in 1984; the share of national income accounted for by wages and salaries correspondingly fell from 60 per cent in 1976 to 47 per cent by 1984, and continued to fall up to 1990 despite an economic upturn in the late 1980s. Unemployment also rose from 6 per cent in 1976 to 11 per cent in 1984, with only around a quarter of the jobless entitled to unemployment benefit. There was also a rapid growth in 'atypical' forms of employment, with fixed-term contracts (of up to three years), which expanded to account for just under 20 per cent of the workforce by the late 1980s.

These developments were accompanied by the fragile framework of employment legislation for those outside the regulated economy: the enormous hidden economy, virtually devoid of legal protection for workers, was estimated to produce around a fifth of gross domestic product in the early 1980s. From the mid-1980s, 'payment in arrears' developed into a mass phenomenon unique in Europe. Private, and even public, companies often failed to pay wages for months on end and only settled their obligations to their workforces after protracted struggles. In 1986, for example, around a 100,000 workers were affected. And the problem has continued into the 1990s. The destruction of the co-operatives established under the agrarian reforms hit agricultural workers hard, especially in the south of Portugal where employment opportunities in the nearby industrial regions of Lisbon and Setubal were drastically reduced as a result of the crisis in shipbuilding.

These grim developments of the early to mid 1980s culminated in moves to a 'new pragmatism' throughout the Portuguese labour and trade union movement, affecting both the relationships between the two confederations and those of the political parties with which they are most closely associated. In January 1988, for example, the two confederations jointly organised a general strike in protest against a legislative package proposed by the Calvaco de Silva Government, which came into office with a free market, deregulationist programme in 1987. Under the proposals, a number of workers' rights established in the 1970s would have been curtailed. However, this unique unity of action could not be reactivated in 1989 when the Government introduced virtually the same package, for a second time: only the CGTP organised protests and strikes. In contrast, following negotiations with the Government, the UGT leadership refused to back joint action with the CGTP and merely allowed its member unions to participate individually in protests. The UGT trade unions representing employees in banking, a major force in the country's union movement, in particular objected to the line pursued by the UGT leaders; but their involvement in the campaign against the proposed law was not sufficient to prevent its acceptance by the Portuguese Parliament. This legislation, while tightening the criteria for the use of temporary workers, introduced the possibility of individual dismissal on economic grounds or grounds of 'low' productivity.

Although there are indications of an easing of the tensions between the two union confederations, the Portuguese trade union movement must now confront the crucial challenges of the 1990s – principally the pressures for modernisation and rationalisation within the single European market – in a weakened condition. Overall membership has fallen since the crisis within the movement of 1976–77. A cautious estimate puts current union density at around 30 per cent. (Reliable independent figures are not available and the two confederations probably overstate their memberships.)

How capably the trade union movement can respond to this demanding environment will depend critically on its ability and willingness to overcome political differences and co-operate in practical ways directed at representing their members' interests, a task which the politically divided Spanish union movement appears to have achieved (see below). Discussions between affiliate unions of the two confederations on collective bargaining issues, and better relations on tripartite bodies, suggest that the legacy of bitterness from the divisions of the past may be fading. And although the CGTP-IN has held back from signing the tripartite Economic and Social Agreements (AES) in the Permanent Council for Social Concertation, it has participated in discussions of the issues. Moreover, the UGT unions have been obliged to assert their autonomy from their political allies, as grass-roots opposition to the positions agreed in the Economic and Social Agreements has made itself felt. These steps towards closer co-operation at national level would almost certainly be facilitated were unions in the ETUC, to which the UGT has belonged since its inception, to work to integrate the CGTP-IN, which remains the largest and most representative confederation.

Spain

According to a public opinion poll carried out in November 1987, the major questions posed by the political transition from the Franco dictatorship to democracy were generally seen as satisfactorily resolved. However, around a third of those surveyed felt that Government policy had proved unequal to the problems of unemployment and income distribution – identified as by far the most important issues confronting the Government. The marked tensions which have emerged since the mid 1980s between the trade union movement and the governing party, the nominally socialist PSOE, also reflect the unease of the Spanish electorate at the Government's social and economic policy. In contrast to developments in Great Britain, however, a number of complicating factors mean that the situation cannot be reduced to a simple pattern of confrontation between Government and trade unions. First, during the 1980s, and particularly since Spain's entry to the European Community in 1986, the Government has been notably successful in driving forward the industrialisation of Spain and raising the overall economic status of the country. Second, the trade union movement is generally weak and organises only around 10 per cent of the Spanish workforce. This weakness is compounded by political divisions, although there have been signs of greater co-operation between the two main confederations in recent years. And third, the PSOE, led by Felipe Gonzalez and in name a socialist/social-democratic party, has continued to dominate the political landscape since the most recent elections, despite some erosion of support in 1991 as a result of internal party disputes and political and financial scandals. Its anti-Fascist credentials and long history in the workers' movement mean that it still commands the support of large numbers of Spanish workers.

Despite trade union hopes of a policy shift after the November 1989 elections, especially following the successful general strike of December 1988, the PSOE has continued to apply a restrictive programme, further tightened in 1992 in the effort to meet the convergence criteria for economic and monetary union established under the Maastricht Treaty.

In addition to curbs on public spending and measures to stifle inflation, the policy also includes controls on bank lending, increases in indirect taxation, and pressure on wages – with a virtual freeze in public sector pay from 1992. The Spanish Government usually also issues a pay recommendation for the private sector, based on its inflation forecast for the coming year.

According to the Government, labour costs in particular have to be kept below those of other EU countries in order to maintain and improve competitiveness. Aside from this objective, the Government's strategy has consisted in promoting economic restructuring and adjustment to EU standards by importing technically advanced capital-goods to modernise Spain's productive base. In recent years, this project has principally been financed through increases in receipts from tourism, transfers from Spaniards living abroad, and foreign direct investment (some of it in property, some in manufacturing itself). Between 1985 and 1988, investment in plant and equipment rose in real terms by around 50 per cent according to the IMF, with heavy involvement by other EC countries. In 1989 the Spanish Government further liberalised the conditions for direct investment, granting foreign partners an equal say in major corporate decisions once their share in the local company exceeds 20 per cent. There are no limits on repatriation of profits and, depending on branch and market circumstances, the foreign partner may also bring in capital, technical know-how, patents and licences.

The accelerated pace of industrialisation in Spain brought about by this policy is not without its disadvantages. Declining employment in agriculture, and the labour-saving impact of new technologies in manufacturing, have pushed unemployment up to among the highest levels in the European Union, at 17 per cent of the workforce. Moreover, high rural unemployment means that the hidden proportion of the unemployed is also probably greater than in other EU states. Deregulation of employment, especially in the area of hiring, has also been pushed ahead. Around a half of Spanish workers are now estimated to be working in precarious forms of employment, either lacking regular work or on fixed-term contracts. At 40 per cent, the rate of youth unemployment is also the highest in the European Union: virtually the only jobs offered to young people are now either fixed-term contracts, often ostensibly for training purposes, or at special lower pay rates.

This gulf between economic and social development has imposed a particularly urgent need for mobilisation on the part of the trade unions. The breach in relations between the Government and unions in the autumn of 1988, during which a common front was achieved between the UGT (socialist oriented) and CC.OO (traditionally communist-leaning), marked an important stage in the growth of opposition to the direction of the PSOE's policy. It also represented an important public rejection of the attempts pursued by the state and employers' organisations since 1975 to embrace the trade unions in a corporatist grip. The demands raised by the unions in the campaign, which culminated in a well-supported general strike in December 1988, were aimed, in particular, at preventing further deregulation of the labour market and reasserting the independence of collective bargaining. Specifically, the union platform called for the withdrawal of plans for employing young people on highly flexible and insecure employment contracts at special low rates of pay, and for an increase in pensions and compensation for previous losses of purchasing power, especially for public employees, and finally for a raising of the minimum pension up to the levels of the minimum wage by 1990.

The moves towards improved co-operation between the two main union confederations played a crucial role in what proved to be the most effective attempt so far to pose an alternative to the Government's economic, industrial and technology policies. In 1986 the UGT won around 41 per cent of all seats in elections to works councils, for the first time overtaking the CC.OO which won about 35 per cent of seats. Both organisations now have around a million members.

The evaporation of members' confidence in the two confederations in the early 1980s – in the case of the UGT because of overly close collaboration with the governing PSOE, and for the CC.OO because of its links with the Spanish Communist Party – led to a major rethink from 1986–87 onwards. Both the UGT and CC.OO, in common with the Government, now advocate a unitary trade union movement. However, as long as each confederation continues to nurse the hope that a single centre would reflect its own political perspective, realising this ambition is highly unlikely.

The vigour of the trade union opposition demonstrated in the 1988 strike was not sustained, although it did serve as a warning to the Government which, following 1988, was more willing to enter into dialogue with the unions on some issues. There have been growing pressures for social dialogue on economic matters, especially from the need to gain union support for the austerity imposed by recession and integration into the Single Market. One sign of this developing relationship was a willingness on the part of the unions to accept new legislation on industrial action, providing for the maintenance of essential services, in return for the Government's establishment of an Economic and Social Council (announced early in 1992 and functioning from November 1992). The unions have also won important concessions in the area of 'atypical' employment: under legislation passed in 1991, employers must show employee representatives any new employment contracts in order to prevent abuse of laws allowing fixed-term employment for training, seasonal or short-term tasks, temporary replacement and work experience. However, in other areas of labour market deregulation – notably on dismissals – the government has pushed ahead without union co-operation.

The readiness of the trade unions from both confederations to pursue dialogue with the Government rests to a considerable degree on the powers now enjoyed by works councils (*comité de empresa*). Under the 1980 Workers' Statute, which borrowed heavily from works council legislation in Northern Europe (and, in particular, Germany), scope has been created for the emergence of independent perspectives on individual employment law, labour market policy and collective bargaining.

For example, competing trade unions in medium-sized and large-scale organisations can each propose their own slate of candidates. In contrast, where only one unified union slate is proposed, candidates must indicate which trade unions they belong to. Elections are also conducted separately for different employee groups (skilled, unskilled, technicians and administrative occupations) with each group represented on the works council in proportion to its share of the total workforce. Works meetings take place on the employers' premises, but usually outside working hours. Non-employees, such as trade union representatives, may be invited. Management representatives are not members of works councils.

However, apart from rights to information disclosure and consultation, which broadly correspond to those which prevail in North European countries with statutory or agreed workplace representation, Spanish works councils do not have effective rights of codetermination. And in contrast to the practice in countries such as France, Germany and the Netherlands, the 1980 Spanish Workers' Statute treats works councils as fully competent partners in collective bargaining. Provided there is no trade union majority on the works council, there are no limits to what subjects can appear on the workplace bargaining agenda. Given the low level of trade union organisation and the relatively high percentage of non-trade union works council members (around 30 per cent), works councils in Spain play a major role in practice in collective bargaining.

In addition, special joint negotiating committees can be set up at the request of either managements or works councils. Decisions require the agreement of at least 60 per cent of the two sides. Beyond the immediate workplace, competence to conclude collective agreements remains the exclusive preserve of the trade unions. However, this right is restricted to those confederations gaining at least 10 per cent of the vote in works council elections in undertakings falling within the scope of the relevant agreement. This provision is intended to prevent the fragmentation of employee representation and operates against the interests of minorities such as the Christian trade union federation, the USO, which at the moment organises around 8 per cent of works council members and 3 per cent of trade union members nationally. The Basque and Galician trade unions, which would not meet the national criteria, enjoy 'most representative status' through their regional strength. Finally, in contrast to the German Works Constitution Act, not only does the Spanish system lack any true codetermination rights, but also no obligation to maintain industrial peace or act in good faith in the interests of the establishment. Such 'peace obligations' can, though, be concluded either by collective or workplace agreement.

The existence of these structures for workplace employee representation, with their orientation towards co-operation and consensus and the right to conclude collective agreements under certain circumstances, combined with weak and divided trade unions, has created pressures for the corporatist approaches which have shaped and limited the scope for trade union activity. Trade union activity in the coming years will not only be influenced by these pressures, but must also take into account the broader context characterised by the limited union strength in the workplace, a low level of representativity in collective bargaining at industry level (because of low levels of union organisation), union participation in corporatist institutions and party political entanglements (both of which are problematic), and the absence of a functioning, socially progressive opposition to the Gonzalez policy of rapid modernisation through a forced pace of technical change, with all its associated social and employment problems.

There is an enormous need for capable and autonomous trade unions, as documented by the successful general strike in December 1988. But the organisational principles and traditions of the trade unions since the demise of Franco have, as yet, prevented them from reconstituting themselves into a powerful force for representing workers' interests. Nonetheless, given public pressure for a better balance between economic and social development, intelligent political use of a two-pronged approach involving the pursuit of consensus through tripartite agreements, but with a readiness to embrace conflict in the form of centrally co-ordinated, large-scale strikes on specific issues, might help the unions to consolidate their position in Spanish society. In turn, this might ease the path to the achievement of a unified trade union movement.

The Future: Structural Change, Internationalisation and the Trade Union Response

The preceding outline of the situation of the national trade union movements in the European Union has highlighted the fact that the main current and future challenges to the trade unions are to be found in structural transformation and internationalisation. Every trade union movement in Europe is suffering under the impact of mass unemployment and the structural transformation of employment (including a fall in the level of trade union organisation), neo-liberal economic and social policies (privatisation, individualisation and the decline of traditional employee solidarity), and the consequences of the introduction of new technologies (increasing flexibility in work organisation and working time, decentralisation, devolution of conduct of industrial relations to plant level). This structural transformation with its, overall, negative impact on the strength and scope of trade unions has been compounded by a longer-term trend towards the extension of infrastructural and service activities ('tertiarisation') compared with production, necessitating a change in the typical trade union clientele from male to female workers. However, white-collar workers and women continue to present major recruitment problems for the trades unions in all EU member-states (as do young people for different reasons).

Although each national setting confers its own unique context, all national trade union movements in the EU are confronted with common problems and dangers. All, for example, are exhibiting organisational fragmentation and increasing internal differentiation, virtually all have had to face economic and distributional policies which are inimical to the interests of working people, and all have proved far from equal to the task of making up membership losses with successful recruitment in new industries and amongst new occupational groups. Given the continuing global economic and social crisis, manifested and shaped by the structural transformation of the world economy and accompanied by persistent and irresolvable high levels of unemployment, the dominance of neo-classical economics and weakened trades unions, the most decisive areas for trade union activity will be at *international* and at *workplace level*.

At *international level*, the key tasks will be to activate and make use of all possible opportunities for information, consultation and communication, together with the creation of a supra-national strategy for collective bargaining able to improve the image and standing of the trade unions in both public awareness and the media. The following suggest themselves at European level:

— Improving trade union contacts with European institutions: the European Commission, Parliament, Permanent Representatives (COREPER), Council of Ministers.
— Joint trade union assessments of country situation reports based on an agreed set of common criteria, the exchange of national bargaining and policy agendas, with coordination at ETUC level and joint action, followed by joint appraisal of any consequent successes and failures.
— Common action towards multinational companies and 'sunrise' industries such as information technology, biotechnology and new materials technology, with the aim of establishing European/international works councils with rights to information and consultation. Initiatives in this field already exist in a number of branches in the form of European-level bodies for consultation and information disclosure (see Part III below).
— Coordination of national trade unions in strategies towards European institutions and employers' organisations with the aim of strengthening union lobbying and negotiating positions.

The primary objective at this level is, therefore, the creation of a common, supra-national context within which trade unions can develop international activities, together with the fostering of an awareness of potential conflicts, both within and outside the trade union movement. These activities must be in accord with the scale of structural change and be matched by effective instruments for exchanging information internationally.

The current problems raised by the pace of technical change, the dramatic transformations in work organisation and the implementation of shorter working hours are all instances of how the focus of industrial relations is increasingly shifting to the level of the *workplace*. Irrespective of the particular orientation of national trade union movements, either corporatist or rooted in free collective bargaining, trade unions must be able to demonstrate that they are able to translate their general policies into workplace realities. Control or merely influence over the direction of technical change, for example, is impossible without effective access to information, scope for consultation, and organisational strength on the part of workplace employee representatives and the workforce itself. The same applies to pursuing and implementing cuts in weekly working hours: only strong workplace union representatives are able to implement agreed policies, limit overtime working, resist the intensified push for productivity increases, and monitor the growing divergence between plant and individual working hours – all of which can undermine the effective realisation of agreed national working time reductions.

As a consequence, one of the most important tasks confronting Europe's trade unions will be that of achieving a *more effective link between the international context and the workplace-level at which policies are implemented*, combined with strengthening workplace level union representation, both organisationally and in terms of access to information. The most systematic steps in this direction are currently represented by the various information and consultative bodies established in multinational companies. These hold out the prospect both of sowing the seeds of a future European level form of codetermination and laying the foundations for European collective bargaining.

Background Statistics

The following tables are divided into four main groups:

— industrial relations (1.1–1.10)
— employment (1.11–1.15)
— social and employment policy (1.16–1.21)
— economic data for European Union actual and prospective member-
  states (1.22–1.29).

Table 1.1 Employees – level of trade union membership (1990/91) (as per cent of labour force)

Belgium	55%
Germany (West)	33%
Denmark	80%
France	10%
Greece	25%
Great Britain	33%
Irish Republic	52%
Italy	39%
Luxembourg	50%
Netherlands	26%
Portugal	30%
Spain	10%

Source: ETUI, Trade Union Membership in Western Europe (Brussels, 1993), authors' calculations

Table 1.2 Employers associations – coverage of workforce

Country	Initial(s)	No. of enterprises	with no. of employees
Belgium	FEB/VDO	30,000	1 million
Denmark	DA & Dansk Industri	22,000	460,000
France	CNPF	1 million	13.6 million
Germany	BDA	1.2 million	18 million
Great Britain	CBI	200,000	10 million
Greece	SEB & GSEBE	2,500	no figures available
Irish Republic	IBEC	3,500	250,000
Italy	Confindustria	100,000	3 million
Luxembourg	FEDIL	250,000	45,000
Netherlands	VNO & NCW	8,000	980,000
Portugal	AIP & CIP	35,700	820,000
Spain	CEOE	1.2 million	5 million

Source: BDA (Confederation of German Employers Associations). See too, Appendix to Part III (p. 288).

Table 1.3 Main trade union confederations in EC member-states

Country	Initial	Date of Info.	Number of employees represented	member of ETUC
Belgium	CSC/ACV	1989	1,431,000	Yes
	ABVV/FGTB		1,014,000	Yes
	CGSLB		213,000	No
Denmark	LO	1992	1,446,000	Yes
	FTF		359,000	Yes
France	CGT	1986–8	1,030,000	No
	CFDT		c.600,000	Yes
	CGT-FO		1,108,000	Yes
	CFTC		250,000	No
	CGC		240,000	No
	FEN		394,000	No
Germany	DGB	1992	11,015,000	Yes
	DBB		1,095,000	No
	DAG		578,000	Yes
Great Britain	TUC	1992	7,760,000	Yes
Greece	GSEE	1991	482,000	Yes
Irish Republic	ICTU	1992	463,000	Yes
Italy	CGIL	1990	5,000,000	Yes
	CISL		3,500,000	Yes
	UIL		1,560,000	Yes
Luxembourg	CGT	1989	44,000	Yes
	LCG		21,000	Yes
	FEP		5,000	No
Netherlands	FNV	1991	1,025,000	Yes
	CNV		308,000	Yes
	RMHP		131,000	No
Portugal	UGT	1990	1,000,000	Yes
	CGTP		1,150,000	No
Spain	UGT	1990	600,000	Yes
	CCOO		600,000	Yes
	ELA-STV			Yes
	USO			No
	CNT			No
	INTG			No

Sources: Belgium: union sources. Denmark: Danish Statistical Office. France: Bibes et Mouriaux, *Les Syndicats européenes à l'epreuve* (Paris, 1990). Germany: WSI. Great Britain: Certification Officer. Greece: GSEE. Ireland: ICTU. Italy: union sources, quoted in IDS/IPM *Industrial Relations* (London, 1991); figures include many unemployed/retired members. Luxembourg: ETUI. Netherlands: union sources. Portugal: claimed membership - but figures are regarded as unreliable. Spain: author's estimates.

Table 1.4 Procedure for extending collective agreements in the EU

In all member-states, collective agreements are dealt with under civil law. This means that they are only binding on the signatory parties (or members of signatory organisations). However, in several countries there are procedures under which collective agreements can be 'extended' – or declared binding – on all employers and employees of a branch or sector, irrespective of whether the employer is a signatory or a member of a signatory organisation.

Belgium
Collective agreements concluded in the National Labour Council or joint industry committee are binding on all employers who are members of an employers' association and apply to all employees in their employment.

Collective agreements can also be extended to cover 'non-organised' employers, unless they have agreed an exception in writing for every employee individually.

The law regulates the system of extension, under which an agreement can be applied to all non-signatories by royal decree on application from the negotiating parties. The vast majority of agreements concluded on the National Labour Council are declared to be generally binding on non-signatories.

Italy
The constitutional provision which allows trade union organisations to conclude generally binding collective agreements is not used.

Under a 1959 statute the government is empowered to issue regulations whose content is identical to that of collective agreements: these are registered on an ad hoc basis with the Ministry of Labour. However, the Constitutional Court has declared this provision to be in contravention of the constitution.

Industry collective agreements are regarded as being generally binding in line with interpretations of the constitutional provision which requires that all employees receive a payment sufficient to ensure a 'free and dignified existence'. Moreover, any employer who implements one term of a collective agreement has been deemed by the courts to be covered by the agreement in its entirety.

Luxembourg
Decrees issued under the authority of the Grand Duke can extend collective agreements to non-signatories provided two conditions are met. Firstly, there must be a recommendation from the tripartite National Conciliation Office; secondly, the collective agreement may not violate any statutory provision.

Denmark
There is no extension procedure as such. In the event of disputes Parliament can intervene to extend the collective agreement in one branch to any sector in dispute. This procedure was resorted to extensively in the 1980s. Many companies who are not members of a signatory employers' association choose to adhere to an existing agreement.

Germany
Collective agreements can be extended to non-signatories by the Federal Minister of Labour on application from either of the negotiating parties to a specific agreement, provided that the employers side represents companies employing at

least half the employees in the relevant industry and region. The practice is largely confined to industries with a preponderance of small employers. In all 4.4 million workers (out of a total workforce of c. 30,000,000) are covered, though extended agreements rarely cover pay.

Great Britain
There are no procedures under which collective agreements can be extended to non-signatory parties.

Netherlands
Under legislation dating from 1937 the Minister for Social Affairs is entitled to extend a collective agreement throughout a sector, on application from one of the negotiating partners. Around 11 per cent of employees are covered by extended provisions.

Irish Republic
Minimum rates of pay in a sector can be established by a Joint Labour Committee and declared to be binding through the Labour Court. Such provisions cover some 5 per cent of the workforce in low-paying and/or weakly organised sectors. Fair Wages Resolutions provide for minimum terms and conditions to be met in companies in receipt of public contracts.

France
Two procedures are available for extending collective agreements.

— extension of agreements into sectors in which trade union organisation is so weak that it is impossible for an industry agreement to be concluded, either throughout the industry or in one geographical area; on application from a concerned party, the Ministry of Labour can apply a collective agreement to employees which most closely meets their interests. This procedure is rarely used.

— a procedure, which may be implemented either at the initiative of the Minister or on application from one of the negotiating parties, subject to an opinion from the National Collective Bargaining Board. This procedure is commonly used.

Greece
Under 1955 legislation there are two procedures for the extension of agreements.

— the Ministry of Labour can declare an agreement to apply to non-signatory employers provided it already covers 51 per cent of the relevant workforce.

— national agreements signed between the central union confederation GSEE and the national employers' associations are directly binding on all private-sector employers.

Spain
There is machinery for the extension of agreements to non-signatory employers; it is, however, rarely used.

Portugal
The Minister can issue an extension order to apply a collective agreement to non-signatory firms within an industry.

Source: Social Europe, Special Issue, 1988. National sources.

Table 1.5 Coverage of workforce by collective agreements in EU member-states

Belgium	No precise figures: over 60% in secondary sector
Denmark	80–100%
France	c. 86%
Germany	c. 90%
Great Britain	c. 45–55%
Greece	All employees
Ireland	Not known
Italy	No precise data, but the vast bulk of employees covered by collective agreements
Luxembourg	70%
Netherlands	75%
Portugal	50%
Spain	80%

Source: Federal German Ministry of Labour, circular (11/4163), authors' research

Table 1.6 Industrial disputes in the EC: number of days lost through strikes and lock-outs, per 1000 employees (annual average)

	1975–9	'80–4	'85	'86	'87	'88	'89	'90	'91	'92
Germany	52	55	2	1	2	2	4	14	6	60
France	217	95	41	32	29	69	50	39	34	25
Italy	1553	938	269	391	278	196	262	298	164	160
UK	517	483	301	89	163	166	183	70	33	24
Spain	1440	660	423	300	643	1422	422	282	478	650
Netherlands	57	20	19	9	13	2	5	50	17	8
Denmark	86	110	990	39	58	40	20	40	31	30
Greece	700	740	620	711	9940	3550	4950	12130	n.a.	n.a.
Portugal	n.a.	199	100	140	40	70	49	47	39	60
Irish Rep.	995	471	495	380	325	180	60	270	100	n.a.

Source: International Labour Office, OECD

Table 1.7 Regulation of strikes and lock-outs in EU member-states

Country	Political strike	Industrial strike	Sympathy strike	Lock-out
Belgium		lawful	lawful	yes, on strict preconditions
Denmark	as for industrial dispute	lawful, appropriate to aims, only in disputes of interests	lawful, if provided for in collective agreement	lawful, as with strike, breach of contract of employment
France	lawful	lawful	lawful	unlawful, save in emergencies
Germany		only lawful if peace obligation is adhered to, ballot requirement	lawful only in exceptional cases	defensive lock-outs permitted under certain circumstances
Great Britain		immunity only if directed at employer, secret ballot required	lawful only under strictly limited circumstances	legally insignificant, may breach contract
Greece	permitted	lawful	lawful, if link to strikers' interests	forbidden by statute
Irish Republic		immunity if legal preconditions met (ballot, permitted trade dispute)	probably lawful	legally not significant, can break/suspend contract
Italy	permitted	lawful	lawful, if link to striking employees	retaliatory lock-out in some circumstances

Luxembourg		lawful if preceded by conciliation	legality doubtful	recognised, but legal status uncertain
Netherlands	permitted	lawful if all affected employees involved and action proportionate to ends	legality doubtful	not regulated, uncertain legal status
Portugal	permitted	lawful, provided certain preconditions met		all forms prohibited by the constitution
Spain	permitted	lawful, secret ballot required	lawful, if link to interests of strikers	defensive lock-outs permitted in emergencies

Source: European Commission, Comparative Study of Working Conditions in the member-states (1989) p. 70.

Table 1.8 Prevention and resolution of disputes in the member-states

Country	Mediation and conciliation	Arbitration
Belgium	Special conciliation committees (sectoral committees) often chaired by government officials	—
Denmark	Negotiations between the parties with participation of public conciliation service	Obligatory procedures set out in collective agreement, for interpretation of agreements
France	Collectively agreed conciliation procedures; possibility of state conciliation rarely used	
Germany	Mediation and conciliation procedures collectively agreed: option of official mediation	Disputes between works councils and employers may go to arbitration committee
Greece	Voluntary mediation and conciliation body run jointly by employers/unions	Arbitration possible on request of parties
Great Britain	Resolution through negotiation, supported by the official arbitration and conciliation service (ACAS)	ACAS can initiate arbitration if requested by one party and with both parties in agreement. Ruling is non-binding but usually accepted.
Irish Republic	Conciliation services offered by Labour Relations Commission, with possible referral to Labour Court	
Italy	Conciliation procedures contained in collective agreements; public conciliation offices	

Luxembourg	Legal provision for compulsory conciliation, with parties free to accept ruling	Voluntary arbitration procedure
Netherlands	Resolution through negotiation assisted by ad hoc committees: no official procedure	
Portugal	Voluntary conciliation if requested by one or both parties, carried out by Employment Ministry	
Spain	Voluntary procedure set up by negotiating parties; state offers conciliation services	Voluntary private arbitration - rarely used; either party can request official arbitration

Source: European Commission, Comparative Study, p. 68. National sources.

Table 1.9 Status of law and collective agreements in various areas of the labour market

	Working time	Part-time	Fixed-term	Agency work	Minimum wage	Pay indexation	Mass dismissal	Individual termination	Vocational training
B	L+ CA+	L+ CA+	L	L+	L+ CA+	L+	L	L+	L+
DK	L+ CA+	- CA+	L	L	- CA	L+	L	L CA	L+ CA+
F	L+ CA+	L+ CA+	L+	L+ CA+	L	-	L+ CA+	L+	L+ CA+
D	L CA+	L+ CA+	L+	L+	CA	not allowed	L+	L+ CA	L
GR	L+ CA+	- CA+	-	tolerated by authorities	L+ CA+	L+ CA+	L+	L CA	L+
IRL	L CA+	- CA+	L	L	L CA	-	L+	L+	L+ CA+
I	L CA+	L+ CA+	L+ CA+	not allowed	- CA	-	L+	L+ CA+	L+ CA+
L	L	- CA+	L	L	L+	L+	L+	L	L+

NL	L / CA+	– / CA+	L	L+	L+	– / CA+	L / CA+	L	L+ / CA+
P	L+ / CA+	L	L	L+	L	–	L+	L+	L+
E	L+ / CA+	L+ / CA+	L+	L+	L	–	L+	L+	L+ / CA+
UK	CA+	CA+	–	–	L+	–	L+	L+	L+ / CA+

Source: European Commission, Social Europe, Special Issue, 1988 (p. 72). Updated from national sources.

Notes: Each field contains two items of information:

1. if there is a statutory provision, there will be a 'L'; if there is a collectively agreed provision, a 'CA'. No provision is indicated by '–',

2. if the provision has been changed since 1982, this is indicated by a '+'.

Table 1.10 Works councils in Europe

Country/ Name	Basis	Composition (a) Chaired by (b)
Germany/ Betriebsrat	statute	(a) 1–31 employees in plants up to 9,000, then 2 for each extra 3,000 (b) employees only
Belgium/ conseil d'entreprise	statute and coordination agreement between social partners	(a) joint body (b) employer
France/ comité d'entreprise	statute	(a) employer and 3–11 employees (b) employer
Great Britain/ joint management and employee consultation committee (term varies)	voluntary agreement/ management decision	(a) usually joint (b) varies
Ireland/ joint industrial council	by agreement	(a) joint (b) usually employer
Italy/ 1. consiglia di fabricca	agreement between national union/ employer confederations	(a) employees only, separate rep. for blue/white collar (b) employee reps.
2. consiglio dei delegati	statute and collective agreement	(a) employees only, mostly trade unionists (b) employee reps.

Election of employee representatives by:	(1) Personnel (2) social and (3) economic rights
Workforce, divided into blue- and white-collar	(1) **Information** on personnel planning, consultation on job design, personnel movements **Codetermination** on appointment /dismissal,vocational training (2) **Codetermination** on company rules, daily working time, holiday planning, pay arrangements, social facilities (3) **Information**: in plants with more than 100 employees, works councils elects economic committee of 3–5 employees for consultation
Workforce on trade union nominations	(1) **Consultation**, establishment of guidelines of appointment/dismissal (2) **Decision-making** on works rules, holiday schedule, administration of social facilities
Workforce on nominations of representative unions in plant: separate electoral colleges for ordinary employees, middle-management and executives	(1) **Consultation, codetermination** on works physicians and social helpers (2) **Administration** of social facilities, award of grants for education courses (3) **Information** on business situation, appointment of 4 representatives to supervisory board
usually whole workforce	usually consultative
usually whole workforce	usually consultative
workforce on union lists	consultative with negotiating rights
homogeneous work groups	(1) **codetermination** on body searches, installation of audio-visual equipment, conciliation on disputes (2) **monitoring** and promotion of health & safety (3) **information**

Table 1.10 (cont.) Works councils in Europe

Country/ Name	Basis	Composition (a) Chaired by (b)
Netherlands/ ondernemingsraad	statute	(a) 3–25 employees (b) employee reps.
Denmark/ samarbejdsudvalg	agreement between national employers/ trade union confed- erations	(a) joint (b) employee
Spain/ comites des empresa	statute	
Greece/ works councils	statute	
Portugal/ commissoes de trabhaladores	statute	

Source: Institut der deutschen Wirtschaft, Dossier 7, Sozialraum Europa (1989).

Election of employee representatives by:	(1) Personnel, (2) social and (3) economic rights
whole workforce: can be on trade union lists	(1) **consultation, consent** required on works rules, pensions and profit-sharing, working time, health & safety; **codetermination** if no legal regulation; **monitoring** of compliance with regulations on working conditions, health & safety; initiation of committees on work environment (3) **information** on business situation, consultation, **veto** on worsening of jobs, including investment and credit policy, **right of recommendation** on seats on supervisory board
shop stewards	(1) **codetermination** on work environment and principles of personnel policy (3) **rights to information**
workforce	(2) **monitoring** rights in social field (3) **rights to information**
workforce	(2) **rights to consultation, codetermination** on holiday planning, accident prevention, vocational training (3) **rights to information**
workforce	(1) right of proposal on (2) social and personnel measures (3) monitoring compliance with legal and agreed norms affecting firm

Updated using local sources.

Table 1.11a Unemployment rates in member-states (annual average rate): all age groups

	EC	B	DK	D	GR	E	F	IRL	I	L	NL	P	UK
Men and women													
1988	9.8	10.2	6.4	6.3	7.7	19.3	9.9	17.3	10.8	2.0	9.3	5.7	8.5
1990	8.3	7.6	8.1	4.8	7.0	16.1	9.0	14.5	9.9	1.7	7.5	4.6	7.0
1991	8.8	7.5	8.9	4.2	7.7	16.3	9.5	16.2	10.2	1.6	7.0	4.0	9.1
1992	9.3	8.2	9.5	4.5	–	18.0	10.0	17.8	10.3	1.9	7.0	4.7	10.0
1993	10.4	9.5	10.6	5.7	–	21.2	10.9	18.2	10.9	2.6	7.9	5.0	10.3
Men													
1988	7.9	6.9	5.4	5.1	4.9	15.0	7.6	16.8	7.2	1.5	7.1	4.0	8.7
1990	6.6	4.8	7.2	4.0	4.3	11.9	6.8	14.0	6.5	1.2	5.5	3.2	7.4
1991	7.3	5.0	7.8	3.7	4.8	12.2	7.4	15.6	6.8	1.3	5.2	2.8	10.0
1992	8.1	5.5	8.4	4.1	–	13.9	8.1	16.9	7.0	1.5	5.3	3.3	11.7
1993	9.3	6.6	9.8	5.4	–	17.6	9.3	17.4	7.5	2.0	6.8	3.9	12.1
Women													
1988	12.6	15.4	7.6	7.9	12.5	27.5	12.8	18.4	17.0	3.0	12.8	8.0	8.3
1990	10.8	11.9	9.1	5.9	11.7	24.0	11.8	15.5	15.6	2.5	10.6	6.4	6.5
1991	10.9	11.4	10.2	4.9	12.9	23.6	12.1	17.3	15.8	2.3	9.7	5.7	7.9
1992	11.2	12.2	10.8	5.1	–	25.5	12.5	19.4	15.7	2.8	8.7	6.5	7.6
1993	12.1	13.9	11.5	6.2	–	27.9	13.0	19.7	16.8	3.7	9.5	6.5	7.9

Table 1.11b Unemployment rates in member-states (annual average rate); aged under 25

	EC	B	DK	D	GR	E	F	IRL	I	L	NL	P	UK
Men and women													
1988	19.6	20.3	8.7	6.8	25.8	40.2	22.1	25.0	32.3	4.8	14.7	13.1	12.4
1990	16.7	17.0	11.1	4.5	23.2	32.0	20.1	20.9	28.9	3.9	11.6	10.6	10.8
1991	17.6	16.7	11.2	3.8	24.6	30.9	21.3	24.5	28.5	3.2	10.8	9.1	14.8
1992	18.2	17.6	11.4	4.0	–	32.5	21.8	24.5	28.4	3.2	10.8	9.2	14.2
1993	19.1	19.6	12.2	4.9	–	36.2	23.1	26.5	27.9	5.7	12.1	10.8	15.2
Men													
1988	17.3	15.1	7.8	6.2	17.0	33.9	18.3	26.8	27.1	4.4	13.9	9.6	13.3
1990	14.7	12.7	10.4	4.3	15.1	26.1	16.5	22.1	23.8	3.2	10.6	8.4	11.9
1991	16.1	13.6	10.2	3.9	17.1	25.5	18.1	25.9	24.2	3.2	10.1	6.6	16.9
1992	17.2	14.8	10.4	4.1	–	27.9	19.1	29.0	24.0	4.0	10.9	8.0	18.6
1993	18.4	17.3	11.3	5.3	–	32.7	21.3	28.3	23.8	6.4	14.1	8.8	17.8
Women													
1988	22.2	25.8	9.7	7.4	35.9	47.7	26.0	22.7	38.4	5.2	15.5	17.6	11.3
1990	19.0	21.6	11.8	4.7	32.4	39.3	23.8	19.5	34.8	4.7	12.7	13.2	9.5
1991	19.3	20.0	12.4	3.8	33.5	37.6	24.6	22.7	33.7	3.1	11.6	12.1	12.3
1992	19.4	20.6	12.4	3.8	–	38.5	24.7	25.8	33.2	3.6	10.3	13.0	12.3
1993	19.9	22.0	13.1	4.5	–	40.9	25.0	24.2	32.9	4.8	10.0	13.2	12.0

Source: Eurostat 1988–92 figures are annual averages; 1993 figure is August (seasonally adjusted)

Table 1.12 Women and the labour market (1991)

	Total labour force	Share of women (%)	Share of women unemployed (%)
Belgium	4,210,000	42.0	59.0
Germany	30,678,000	41.0	47.0
Denmark	2,912,000	46.0	51.0
France	24,619,000	43.0	56.0
Greece (1990)	3,951,000	–	62.0
Ireland	1,334,000	32.0	25.0
Italy	24,598,000	37.0	57.0
Luxembourg	165,000	36.0	52.0
Netherlands	7,011,000	40.0	54.0
Portugal	4,869,000	44.0	63.0
Spain	15,382,000	35.0	52.0
United Kingdom	28,264,000	43.0	24.0
EC	147,993,000	40.0	49.0

Source: OECD, *Employment Outlook* (1993)

Table 1.13 Women in Europe's trade unions (1985)

Country	Organisation	% of all trade union members	% of conference delegates	% of officials
Belgium	CSC & FGTB	33	10–15	8
Germany	DGB	22	15	11
Denmark	LO	46	18	12
France	CFDT	32	19	18
Greece	GSEE	n.a.	n.a.	4
G.Britain	TUC	n.a.	15	18
Ireland	ICTU	32	n.a.	7
Italy	CGIL	32	16	4
Luxembourg	CGT	17	4	3
N'lands	FNV & CNV	16–20	n.a.	12
Portugal	UGT	46	20	3
Spain	UGT	12	7	5

Source: ETUI, quoted from CFDT *Aujourd'hui* No. 91, December 1988.

Table 1.14 Growth in number of pensioners: percentage of population aged 65 or over

Country	1990	2040
Germany	15.5	27.6
Netherlands	12.7	24.8
Denmark	15.3	24.7
Italy	13.8	24.2
France	13.8	22.7
Spain	12.7	22.7
Belgium	14.2	21.9
Greece	12.3	21.0
Portugal	11.8	20.4
UK	15.1	20.4
Ireland	11.3	16.9

Source: OECD, Ageing Populations (1988)

Table 1.15 Percentage of population no longer in employment at age:

55–59 years		60–64 years	
Belgium	63	Luxembourg	88
Luxembourg	62	Belgium	87
Netherlands	57	Netherlands	82
Italy	56	France	81
Irish Republic	50	Germany	80
Spain	50	Italy	77
France	49	Spain	68
Greece	48	Great Britain	64
Portugal	47	Greece	64
Germany	41	Portugal	62
Great Britain	34	Irish Republic	62
Denmark	28	Denmark	59

Source: Eurostat, ILO (data applies to 1986)

Table 1.16 Statutory working time regulation in EU member-states

Country	Weekly working time	Overtime	Nightwork
B	40 hours	65 hours within 3 month period	20.00–06.00
DK	no statutory provision	regulated by collective agreement	no statutory provision
D	48 hours	2 hours daily up to 30 days per year based on a 48-hour week	20.00–06.00
GR	5 day week	Sectoral annual overtime quotas set by Labour Ministry	22.00–07.00
E	40 hours in private sector 40 hours	Incurs higher social insurance contributions	22.00–06.00
F	39 hours	9 hours a week, 130 hours a year, more with permission	22.00–05.00
IRL	48 hours	2 hours per day, 240 hours per year	no statutory provision
I	48 hours	no statutory provision	24.00–06.00
L	40 hours	2 hours per day	no general statutory provision; pregnant and nursing mothers, 22.00–06.00
NL	48 hours	0.5–3.5 hours a day	20.00–07.00
P	44 hours	2 hours per day, max. 200 hours per year	20.00–07.00, at least 7 hours during this period
GB	no statutory provision	no statutory provision	no general statutory provision

Source: EC Commission, Comparative Study, op.cit. p. 33, Incomes Data Services

Table 1.117 Agreed working hours and holidays

Country	Agreed weekly working hours	Annual leave & public holidays
Belgium	38 hours or less	Minimum 4 weeks' leave: 10 public holidays
Denmark	37 hours	Minimum 4 weeks' leave: 10 public holidays
France	39 hours	Minimum 5 weeks' leave: 11 public holidays
Germany	36–38 in West: 38–40 in East. 'Time-banking' with additional days by plant agreement in West German manufacturing	25–30 days' leave: 10–14 public holidays (variation by *Land*, depending on religion)
Great Britain	35–40 hours	Average 25 days' leave: 8 public holidays
Greece	40 hours in industry: 37–39 in services	21–30 days' leave (often by service): 4–6 public holidays + further 8 bank/government holidays
Irish Republic	39 hours in industry	20–25 days' leave: 8 public holidays
Italy	40 hours (but with additional 'banked' days off)	25–30 days' leave: 10 public holidays + some local saints' days
Netherlands	39.5 on average in industry (with additional 'banked' days off)	25–32 days' leave, by age and seniority: 8 public holidays
Portugal	38–42 hours	21–30 days' leave: 13 public holidays
Spain	Annual agreed hours in large companies, 1,748 (1990)	22–27 days leave: 14 public holidays

Source: Incomes Data Services, *European Report*, various issues. Under 'time-banking', working time reductions are effected through reductions in annual (or six monthly) average hours rather than per week. That is, if the agreed working week falls from 40 to 37 hours, the previous 40 hours continue to be worked but workers 'bank' three hours a week and take extra days off. Such arrangements are common in Italy, the Netherlands and Germany where workers accumulate up to 15 days off a year in addition to annual leave.

Table 1.18 Working time flexibility in selected countries in the European

Country	Weekend work
Belgium	— inclusion of Saturdays and Sundays in working schedules: two 12-hour shifts at weekends, of which 24 usually paid as 36 hours — inclusion of all 7 working days into regular schedules: 3- or 4-day weeks on 12-hour shifts with varying weekly rest-days — inclusion of Saturdays into schedules: 4-day week on 9.25-hour shifts with varying weekly rest-days ['working time experiments']
Germany	Saturday shifts agreed at BMW as part of revised working time plan under which employees work some Saturdays in return for longer blocks of time-off.
France	— two shifts of 12 hours on Saturday and Sunday (with the rest of the week off) or, — a shift lasting 16 hours: 6 hours on Friday p.m. and 10 hours on Saturday or 10 hours on Saturday and 6 on Sunday, or, — choice between two working time blocks: Friday-Saturday-Sunday or Saturday-Sunday-Monday or, — regular alternation between shortened working time at weekends and normal working hours during the week. — distribution of working hours over 5 or 6 days of the week. Maximum: 10 hours per day and 46 hours per week, or an average of 44 hours spread over 12 weeks. [applies in the metalworking industry]

Union

Weekly working time	Annual working time	Other provisions
— unequal distribution of weekly working time (35-40 hours) over working days [applies in metalworking industry]	— Flexible working week: • daily working time can be varied by +/- two hours (up to 9 hours per day), weekly working time can be varied by +/- five hours (up to 45 hours a week) without incurring overtime rates; • work on Sundays and public holidays, previously only allowed under special circumstances, is generally permitted; • daily working time can be extended to 12 hours. Condition: agreed or statutory working hours (40 hours) must be complied with on average over a reference period of up to one year, depending on agreement. [All undertakings are legally entitled to negotiate corresponding provisions in industry or company agreements]	
Up to 17 per cent of a workforce can work up to 40 hours a week, deviating from the agreed 36 hour week. [metalworking industry] Agreed working hours can be attained on average over a one year reference period, to be extended to three years for project related activities, subject to a maximum 10 hour day. [chemical industry]	Plants may continue to operate a 40 hour week for employees with the difference between this and agreed hours (36 in metalworking) 'banked' and taken as additional time off in blocks.	
Cyclical working time: regular alternation of weekly working time (e.g. 41-36–36 hours) with an average over the cycle of 39 hours) [applies in several branches]	— modulated working time. Weekly working time is mostly between 37 and 41 hours, with an upper limit of 44 hours a week. No lower limit, in order to facilitate use of free shifts [unrostered days]. Condition: must comply with statutory 39-hour working week over a one year period. [applies in several collective agreements]	Time off in lieu: reductions in weekly working hours in the form of Friday afternoons off or bundled into half or whole days off within 6–8 weeks or in the form of bridging days. [applies in metalworking]

Table 1.18 (cont.) Working time flexibility in selected countries in the European

Country	Weekend work
Denmark	
Netherlands	
Italy	

Source: IW-Zusammenstellung, Dossier 7, Sozialraum Europa, 1988/89; national

Community

Weekly working time	Annual working time	Other provisions
— fixed number of working hours per week, with the possibility of agreeing the number of working days and the daily hours per day in accordance with the requirements of production. — uneven distribution of working hours over different departments, work-teams and/or individual employees so that the agreed working time is arrived at on average. [applies throughout the economy]		Time off in lieu: working time surpluses can be taken as time off in lieu within a reference period of six months. [applies throughout the economy]
— with an agreed weekly average working time of 37 hours, actual weekly hours can diverge upwards or downwards depending on available work: 4 or 5 day week is possible e.g. 4 x 8.5 = 34 with little work available or 5 x 8.5 = 42.5 when required. Condition: the agreed weekly time must be achieved over a quarter or a year.	— annual hours: the working week can be extended or reduced from the normal 40-hour week depending on requirements (four day week possible) Condition: annual agreed hours, currently 1,752, must be complied with. [applies in metalworking] — Roster free days: agreed annual hours contains 'roster free days' which are blocks of days off adding up to 26 days in all. When they are to be taken is negotiated between employee or works council and employer, with due regard for exigencies of production. [applies in many collective agrements]	Young workers can claim additional days off [applies in metalworking]
	— annual hours agreed at plant level. Agreed annual working hours contains blocks of time-off, to be taken by agreement between employer and employee with due account of needs of production.	Time off in lieu: reduction in weekly hours in the form of days off. [applies in most collective agreements]

sources

Table 1.19 The law and industrial relations in the European Community

Country	Separation between law and collective agreement State intervention
Belgium	Close link between the law and collective agreement. State involvement, depending on issue
Denmark	Autonomy of social partners, although state may become involved through incomes policy
Germany	Law underpins collective bargaining. State does not intervene in collective bargaining
Greece	Social partners tied to parties. Move from high state regulation to free collective bargaining
Spain	Collective bargaining provided for in constitution and workers statute. Autonomy of social partners with state involvement in tripartite discussions
France	Centralised system for provision of minima, with greater decentralisation of bargaining since 1982 'Auroux' laws
Ireland	Voluntaristic system, with incomes policies regulating bargaining since 1987
Italy	Law underpins collective bargaining, with progressive state withdrawal from direct intervention but involvement in framework setting negotiations
Luxembourg	Close link betwen law and collective agreements
Netherlands	Link between law and collective agreements, with diminishing involvement of state
Portugal	Principle of free collective bargaining, although state still plays an important role
United Kingdom	Voluntarist system, with law not playing role in bargaining and developed system of individual contract

Source: European Commission, *Social Europe*, Special Issue (1988); national sources

Coordination between industry collective agreements and plant agreements	Main level of bargaining
General agreement gives minimum provision. Additional payments etc. negotiated at sectoral or establishment level	General agreement and branch agreements
A general collective agreement provides the framework for branch agreements. Greater decentralisation from branch to workplace bargaining	Branch
Strong coordination between collective agreements and plant agreements	Branch
National general agreement sets framework for other levels of bargaining	Branch/ Occupation
Branch agreements set framework for company agreements	Branch
Attempted strict division by levels (through Auroux laws)	Branch
Incomes policy agreement regulates work-place level settlements	Company
Attempts to harmonise industry agreements and company bargaining	Branch
	Branch and undertaking
Branch agreements set framework; large companies negotiate separately	Branch
	Branch
Co-ordination on some issues, e.g. hours, via trade union	Company, with declining branch

Table 1.20 Expenditure on social protection in the EC (1991)

	As % of Gross Domestic Product	Per capita (adjusted for purchasing power)	Per capita (% of EC average)
Netherlands	32.4	5,101	129
Denmark	29.8	4,608	117
France	28.7	4,803	122
Luxembourg	27.5	5,797	147
Belgium	26.7	4,191	107
Germany	26.6	4,952	126
United Kingdom	24.7	3,653	92
Italy	24.4	3,991	101
Spain	21.4	2,432	61
Ireland	21.3	2,240	57
Greece (1989)	20.7	1,367	34
Portugal	19.4	1,616	41
European Community 12	26.0	3,930	100

Source: Eurostat, *Social protection expenditure and receipts 1980–91* (Luxembourg, 1993). Units for per capita expenditure are expressed in Purchasing Power Standards (PPS) in order to eliminate distortions caused by different price levels in EC countries.

Table 1.21 Financing social protection expenditure (1987)

	Employers	Employees	Public funds	Other
Italy	52.6	15.8	28.6	3.0
Spain	52.2	19.4	26.0	2.4
France	52.2	27.0	18.2	2.6
Portugal	51.9	19.3	24.7	4.1
Belgium	42.1	19.7	27.5	10.8
Germany	41.1	30.4	25.2	3.2
Luxembourg	33.4	23.3	36.8	6.4
Netherlands	33.2	35.8	14.2	16.8
United Kingdom	27.9	17.0	43.4	11.8
Greece (1989)	23.0	23.9	49.0	4.2
Ireland	22.1	13.1	63.9	0.9
Denmark	10.9	4.3	77.9	6.8
European Community 12	42.3	23.9	28.1	5.7

Source: Eurostat

Table 1.22 Gross Domestic Product: 1967–76 to 1992, estimate and projection for 1993/4 (annual change in real GDP)

	1967–76	1980	1981	1982	1983	1984	1985	1986	1987	1988	1989	1990	1991	1992	1993	1994
Austria	4.5	2.9	-0.3	1.1	2.0	1.4	2.5	1.2	1.7	4.1	3.8	4.6	3.0	1.5	-0.5	1.0
Belgium	4.5	4.1	-0.9	1.5	0.5	2.1	2.5	1.6	1.7	5.0	3.8	3.3	2.1	0.8	-1.2	0.9
Denmark	3.2	-0.4	-0.9	3.0	2.5	4.4	4.3	3.6	0.3	1.2	0.6	2.0	1.2	1.0	0.2	2.5
Finland	4.5	5.3	1.6	3.6	3.0	3.1	3.3	2.8	3.3	5.4	5.4	0.0	-7.0	-4.0	-2.0	-0.3
France	4.3	1.6	1.2	2.5	0.7	0.7	1.9	2.5	2.3	4.5	4.3	2.5	0.7	1.4	-0.9	1.1
Germany	3.8	1.0	0.1	-0.9	1.8	2.8	2.0	2.3	1.5	3.7	3.6	5.7	4.5	2.1	-1.5	0.8
Greece	6.3	1.8	0.1	0.4	0.4	2.8	3.1	1.6	-0.5	4.4	3.5	-1.1	3.3	0.9	0.5	0.9
Ireland	4.6	3.1	3.3	2.3	-0.2	4.4	3.1	-0.4	4.6	4.2	6.5	9.1	2.6	4.9	2.7	3.1
Italy	4.3	4.1	0.6	0.2	1.0	2.7	2.6	2.9	3.1	4.1	2.9	2.1	1.3	0.9	-0.1	1.7
Luxembourg	3.7	0.8	0.8	1.1	3.0	6.2	2.9	4.8	2.9	5.7	6.7	3.2	3.1	1.8	1.0	1.5
Netherlands	4.4	0.9	-0.7	-1.5	1.4	3.1	2.6	2.0	0.9	2.6	4.7	4.1	2.1	1.4	-0.2	0.6
Portugal	5.5	4.6	1.6	2.1	-0.2	-1.9	2.8	4.1	5.3	3.9	5.2	4.4	2.1	1.6	-0.4	2.0
Spain	5.5	1.3	-0.2	1.6	2.2	1.5	2.6	3.2	5.6	5.2	4.7	3.6	2.2	0.8	-1.0	0.8
Sweden	3.2	1.7	0.0	1.0	1.8	4.0	1.9	2.3	3.1	2.3	2.4	1.4	-1.7	-1.7	-2.7	1.5
United Kingdom	2.3	-1.9	-1.2	1.6	3.6	2.3	3.8	4.1	4.8	4.4	2.1	0.5	-2.2	-0.6	2.0	2.9
EC	4.0	1.4	0.1	0.8	1.6	2.3	2.5	2.8	2.9	4.1	3.5	3.1	1.5	1.1	-0.3	1.4

Source: OECD, *Economic Outlook*, December 1993.

Table 1.23 Investment: 1970–76 to 1992, estimate and projection for 1993/4 (percentage change on previous year). (Gross private non-residential fixed capital formation)

	1970–76	1980	1981	1982	1983	1984	1985	1986	1987	1988	1989	1990	1991	1992	1993	1994
Austria	5.6	4.6	-2.7	-10.2	-0.9	4.1	8.6	3.7	5.7	7.3	8.6	8.7	5.1	-1.6	-4.6	0.1
Belgium	2.3	8.7	-4.3	1.7	-5.3	6.7	2.4	6.5	7.4	14.9	15.3	8.7	-0.4	-3.5	-7.5	0.5
Denmark	3.9	-9.6	-16.5	19.9	2.7	12.1	18.9	18.8	-5.4	-7.3	5.8	3.9	-2.7	-13.4	-2.5	5.0
Finland	3.6	14.7	4.5	2.8	6.3	-1.8	5.7	2.9	6.6	11.0	15.5	-6.4	-24.6	-21.0	-15.0	-5.0
France	2.9	4.2	-2.5	0.0	-4.1	-2.1	4.4	6.6	6.0	9.6	8.6	4.4	-1.8	-4.2	-8.5	-1.0
Germany	-1.0	2.8	-3.9	-4.7	4.5	-0.4	5.0	4.3	3.8	5.6	7.4	10.1	7.5	-1.8	-11.9	-0.8
Greece	3.2	1.0	-4.2	0.2	-8.4	-6.6	7.2	-11.4	-4.1	-12.4	13.7	11.3	-5.9	2.7	1.7	-1.5
Ireland	5.6	-3.0	10.6	-4.7	-11.4	-2.7	-13.1	1.1	2.9	7.3	14.7	14.9	-11.5	-4.9	-0.4	3.1
Italy	1.5	9.7	-8.4	-8.9	-6.6	4.3	0.0	4.0	9.1	9.5	4.7	2.3	-2.9	-3.3	-12.	2.5
Luxembourg [1]	–	12.7	-7.4	-0.5	-11.8	0.1	-9.5	31.2	14.7	14.1	8.9	2.5	9.8	-2.2	4.0	-2.0
Netherlands	-1.1	-4.7	-12.6	-2.3	7.3	5.0	-19.4	12.3	1.5	1.6	7.8	2.4	4.4	-0.8	-4.8	-1.8
Portugal [1]	–	8.5	5.5	2.3	-7.1	-17.4	-3.5	10.9	15.1	15.0	5.6	5.9	2.4	5.7	1.0	4.0
Spain	5.5	1.4	-5.5	-2.1	-0.3	-10.6	0.1	14.0	21.1	13.9	13.9	3.3	3.0	-2.0	-11.1	-3.0
Sweden	5.5	8.7	-6.8	1.6	3.9	7.7	12.2	2.7	8.8	5.0	14.4	-0.9	-15.5	-16.4	-10.0	3.0
United Kingdom	1.3	-4.2	-5.6	8.0	-0.9	14.6	13.5	0.9	16.9	18.4	8.2	-2.8	-9.0	-2.7	-1.1	2.9
EC	1.5	2.6	-5.4	-1.3	-1.2	2.3	5.4	5.5	8.8	10.1	8.3	4.3	-0.4	-2.9	-8.6	0.3

Source: OECD, *Economic Outlook*, December 1993

Notes: 1. Figures are for total gross fixed capital formation.

Table 1.24 Consumer price inflation: 1979–93

	1979	1980	1981	1982	1983	1984	1985	1986	1987	1988	1989	1990	1991	1992	1993
Austria	3.7	6.3	6.8	5.4	3.3	5.7	3.2	1.7	1.4	1.9	2.6	3.3	3.3	4.0	3.6
Belgium	4.5	6.7	7.1	8.7	7.7	6.3	4.9	1.3	1.6	1.2	3.1	3.4	3.2	2.4	2.8
Denmark	9.6	12.3	11.7	10.1	6.9	6.3	4.7	3.6	4.0	4.6	4.8	2.7	2.4	2.1	1.3
Finland	7.5	11.6	12.0	9.6	8.3	7.1	5.9	2.9	4.1	5.1	6.6	6.1	4.3	2.9	2.2
France	10.8	13.6	13.4	11.8	9.6	7.4	5.8	2.7	3.1	2.7	3.6	3.4	3.2	2.4	2.1
W. Germany	4.1	5.5	6.3	5.3	3.3	2.4	2.2	-0.1	0.2	1.3	2.8	2.7	3.5	4.0	4.1
Greece	19.1	24.7	24.5	21.0	20.2	18.5	19.8	23.0	16.4	13.5	13.7	20.4	19.5	15.9	14.4
Ireland	13.2	18.3	20.4	17.1	10.5	8.6	5.5	3.8	3.1	2.1	4.1	3.3	3.2	3.1	1.4
Italy	15.7	21.1	18.7	16.3	15.0	10.6	8.6	6.1	4.6	5.0	6.6	6.1	6.5	5.3	4.2
Luxembourg	4.5	6.3	8.1	9.4	8.7	5.6	4.1	0.3	-0.1	1.4	3.4	3.7	3.1	3.2	3.6
Netherlands	4.2	6.5	6.7	5.9	2.7	3.3	2.3	0.1	-0.7	0.7	1.1	2.5	3.9	3.7	2.6
Portugal	23.9	16.6	20.0	22.4	25.5	28.8	19.6	11.8	9.4	9.7	12.6	13.4	11.4	8.9	6.5
Spain	15.7	15.6	14.5	14.4	12.2	11.3	8.8	8.8	5.2	4.8	6.8	6.7	5.9	5.9	4.6
Sweden	7.2	13.7	12.1	8.6	8.9	8.0	7.4	4.2	4.2	5.8	6.4	10.5	9.3	2.3	4.6
United Kingdom	13.4	18.0	11.9	8.6	4.6	5.0	6.1	3.4	4.1	4.9	7.8	9.5	5.9	3.7	1.6
EC	10.8	13.7	12.4	10.9	8.6	7.2	6.1	3.7	3.3	3.6	5.3	5.6	5.1	4.3	3.3

Source: OECD, *Economic Outlook*, December 1993; OECD, *Index of Consumer Prices*.

Table 1.25 Pay: 1970–76 to 1992. Estimates and forecasts for 1993/4. (Compensation per employee in the business sector: percentage change on preceding year)

	1980	1981	1982	1983	1984	1985	1986	1987	1988	1989	1990	1991	1992	1993	1994
Austria	7.9	7.8	5.6	5.7	5.4	5.3	7.5	4.3	3.5	4.6	3.9	6.2	4.8	5.0	2.7
Belgium	8.7	7.8	7.5	5.7	8.6	5.2	4.4	2.4	2.4	4.7	5.5	6.3	5.3	4.2	3.4
Denmark	11.1	8.7	11.2	9.0	6.0	4.8	5.1	7.2	3.5	4.6	4.1	3.8	3.0	2.9	3.6
Finland	14.4	14.6	9.6	9.5	10.3	10.6	7.8	8.5	10.9	11.4	9.4	4.9	-1.9	3.4	2.8
France	15.2	14.5	13.9	10.3	8.3	4.2	4.2	4.1	4.5	4.2	5.0	4.6	3.4	3.4	2.3
Germany[1]	6.9	4.8	4.8	3.9	3.8	3.1	3.7	3.3	3.2	3.0	4.2	4.7	W: 5.7 E: 37.9	W: 3.3 E: 13.7	W: 1.3 E: 8.4
Greece	14.6	20.4	26.4	21.4	18.1	22.4	12.8	9.4	16.7	16.7	17.6	14.7	12.1	13.4	11.5
Ireland	20.0	17.4	14.0	13.9	11.6	9.8	5.2	6.0	7.2	6.8	4.2	4.3	5.4	5.3	5.4
Italy	20.2	20.5	16.6	15.9	11.9	10.4	7.0	7.7	7.9	9.5	8.9	8.8	6.1	4.3	4.0
Netherlands	6.0	4.1	6.5	3.9	0.3	1.7	2.7	1.8	1.1	0.7	3.1	4.5	4.4	3.4	2.9
Portugal	20.1	20.2	19.1	20.4	21.0	17.9	18.0	17.8	7.2	10.4	17.2	15.5	12.7	8.5	6.0
Spain	15.7	16.8	15.2	15.6	10.3	7.7	7.1	5.4	6.1	5.3	7.6	8.6	8.6	7.8	4.5
Sweden	14.7	10.5	5.5	8.0	9.8	8.4	8.3	7.4	8.1	12.6	9.5	6.4	4.6	3.8	3.3
United Kingdom	19.1	13.2	8.9	7.9	6.1	8.6	8.3	6.3	8.1	8.4	10.0	8.2	5.7	3.4	3.7

Note: 1. Figures for Germany are for West Germany until 1991. OECD figures have been supplemented by official earnings data for the years 1991–93. Data refers to gross income per employee.

Source: OECD, *Economic Outlook*, December 1993. 1993 and 1994 figures are forecasts.

Table 1.26 Productivity. (Productivity in the business sector: percentage change at annual rates)

	Total factor productivity			Labour productivity			Capital productivity		
	1960–73	1974–79	1980–91	1960–73	1974–79	1980–91	1960–73	1974–79	1980–91
Austria	3.3	1.2	0.9	5.8	3.2	2.0	-2.0	-3.1	-1.5
Belgium	3.9	1.4	1.4	5.2	2.8	2.3	0.6	-1.8	-0.7
Denmark	2.8	1.1	1.4	4.3	2.6	2.3	-1.0	-2.4	-0.8
Finland	3.3	1.6	2.1	4.9	3.2	3.2	0.0	-1.8	-0.5
France	3.9	1.7	1.4	5.4	3.0	2.3	0.9	-1.0	-0.4
West Germany	2.6	1.8	1.0	4.5	3.1	1.6	-1.4	-1.0	-0.4
Greece	5.8	2.1	0.5	8.8	3.3	0.9	-8.8	-4.2	-1.8
Ireland	3.7	2.4	3.3	4.9	3.4	4.2	-0.8	-1.8	-0.1
Italy	4.4	2.1	1.2	6.3	2.9	1.8	0.4	0.3	-0.2
Netherlands	3.4	1.8	0.8	4.8	2.8	1.3	0.6	-0.2	-0.2
Portugal	5.0	-0.4	1.0	7.5	0.5	1.7	-0.6	-2.5	-0.7
Spain	3.4	1.0	1.9	6.0	3.3	2.8	-3.6	-5.1	-0.8
Sweden	2.7	0.4	0.6	4.1	1.5	1.3	-0.8	-2.3	-1.4
United Kingdom	2.3	0.6	1.3	3.6	1.6	2.0	-0.6	-1.5	-0.1
OECD Europe	3.3	1.4	1.2	5.1	2.6	2.0	-0.7	-1.4	-0.5

Notes on years: 1960–73, or earliest year available (1961 for UK, Finland, Greece and Ireland; 1963 for France and Sweden; 1970 for Belgium and the Netherlands).

Source: OECD, *Economic Outlook*, December 1993.

Table 1.27 Employment growth with estimates and forecast for 1993/4 (percentage change on preceding year)

	1980	1981	1982	1983	1984	1985	1986	1987	1988	1989	1990	1991	1992	1993	1994
Austria	0.7	0.6	1.2	-1.0	0.1	0.0	1.4	0.6	0.3	1.0	2.1	1.7	2.1	-0.5	-0.1
Belgium	-0.1	-1.9	-1.3	-1.0	-0.2	0.6	0.7	0.5	1.5	1.6	1.4	0.1	-0.4	-1.5	-0.8
Denmark	-0.5	-1.3	0.4	0.3	1.7	2.5	2.6	0.9	-0.6	-0.6	-0.5	-0.9	-0.1	-0.9	-0.5
Finland	3.2	1.1	1.0	0.6	1.0	1.0	-0.3	-0.3	0.3	1.6	-0.1	-5.2	-7.1	-6.9	-3.2
France	0.1	-0.6	0.2	-0.3	-0.9	0.5	0.3	0.4	1.0	1.4	1.0	0.1	-1.0	-1.2	-0.4
Germany	1.6	-0.1	-1.2	-1.4	0.2	0.7	1.4	0.7	0.8	1.5	3.0	2.6	-1.7	-2.3	-1.7
Greece	1.4	5.2	-0.8	1.1	0.3	1.0	0.3	-0.1	1.7	0.4	0.6	-1.3	1.9	-0.4	-0.4
Ireland	1.0	-0.9	0.2	-2.1	-1.8	-2.5	0.5	0.6	0.3	-0.1	3.3	-0.1	0.0	0.2	0.5
Italy	1.3	0.2	-0.3	0.2	0.4	0.4	0.5	-0.2	1.1	0.1	1.8	0.9	-0.6	-3.8	-0.8
Luxembourg	0.7	0.3	-0.3	-0.3	0.6	1.5	2.6	2.7	3.1	4.0	4.2	4.4	1.9	1.7	0.0
Netherlands	1.2	-1.1	-2.1	-1.3	0.5	1.3	2.5	1.6	2.9	2.0	3.3	2.6	1.0	-0.7	-0.6
Portugal	2.2	0.5	-0.1	3.9	-0.1	-0.5	0.2	2.6	2.6	2.2	2.2	3.0	-6.4	-1.0	-0.6
Spain	-3.0	-3.0	-1.3	-1.1	-1.8	-0.9	2.2	3.1	2.9	4.1	2.6	0.2	-1.9	-4.5	-1.1
Sweden	1.3	0.2	-0.1	0.1	0.7	1.0	-0.7	1.6	1.4	1.5	0.9	-1.7	-4.1	-6.7	-1.2
United Kingdom	-1.0	-3.4	-1.9	-0.2	2.2	1.1	0.3	2.3	3.3	2.7	0.3	-3.2	-2.7	-1.0	1.1
EC	0.2	-1.0	-0.9	-0.4	0.2	0.6	0.9	1.1	1.7	1.7	1.7	0.3	-1.5	-2.1	-0.6

Source: OECD, *Economic Outlook*, December 1993.

Table 1.28 Public expenditure (as percentage of GDP) 1980–92, estimate for 1993

	1980	1981	1982	1983	1984	1985	1986	1987	1988	1989	1990	1991	1992	1993
Austria	48.1	49.5	50.1	50.4	50.0	50.9	51.6	51.9	50.2	49.0	48.7	49.9	50.7	52.2
Belgium	51.9	56.4	56.3	55.9	54.9	54.5	54.1	52.6	50.5	49.3	49.1	49.9	50.7	51.9
Denmark	56.2	59.8	61.2	61.6	60.4	59.3	55.7	57.3	59.4	59.6	58.3	58.7	59.8	62.0
Finland	35.5	36.3	37.9	39.1	38.7	40.4	40.7	41.2	39.0	37.5	45.5	54.1	59.5	62.5
Germany	47.9	48.7	48.9	47.8	47.4	47.0	46.4	46.7	46.3	44.8	45.1	48.5	49.0	50.8
Greece	33.1	39.1	39.7	41.7	44.4	48.3	47.6	47.6	47.5	49.3	53.3	50.8	50.7	53.2
Spain	32.2	34.9	36.6	37.7	38.1	41.1	40.7	39.6	39.5	40.9	41.8	43.3	44.5	46.9
France	46.1	48.6	50.3	51.4	51.9	52.2	51.3	50.9	50.0	49.1	49.8	50.6	51.8	54.3
Irish Rep.	48.9	50.4	53.2	53.2	51.4	52.5	52.3	50.4	47.1	40.5	41.0	42.1	43.7	44.6
Italy	41.9	45.9	47.6	48.7	49.3	50.9	50.7	50.2	50.3	51.3	53.2	53.6	53.2	53.2
Luxembourg	54.8	58.5	55.8	55.1	51.8	51.7	51.0	54.2	50.8	47.1	49.7	53.4	53.9	54.0
Netherlands	54.9	56.8	58.7	59.3	57.8	56.1	56.1	57.7	56.3	53.8	54.1	54.5	55.2	55.8
Portugal	25.9	43.9	43.0	47.9	44.4	43.4	43.9	43.5	43.5	41.7	42.9	49.7	51.6	50.7
Sweden	60.1	62.6	64.8	64.5	62.0	63.4	61.6	57.8	58.1	58.3	59.1	61.5	67.3	72.0
United Kingdom	43.0	44.2	44.6	44.7	45.2	44.0	42.5	40.7	38.0	37.6	39.9	40.8	43.2	44.9

Source: OECD, *Economic Outlook*, from 1987, Luxembourg figures from European Commission

Table 1.29 Public indebtedness (Gross public debt as percentage of nominal GDP), 1980–93

	1980	1981	1982	1983	1984	1985	1986	1987	1988	1989	1990	1991	1992	1993
Austria	37.2	39.3	41.6	46.0	47.9	49.6	53.8	57.3	57.6	56.9	56.4	57.0	55.8	57.0
Belgium	79.9	93.2	102.3	113.3	118.2	122.3	126.7	131.5	132.9	130.2	130.7	133.9	136.0	141.6
Denmark	33.5	43.7	53.0	61.6	65.9	64.1	58.3	55.9	58.0	58.5	59.5	60.7	62.4	66.2
Finland	13.9	14.6	17.1	18.7	19.0	19.0	18.8	20.1	18.8	16.6	16.6	25.4	44.0	60.0
France	37.3	36.4	40.1	41.4	43.8	45.5	45.7	47.2	46.8	47.5	46.6	48.6	51.6	57.1
Germany	32.8	36.5	39.6	41.1	41.7	42.5	42.6	43.8	44.4	43.2	43.5	41.8	42.8	46.2
Greece	27.7	32.8	36.1	41.2	49.5	57.9	58.6	64.5	71.1	76.0	89.0	96.3	94.6	98.4
Ireland	72.5	77.2	83.0	97.0	101.3	104.3	116.0	117.1	115.2	105.4	98.7	96.7	93.8	92.1
Italy	59.0	61.1	66.4	72.0	77.4	84.3	88.2	92.6	94.8	97.9	100.5	104.0	108.0	114.0
Netherlands	44.8	49.1	54.2	60.4	64.5	67.9	69.6	73.5	76.2	76.3	76.5	76.6	78.0	80.6
Portugal	37.5	47.3	50.7	56.5	63.0	66.5	64.3	72.4	75.2	71.7	66.6	67.5	62.6	67.6
Spain	18.3	24.0	30.4	36.4	43.5	48.8	49.9	49.4	45.7	46.9	46.8	49.3	51.4	57.4
Sweden	44.3	52.1	61.7	65.5	67.0	67.6	67.1	59.1	53.5	48.4	44.2	45.7	52.9	67.6
United Kingdom	54.1	54.3	53.0	52.9	54.4	52.7	51.1	48.6	42.2	36.8	34.7	35.4	40.5	47.3

Source: OECD, *Economic Outlook*, December 1993.

PART II

Trade Union Organisation and Employee Representation

SIEGFRIED MIELKE, PETER RÜTTERS
& KURT P. TUDYKA[1]

Introduction

The significance of structures of employee representation, both for working people and their organisations, depends crucially on the strength and effectiveness of trade unions. This is true not only of countries such as Great Britain, which lack any statutory basis for workplace level employee representation, but also of France and Germany where such institutions are subject to detailed legal regulation. Without trade unions which are representative and have the financial strength, willingness and scope to support workplace bodies and make full use of their available rights, systems of workplace representation cannot function effectively as institutions serving employee interests.

Consequently, the individual country chapters which follow begin with an overview of national *trade union organisations and structures*, followed by a description of *structures of employee representation* at company and at company and workplace level. Each chapter concludes with a consideration of the extent to which trade unions are able to represent employee interests at *national level*.

Two immediate issues are of concern here, each of which will be explored in the individual chapters. Firstly, at what level are rights of representation granted and to whom (the individual plant or establishment, the firm or group etc.)? Secondly, how are these rights secured and protected (for example, by local agreements, legally binding collective agreements for an industry, laws or national constitutional provisions)? A further important yardstick is whether such representative institutions are established only when the employees concerned, or their trade unions, demand it (as in Germany), or whether there is a mandatory obligation for them to be set up (as in France and the Benelux countries). It is also important to look at whether the various structures of representation provide scope for the co-ordinated exercise of influence and co-determination. Finally, and by way of a broader international comparison, we turn briefly to the issue of whether, despite national differences, the common features shared by national systems and structures make it possible to speak of a 'European model' of employee representation.

Notes

1. The country chapters in this section covering Belgium, Luxembourg, the Netherlands and the Irish Republic were written by Kurt P. Tudyka, and the other chapters by Siegfried Mielke and Peter Rütters.

Belgium

Trade unionism in Belgium is pluralistic in structure, with a high overall level of union membership. Around 75 per cent of the labour force are trade union members (80–90 per cent of blue-collar workers, 70 per cent of civil servants, and 40 per cent of white-collar employees), with the bulk of the organised workforce in one of the three main trade union centres which are based on different political and religious standpoints. They are: the socialist General Federation of Belgian Workers (FGTB/Fédération Générale du Travail de Belgique; ABVV/Algemeen Belgisch Vakverbond) with 1.1 million members; the catholic Confederation of Christian Trade Unions of Belgium (CSC/Confédération des Syndicats Chrétiens de Belgique; ACV/Algemeen Christelijk Vakverbond) with 1.3 million members; and the liberal General Confederation of Liberal Trades Unions of Belgium (CGLSB/Centrale Générale des Syndicats Liberaux de Belgique; ACLVB/Algemeen Centrale der Liberale Vakverbonden van Belgie) with 200,000 members. There are also a number of smaller employee organisations. Regionally, the FGTB/ABVV is broadly equally represented in the two main regions – Flemish-speaking Flanders and French-speaking Wallonia. In contrast, the CSC/ACV has about 70 per cent of its membership in Flanders. The CSC/ACV also has a higher proportion of women members, around 45 per cent, which reflects its stronger presence in the service sector.

Organisational structure

The ABVV/FGTB and ACV/CSC have a similar, dual structure. In each case, individual members join one of their confederation's industry federations (eleven in the ABVV/FGTB and seventeen in the ACV/CSC) together with local and regional sections of the confederation itself, which organise employees regardless of occupation or status. Blue-collar and white-collar employees each have their own sections, and white-collar workers in the public and private sectors have their own separate federation. Nationally, and in accordance with Belgian federalist principles, both confederations and their affiliated industry federations have divisions corresponding to the three major administrative subdivisions of the country (for Brussels, Flanders and Wallonia), a number of regional organisations (twenty-four in the ABVV/FGTB and thirty-two in the ACV/CSC), and hundreds of workplace branches, and, in the case of ACV/CSC, independent local secretariats.

The most important level for practical membership-related activity in both ABVV/FGTB and ACV/CSC is that of the region. Its task is to run the union's administrative services at regional, district and local level, provide legal support and advice, carry out membership training, collect dues and pay out strike pay and unemployment benefit. They also have a particular responsibility for issues relating to women and young people.

The industry federations are primarily concerned with concluding collective agreements and overseeing any other agreed provisions. They also carry out membership training and education, and provide information, often in collaboration with the appropriate regional office of their confederation.

Only the liberal ACLVB/CGLSB has no industry federations, and is organised solely through multi-industry and local sections, and union representation at company level. But like the other confederations, it does have a specialist union for public sector employees.

Despite these basic similarities, there are some organisational differences between the two major confederations, the ABVV/FGTB and ACV/CSC. For example, compared with the centralised ACV/CSC, the ABVV/FGTB is characterised by greater authority at regional level. In addition, the most basic level of organisation in the ABVV/FGTB consists of workplace branches; the membership only becomes divided into industry federations and the confederation's own structures at regional level and above. In contrast, the ACV/CSC's membership joins both a works branch of the relevant industry federation and the confederation's own local section.

In each confederation, there is an annual congress at regional level which sets the overall direction of policy to be implemented by the executive committee and influential regional secretary. The regions are organised into three broader administrative regional committees (corresponding to the three-fold national regional division) which form the link to the national organisations. The national congress in both confederations usually meets every four years, although in recent years extraordinary conferences have been called almost every year in response to particular events or developments in social and economic policy. The National Committee (in the case of the ABVV/FGTB) and General Council (ACV/CSC) meet eight to ten times a year to set policy between conferences. In the ABVV/FGTB, the National Committee consists of 150 members, of which two thirds are from the industry federations and one third represents the inter-regional committees (corresponding to the main national administrative regions). In the ACV/CSC, the General Council has 300 members, again with two thirds from industry federations and one third from regional bodies. Overall direction in the ACVV/FGTB is in the hands of a National Bureau, composed of equal numbers of representatives of industry federations and inter-regional committees. The Executive Committee of the ACV/CSC has a similar make-up. In the two main confederations, day-to-day administration is dealt with by small executives, both of which are located in Brussels. The ACLVB/CGLSB has its main office in Ghent.

The trade union confederations are both formally and organisationally independent of political parties. However, the various vertical divisions of Belgian society – its religious and political 'pillars' – especially within the Catholic community, mean that effective links are maintained. Contacts between the two major confederations take place at a number of levels; both ignore the small liberal confederation.

The integration of social forces in Belgium into these three vertical pillars – Catholic, Socialist and Liberal – therefore embraces the various institutions through which employee interests are expressed. The outcome is a diverse and complex network of bodies for airing grievances, exchanging information, opinions, plans and demands, and giving notice of proposed actions and responses to events. This structure also provides a variety of mechanisms for the exchange of information and consultation between employers and employees, as well as with state or other public bodies at national, regional, occupational and sectoral levels. Such a dense culture of consultation consequently presupposes the existence of parties prepared to adopt a pragmatic negotiating stance.

Employee representation at workplace level

There are three forms of employee representation at company or workplace level. Each grew up at a different historical period and their roles sometimes overlap in practice.

As early as the pre-war period, enterprises in Belgium with more than fifty employees were required to have Committees for Safety, Health and the 'Embellishment' of the Workplace (abbreviated to SHEs), consisting of equal numbers of employer and employee representatives. (These committees are currently regulated by legislation passed in 1952.) The SHEs have rights to information and consultation on workplace health and safety issues, including the appointment of plant safety specialists, and can make decisions on immediate grievances in these fields.

The second form of workplace representation is the trade union delegation (*délégations syndicales/vakbondsafvaardiging*) which has a direct negotiating role at workplace level. Union delegates, who are protected against most forms of dismissal, are recognised and operate on the basis of the 1947 national agreement between employers and trade unions, and since 1971 on the basis of formal national collective agreement. Their origin lies in the special circumstances of the Occupation, when trade unions were banned but collaborationist corporatist structures largely rejected. This provided some scope for employers and employee organisations to come to agreement on the basis of a position of national resistance (see below).

The tasks of the delegations are not precisely defined. They were originally conceived as a trade union body with rights to submit and pursue claims at workplace level on issues such as pay, working time, breaks and holidays, health and safety and other working conditions. In practice, they also play a central role in consultations between employers and employees, assessing how close respective positions are before issues pass formally onto the agendas of the works council (see below).

The 1944 Social Pact between the employers and trade unions, whose origins lay in the experiences of national resistance and reconstruction, included an agreement to establish forms of industrial co-operation through joint organisations at company level. Under the 1948 Law on Economic Organisation, enterprises with more than fifty employees were required to set up works councils (*conseils d'entreprise/ondernemingsraad*), an obligation extended to non-commercial organisations in 1975. In practice, only enterprises employing on average more than 100 employees have moved to establish works councils – a task, in law, entrusted to the employer.

Works councils consist of the employers and their representatives and members representing the employee side elected by the workforce. Elections take place every four years. Candidates are nomintated by the main union confederations, together with the national confederation of managers (CNC). In the 1991 elections, the FGTB/ABVV won 38 per cent of the vote, the CSC/ACV 52 per cent, CGSLB/ACLVB 8 per cent, the CNC 3.1 per cent. The vote for the CSC/ACV has been rising steadily for several years, reflecting its greater strength among white-collar employees and in the service sector. In contrast, the FGTB/ABVV, with its concentration in heavy industry, has seen a progressive decline in its share of the vote. As with union membership, the stronghold of the CSC/ACV is in Flanders, where it far outstrips the FGTB/ABVV in the number of works council seats held. Works councils have rights to information, consultation and – in exceptional cases and generally provided there is unanimity – rights of decision-making. Their powers to make decisions are confined to the social aspects of the work environment, such as works rules, selection criteria for hiring and dismissal, setting dates for holidays, and monitoring compliance with employment and social legislation. The employer's primary obligation is to provide information on financial and other economic matters related to the business. The works council has a right to regular information on developments which affect the workforce and which fall within the competence of the council, as well as a right to be informed when special circumstances warrant it. Rights to information were more precisely defined in the early 1970s. However, studies have shown that the information disclosed on economic and social issues is often insufficient to allow a works council to conduct a satisfactory discussion of the employer's business situation. The works council has a right and obligation to consult with the employer on issues and information brought to them, and to offer their own proposals or raise grievances. In contrast to the trade union delegations, works councils are intended to co-operate rather than bargain with the employer. They do not enjoy rights of codetermination in the strict sense of the term.

Regional and national representation

Regional economic commissions, set up in 1970, are entrusted with the task of dealing with the specific problems of Wallonia, Flanders and Brabant. The federalisation of Belgium in the 1980s, combined with the divergent economic development in the regions, has enhanced the importance of these bodies.

Industry councils (*bedrijfsraden*), on which the trade unions are represented, have existed since 1948. Their task is to look at the situation at branch level, make recommendations and provide advice to government ministries and the Central Economic Council (see below) on sectoral questions.

The Central Economic Council (*Conseil Centrale de l'Economie / Centrale Raad voor het bedrijfsleven*), also established in 1948, is made up of representatives of employers, employee organisations and co-operatives, and independent experts. It issues a twice-yearly report on the state of the economy, in part based on the submissions of the industry councils. Its role has been enhanced since 1989 when, under national legislation aimed at boosting industrial competitiveness, it was given the task of assessing Belgium's comparative position on a range of economic indicators. The legislation empowers the government to take measures to rectify any decline in international competitiveness, including making changes to the system of wage indexation.

The National Committee for Economic Growth, set up in 1960, consists of the government and five employer and five employee representatives. Chaired by the Economics Minister, it issues opinions on the overall direction of economic policy, in particular investment, employment and pay. Resolutions must be agreed unanimously. The Committee was originally intended to provide consultation and support for the government's long-term economic planning, but it was soon adapted to deal with more short-term problems.

Where national economic crises, either cyclical or structural in nature, have warranted it, representatives of government, trade unions and employers have met at irregular intervals in National Labour Conferences (first convened in 1936). This particular tripartite institution has not functioned in recent years, with many of its roles taken over by the National Labour Council. In addition, the government has sometimes decided to press ahead with measures without first seeking an accord between the two sides of industry. Similar tasks were envisaged for the National Employment Conferences, which have also not been summoned in recent years.

The first organisational form for the representation of employee interests via trade unions developed at industry level, and only then subsequently at enterprise level. This is reflected in the important role played in the Belgian economy since the First World War by the negotiation of collective agreements for every branch by the Joint Committees (*paritaire comités*) of employers and trade unions. The Joint Committees also have the right to set up conciliation commissions to assist in mediation in the event of industrial disputes. In 1919 there were only three such committees; this rose to twelve by 1920, sixteen by 1922, forty-seven by 1939, with the current total close on 100. They cover virtually every branch, with the exception of the public sector. Their operation was regulated by legislation passed in 1945, and subsequently amended in 1962 and 1968.

The Joint Committees function in a national context shaped by a higher negotiating body, the National Labour Council (*Conseil National du Travail/Nationale Arbeidsra[a]d*), sometimes termed Belgium's 'social parliament'. This consists of twelve employer and employee representatives drawn from the nationally recognised employers' organisations and trade unions. The Council, established under public law in 1952, is the successor to a number of national organisations, some of them dating from the mid-nineteenth century. The Council has an important role in collective bargaining, exercised through various mechanisms. In the first place, it can conclude collective agreements at national level covering either the whole of the private sector or, if appropriate, a number of individual branches of industry. These can be extended to cover all employers in an industry, whether a member of a signatory organisation or not. It can also negotiate agreements for branches in which no Joint Committees have been set up. The Council also has a broader role in social affairs and can issue advice to the government, in particular the social and labour ministry or Parliament, either on request, or on its own initiative. For example, between 1952 and 1988 it prepared a total of 800 opinions and reports, and exercised a significant influence on labour and social legislation.

In all, it is estimated that there are some 120 joint bodies on which employers and trade unions meet. Compared with other European Union member states, the representation of employee interests in public bodies and in the private sector has been effected through a high degree of institutionalisation and centralisation, with a large measure of incorporation into officially established institutions in which the employee side retains a major role. However, despite the scope for trade union views to be expressed in national forums, there is no joint decision-making – codetermination – at workplace or company level in the form found in Germany, for example.

Both these facets are a product of the particular experience of wartime Occupation and the post-war period. Active and passive resistance nourished a sense of common purpose, leading to the establishment, or agreement to establish, a number of essentially consensual institutions. Following the end of the war, national economic reconstruction posed similar demands for national unity and social cohesion. In addition, as in the Netherlands and Luxembourg, the Belgian labour movement has always had a strong trade union current committed to a Christian social doctrine and emphasising a co-operative approach to the representation of employee interests rather than polarisation and conflict. Finally, the corporatist compromise survived because more radical ideas for introducing greater economic democracy in the post-war period were thwarted by the politics of the Cold War.

Denmark

The origins of the Danish trade union movement, which grew up in close association with the socialist and social democratic movements but later avoided any major political division, lie in the last three decades of the nineteenth century. Spurred on by the parallel organisational efforts of the employers, who established a central association in 1896 (*Dansk Arbejdsgiverforening*–DA), a number of national craft unions were established in the 1890s, culminating in 1898 with the foundation of a central confederation, *De Samvirkende Fagforbund* (DSF), forerunner of the current union centre, the *Landsorganisation* (LO).

This initial phase was concluded with an arrangement which has continued to shape Danish industrial relations until the present day. In 1899, following several months of industrial action, the DSF and DA signed the 'September Compromise' under which each side recognised a set of mutual rights and obligations. Trade union rights to organise, the right to strike and the employers' lock-out were acknowledged as legitimate weapons provided certain procedures were complied with; and each side agreed to conclude, recognise and abide by collective agreements and ensure their implementation. In return, the unions recognised management's prerogative over the production process, together with a fundamental and reciprocal commitment to industrial peace. This accord initiated a regulated approach to dealing with industrial conflicts which was further developed in the following decade through agreements on arbitration and conciliation procedures, the establishment of a system of labour courts, and the setting-up of a national conciliation board.

Although the 1899 September Accord enshrined the principle of free collective bargaining, the state has been active as a third party in the industrial relations system. In part, it has merely offered legislative ratification to arrangements already agreed between unions and employers. However, it also retained the right to intervene directly in bargaining – a process which has continued to the present day under both Social Democratic and Conservative-Liberal administrations.

Organisational structure

In addition to the *Landsorganisation i Danmark* (LO), which with 1.4 million members organises the majority of blue- and white-collar employees in national industry, craft and general unions, there are two other significant national organisations. The FTF (*Funktionärernes og Tjenestemändenes Fällesrad*), with 350,000 members, was established in 1952 as a non-politically affiliated union centre for civil servants and white-collar workers, with the particular aim of contesting the egalitarian policies pursued and encouraged by the LO, and of maintaining these member groups' special status within the labour force. Secondly, in 1972, the merger of a number of professional organisations led to the formation of the *Akademikernes Centralorganisation* (AC), with around 100,000 members. Like the LO and FTF, the AC is involved in collective bargaining at local government and national levels through its participation in the appropriate collective bargaining forums.

In 1990, the LO consisted of twenty-nine affiliated unions operating on a number of organisational principles. As well as two unions which organise unskilled and semi-skilled workers (SiD, with 320,000 members, and the Union of Women Workers with 102,000), both of which are amongst the five largest LO affiliates, there are a number of craft unions, the most influential of which is the 140,000-strong engineering workers' union, *Dansk Metalarbejderforbund*, and several industrial unions and organisations for white-collar workers and public sector employees. Of this latter group of unions, the Commercial and Salaried Employees Union (HK), with 320,000 members, forms one of the largest LO unions.

Although LO congresses in 1971 and 1987 agreed resolutions intended to streamline organisational and bargaining arrangements by establishing industry unions, with an initial grouping into five sectoral 'cartels', these have not yet accelerated the process of concentration. What reduction has taken place in the number of unions (from fifty-six in 1970 to twenty-nine by 1990) has been the result of merger rather than reorganisation. One pressure towards merger, at least for smaller organisations, has been the requirement in force since 1985 that only unions with more than 5,000 members can claim state support in the running of unemployment insurance funds.

The first functioning industrial cartel was in the engineering industry, and was established primarily through direct links between the unions involved – the skilled workers' union Dansk Metal, the SiD and various craft unions – rather than through the official LO process, which has stalled. The cartel, which changed its name from 'CO-Metal' to 'CO-Industri' in 1992, has become an important force in the reshaping of bargaining in Denmark away from centralised bargaining and towards the conclusion of industry agreements with considerable scope for additional workplace negotiation. In 1993, bargaining was further streamlined by the incorporation of seven branch agreements into one 'Industrial Agreement' for manufacturing industry.

The basic unit of the individual unions in the LO is the local association. In larger firms or plants, these are often supplemented by 'clubs' embracing members of several craft or union branch organisations, led by an elected steward who also serves as a trade union representative. If there are clubs made up of several unions in one establishment, the shop stewards will form a joint club and elect a representative.

At district level, the local associations of the LO's affiliated unions also come together in joint cartels. Cartels between individual unions also operate at the level of government districts, with representatives of local joint organisations and full-time regional officials of the LO. Co-ordination between trade unions at local and regional level, and the direct representation of the LO, are increasingly aimed at influencing local government decisions and obtaining a voice in other decision-making bodies at these levels – a process bolstered by the decentralisation of 1970 local government reform and 1976 social security reform.

As with its constituent unions, the LO's decision-making bodies embrace, firstly, a Congress which meets every four years and consists of members of the Executive Committee, together with the central executives of the constituent unions supplemented by one delegate for every 2,000 members, and representatives of the local and regional joint organisations. Apart from electing the President and Executive Committee of the the LO, Congress's main task involves amending the confederation's constitution, setting contribution levels, passing resolutions on the admission of new organisations, and determining overall union objectives.

The Committee of Representatives, which meets annually between Congresses and is composed of the Executive Committee and representatives of the constituent unions in proportion to their membership, supervises the activity of the Executive Committee, deals with administrative issues and ensures that the aims and priorities of the LO are put into practice.

The real decision-making centre of the LO is the twenty-one-strong Executive Committee, sixteen of whom are representatives of the constituent unions elected by Congress, ensuring domination by the largest unions (and in particular the SiD and Dansk Metal).

Despite signs of centralisation, and bureaucratisation, the LO is characterised neither by its dominance of constituent unions (whose contributions finance it), nor by the unrestrained autocracy and autonomy of the individual trade union leaderships. The main factor limiting the power of union leaderships is the substantial scope for member participation at local branch level combined with a requirement that changes to collective agreements must be confirmed by a mandatory ballot of members. Furthermore, the differences of interest and policy which arise between the constituent unions, and in which the LO exercises a mediating role, militate against excessive centralisation.

Ultimately, the real power of the LO lies in its power to conduct collective bargaining and sign agreements. Whereas the LO exercises competence on general matters, especially those which entail provisions (such as pensions), which affect the whole workforce, bargaining on industry-specific matters, including the regulation of industrial disputes and the maintenance of strike funds, is left to the constituent unions. Collective bargaining on pay has alternated between centralised rounds (between the LO and the national employers association DA) and decentralised rounds (that is, at industry level) since the mid 1980s, with occasional direct government intervention to resolve protracted disputes. The most recent trend is towards greater decentralisation, with looser industry agreements leaving greater scope for company level bargaining. However, the shift to industry bargaining has not functioned entirely smoothly, and the LO has still found an important role in mediating between organisations and agreeing national provisions.

The FTF confederation consists of forty-two individual unions divided into three sections: one section embraces white-collar employees in the private sector and accounts for around 25 per cent of the FTF's membership; another section brings together organisations representing employees in local and regional government, totalling around 35 per cent of the membership; and the third section is a confederation of central government employees, accounting for the remaining 40 per cent of the FTF's membership.

The FTF also has the usual decision-making bodies: a Congress which meets every two years and consists of representatives of the constituent organisations in proportion to their membership; a General Council which makes decisions between Congresses and which, in addition to members of the FTF's Executive Committee, contains thirty representatives from the three sections, weighted accorded to membership; and an Executive Committee which is elected by Congress (though with a composition which must reflect the membership strength of the three sections). The Executive Committee is the most important body both for co-ordinating and managing the FTF.

The sections' main functions are to act as a link between the constituent unions, to elect members for the General Council and to elaborate proposals for the members of the Executive Committee. Apart from this, they primarily exercise an advisory and consultative role.

Since the mid 1980s, a structure has been created at district level to enable the confederation to respond to the growing powers now enjoyed by the lower tiers of local government. This is especially important in securing and representing union interests in local and regional bodies on issues such as labour market policy, training and education, and policy on technology and the environment.

The FTF does not have any particular competence vis-à-vis its member unions; its activities in the field of collective bargaining – that is, its involvement in the joint union committee of all central government employees (CFU) and the committee of local government employees (KTU) are based solely on powers ceded, and renewed at regular intervals, by the member unions.

When originally founded in 1952, the FTF was repudiated by the LO as an organisation set up as conservative competition to itself. However, growth in the FTF's membership and the importance of white-collar workers in the electorate led to recognition by the Social Democratic Party. This, together with the exigencies of collective bargaining, finally led to an agreement in 1972 between the LO and FTF which provided for mutual recognition and a demarcation procedure. This defused what had been the source of considerable tension and, despite differences, opened the way to co-operation in bargaining. Since then, the LO, FTF and AC have presented joint claims to both private and public employers.

Membership trends and structure

With a total of 2.1 million members, the LO, FTF, AC and other employee organisations account for more than 80 per cent of Denmark's labour force. This would appear to have virtually exhausted the potential for trade union membership, especially since there is now practically no variation in the willingness of different employee groups (blue-collar; white-collar; unskilled women – who make up 46 per cent of the LO and 55 per cent of FTF) to join trade unions. A number of reasons underlie the high level of union density. In part, the success of the Danish union movement can be attributed to the diversity of organisations and services, with scope for maintaining existing employee status as well as extending opportunities for acquiring skills and participating in vocational training. Job insecurity – especially among white-collar workers – also plays a role, and was especially marked in the 1970s when the readiness of this group to join unions increased substantially. Danish unions also play a role in the provision of services undertaken elsewhere solely by the state. For example, unions are closely associated with the administration of the state-subsidised unemployment benefit funds and, until reform of the public employment exchange system, were also involved at local level in the operation of job placement services.

Despite the multiplicity of organisations within the LO and FTF, the bulk of the membership is concentrated in a small number of trade unions who, as a consequence, exercise considerable, but by no means always congruent, influence on trade union policy. This divergence does serve to contain their power over smaller organisations – a fact illustrated in the debate on organisational reform and consolidation which has been continuing in the LO for around two decades. Within the LO, the commerce and office workers' union HK (310,000 members), the women's trade union (102,000), the semi-skilled workers' union SiD (320,000), the metalworkers' union Dansk Metal (138,000) and the local government union (120,000), account for around 70 per cent of the membership. The FTF exhibits a similar degree of concentration, with three organisations (the teachers' association, the bank employees' unions and the nurses' council) accounting for over 40 per cent of the membership.

Workplace employee representation

Industrial relations in Denmark are characterised both by a long tradition of institutionalised arrangements and a high degree of autonomy from the state in the field of collective bargaining. These two factors also go some way to explaining why the main institutions of workplace employee representation are based not on statutory provisions but rather on national agreements concluded between the LO and DA. There are four forms of employee representation at workplace and enterprise level. Workplace level representation through shop stewards and 'co-operation committees' are both based on framework agreements between the LO and DA; in contrast, workplace health and safety committees, and representation on the supervisory boards of public limited companies, are provided for in legislation.

Arrangements between trade unions and employer associations for the election of shop stewards (m. *tillidsmand;* f. *tiilidskvinde*) at the workplace extend back to the beginning of this century. They are now all embraced by a national agreement between the LO and DA, with appropriate modifications at industry level. On average, one shop steward is elected for every fifty employees. They function as representatives of the trade unions at the workplace, have special protection from dismissal and are entitled to time-off to carry out their duties. Stewards thus serve as a link between management and workforce through their role in handling the whole range of issues affecting workplace terms and conditions. However, since stewards are also usually active trade unionists, they play an important role in linking the workplace with the broader organisations of the trade unions. Their specific tasks are usually regulated in collective agreements, although they do not enjoy any special rights of participation or codetermination. Rather, they are principally a mediating and consultative institution, required by collective agreements to contribute to co-operative and peaceful industrial relations at the workplace.

In the private sector, 'co-operation committees' have been operating under an agreement between the DA and LO since 1947. They may be set up either on the initiative of management or the majority of employees in workplaces with more than thirty-five workers. Committees consist of equal numbers of employer and employee representatives, with the chair appointed by management and the deputy chair by the employees. Committee size depends on the number of employees in the establishment. Employee representatives are elected by all employees every two years, although a proportion of committee places are reserved for trade union shop stewards in order to facilitate co-ordination with general trade union objectives.

Co-operation committees are not empowered to deal with matters which are already regulated by an industry or by national collective agreement or company pay agreements. They also have no guaranteed rights to influence managerial decisions as such. Rather, the LO/DA 'Co-operation Agreement', most recently amended in 1986, provides for a set of broad rights to information and involvement in establishing basic principles for a wide range of workplace issues. For example, there is a right to information on the financial situation and economic outlook of the company, the employment situation and its future development, and any planned changes to the organisation of the workplace. There are consultation rights on general production and personnel planning, as well as on more extensive changes to the establishment. Since 1986, greater powers have existed over the introduction of new technologies, with extensive information and consultation rights. The participation of co-operation committees in establishing basic principles for the structuring of the working environment, general personnel matters, training and retraining in the field of new technology, and the storage of and access to personal data, means that they enjoy effective rights of codetermination in these fields. Disputes can be resolved through a multi-stage conciliation procedure.

Independent workplace health and safety committees exist on the basis of health and safety legislation first passed in 1975. They consist of representatives of management and elected employee representatives. The committees basically have a consultative role, but may carry out independent inspections and call directly on the official health and safety executive.

Employees have had statutory rights of representation on the supervisory boards of companies with more than fifty employees since 1974, should the workforce wish it. Although initially confined to two employee board representatives, employee representation was raised to one-third of the supervisory board (at least two members) in 1980. Employees elected to the supervisory board have the same rights and duties as other board members, and are also protected from dismissal under most circumstances.

Trade unions and the state

The LO's influence on government policy has traditionally been exercised through the organisation's close links with the Social Democratic Party – a connection secured through mutual membership of each organisation's highest level decision-making bodies, a joint ad-hoc committee for policy co-ordination and close personal connections. Nevertheless, the relationship is not entirely free of conflicts and difficulties. The scope for the LO to promote its interests during the periods of Social Democratic participation in government between 1930 and the early 1980s was limited by the fact that the Social Democrats were involved either in coalitions or as a minority party. And, for most of the 1980s and up to 1993, Denmark has been governed by a conservative-liberal coalition often in in overt conflict with the unions. Both these circumstances have served to emphasise the importance of the provisions and arrangements negotiated with the DA, rather than the LO's political contacts.

Above and beyond these established institutions in the industrial relations field, there is also a long and accepted tradition that employer and employee organisations should be brought into the processes of political decision-making. In addition to participation in various official bodies, the LO and FTF (as well as the employer organisations) sit on the tripartite National Economic Council which provides a forum within which union influence can be exerted on issues such as incomes policy, economic policy and social policy. There are also numerous national and local consultative bodies in the fields of employment, training and education policy.

France

The French trade union movement has always been characterised by a high degree of fragmentation, combined with a marked political and religious pluralism. Its origins lie partly in the Labour Exchanges (*bourses du travail*), which brought together different associations of craftworkers at local level during the 1880s, and partly in the numerous branch and industry unions which joined together in the *Fédération Nationale des Syndicats* in 1886. For much of its history the movement has been regarded as strong, combative, and capable of mobilising masses of workers. But large-scale losses of membership since the mid 1970s, especially on the part of the CGT and CFDT (formerly the two most powerful confederations), have brought about a steep reduction in the level of union density and necessitated a re-evaluation of the status and influence of the French trade union movement.

The trade union confederations

The oldest French confederation, the *Confédération Générale du Travail* (CGT), was initially established in 1895 as a syndicalist organisation, independent both of broader political positions and parties and of the state. Following the First World War and Russian Revolution, it became a battleground for communist, reformist and anarcho-syndicalist factions. It became clear that these divisions could not be contained within a single confederation, and one of the immediate effects was the establishment of the Christian *Confédération Française des Travailleurs Chrétiens* (CFTC) in 1919. During the 1920s the CGT remained beset by conflicts between its various political tendencies, with one faction, the CGT-U, breaking away to join the Red Trade Union International in 1923. In 1936, during the period of the Popular Front government, these divisions were successfully surmounted for a while, only to re-emerge in the wake of the Second World War. The Cold War, during which the CGT executive adopted an unambiguously pro-communist stance, led to the breakaway of social democrats in the union to establish, in 1947-

Table 2.1 Overview of the French trade union confederations

Name	Year of formation	Number of members (1986–88)	Political outlook	Main areas of organisation
CGT (*Confédération générale du travail*)	1895	c. 1 million	Communist	Metalworking, construction, printing, paper, mining, docks, public sector (electricity, railways, post)
CFDT (*Confédération française démocratique du travail*)	1964	600,000	Socialist	Metalworking, health service, food, education, chemicals, transport, technical workers
CGT-FO (*Confédération générale du travail – Force ouvrière*)	1948	c. 1 million	Reformist	Public sector, banks, insurance
CFTC (*Confédération française des travailleurs chrétiens*)	1919/64	250,000	Christian, reformist	Coal mining, religious schools, health service, banking, chemicals
CGC (*Confédération générales des cadres*)	1944	250,000	Moderate, reformist, status-oriented	Senior, middle and lower level white-collar workers; chemicals, metalworking and energy
FEN (*Fédération de l'éducation nationale*)	1948	395,000	Socialist	Education, training, science

Source for membership figures, Bibes and Mouriaux (eds) *Les Syndicats européens à l'épreuve* (Paris, 1990).

48, their own confederation, the *Confédération Générale du Travail – Force Ouvrière* (CGT-FO) often abbreviated to FO. The same period also saw the formation of another important, independent sectoral union in education, the *Fédération d'Education Nationale* (FEN). The CGT-FO, initially strenuously anti-communist, has generally followed a reformist and pragmatic course of 'pure trade unionism' since its break with the CGT. In contrast to the CGT, which remains overwhelmingly blue-collar, the CGT-FO has successfully recruited in the growing service sector. One consequence has been that over the past ten years, the CGT-FO has survived the crisis in French trade unionism in generally better shape than either the CGT or CFDT federations (see below). In terms of membership, the CGT-FO now broadly equals the CGT, which has shrunk considerably.

The third confederation, the *Confédération française démocratique du travail* (CFDT), which grew out of the Christian and in particular the Catholic trade union movement, loosened its ties with the Catholic church after the Second World War. After protracted internal disputes, it emerged in the mid 1960s as a radical socialist confederation with a particular emphasis on grass-roots democracy and a commitment to class struggle (leaving its religious rump to reconstitute itself as the CFTC in 1965). Despite a number of policy differences, it established an informal alliance with the CGT in the 1960s and 1970s. However, during the late 1970s the CFDT decided to abandon a number of its more radical, anti-capitalist positions and embrace 'profit and the market place as the pillars of the capitalist economy' (Leggewie, 'Französische Gewerkschaften auf dem wege in die postindustrielle Gesellschaft?', in W. Müller-Jentsch (ed.) *Zukunft der Gewerkschaften*, (Frankfurt, 1988)). The traditional dual structure of French trade unions is most easily seen in the simplified diagram, Figure 2.1.

In general, common histories have meant that the similarities in structure are greatest between the CFDT and CFTC on the one hand, and the CGT and CGT-FO on the other. Nevertheless, within this overall pattern, the differences can be quite considerable. For example, the FO has 16,000 local trade unions (*syndicats*) as its basic unit of organisation, composed of workers in the same locality working in similar types of employment: these are combined into its twenty-eight national industry federations. In contrast, the CFDT has only 2,000 constituent *syndicats*. And whereas the 500 odd local unions (*unions locales*) of the CDT-FO highlight the decentralised operation of its *départmental* level unions (*union départementale*), this does not apply in the case of local and regional sections within the CGT. The basic unit of organisation in the CFDT is the local trade union, which forms the foundation for both industry unions and occupational unions. It is geographically defined and must be constituted so as to 'be compatible with the demands of

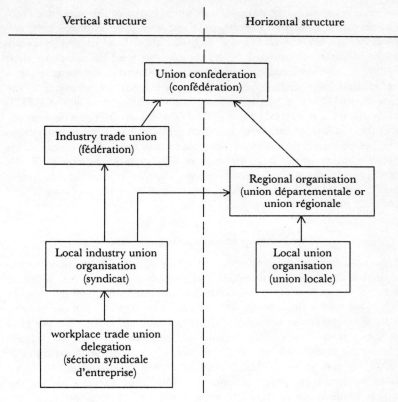

Figure 2.1 Dual structure of French trade unions

continuing action and democratic [functioning]' (ETUI, *The trade union movement in France*, Brussels, 1987, p35).

There are few differences between the leadership structures of the national industry federations, occupational unions and the main confederations. The FO has twenty-eight national federations, the CFDT twenty-three, the CGT thirty-seven including three professional and managerial unions, and the CFTC fifty-one. They are all governed by their respective federations' congresses, which usually meet every two to three years, the national confederal committees which determine the policies and day-to-day running of the national individual unions and are elected by the congresses or executive committees, and the administrative or executive committees, also elected by congress, which are responsible for implementation of congress decisions.

At the level of the confederations, the most important bodies are the national congresses, the national confederal bureaus, the executive committees and the national executives. In line with their emphasis on grass-roots democracy, the CFDT and FO only allow local unions (*syndicats*), and not *département* unions or federations, to send delegates to their congress. The national executives are of particular significance: they are elected and monitored by the national confederal committee in the case of the FO, and by the national council in the case of the CFDT, and include a secretary or a member of the board from a federation; members of the national executive are ordinary members of the executive commissions, which are responsible for the conduct of union affairs between national committee meetings. The general secretaries of the confederations' national executives have a special role in that they meet and negotiate at national level with the government, Parliament and political parties.

Membership trends and composition

Economic and political changes since the mid 1970s have led to a dramatic loss of union membership. Trade union density has now fallen to around 10 per cent of the workforce, compared with 25–28 per cent in the 1970s and a peak of 55 per cent in 1946. Pessimists have put the level of organisation at less than 9 per cent overall, and only 6 per cent in the private sector. This overall development has also altered the relative membership levels of the individual confederations, with politically reformist and negotiation-oriented unions gaining ground relative to more conflict-oriented unions. The CGT, for decades by far the largest confederation, has been most badly hit. Having lost members through job losses in traditional industrial sectors such as coal and steel, where the CGT had always been the leading union, it was unable to offset this by developing successful strategies for recruiting among female and younger employees, and white-collar and more technically skilled employees. The CGT's main area of recruitment remains male, middle-aged, skilled blue-collar workers. In particular, the difficulties experienced by the CGT in responding to the increasing number of women in the workforce, the growing tertiary sector and the pace of technological change, have served as a barrier to recruiting new potential members in the labour force.

From a membership of around 4 million in the early 1950s, the CGT was down to a mere 835,000 in 1985, according to the French employers' organisation, or 1.6 million on the CGT's own estimates, which are probably somewhat optimistic. A 1990 study put its membership at about 1 million (see above). Developments in the former Eastern bloc countries, and the inability of the CGT to liberate itself from the authoritarian socialism of the French Communist Party and thus attract new members in the growing service sector, presage further membership losses in the medium term. According to the same 1990 study (see table above), the CFDT's membership fell from 830,000 in 1976 to an estimated 600,000 by 1990.

In contrast, unions which have pursued a more conventional bargaining approach, such as the CGT-FO and the CFTC, have retained and in some cases increased their memberships and grown in importance in relation to the other confederations. Loss of membership, poor levels of dues collection, and high membership turnover have resulted in a generally catastrophic financial situation for most French trade unions. It is estimated that union dues provide only 12 per cent of the money needed by confederations for their activities. Continuing declines in membership will undoubtedly lead to greater union dependence on the state, narrowing the scope for unions to act independently. (State funds are available to cover election costs to bodies such as industrial tribunals, and for training.)

Company level representation

There is a dual structure of employee representation at workplace level. On the one hand, statute law provides for two types of body to be set up and elected for the representation of the workforce as a whole, depending on the size of establishment: staff representatives (*délégués du personnel*) and/or works committees (*comité d'entreprises*). On the other hand, trade union delegates (*délégués syndicaux*), who also enjoy legal recognition and workplace bargaining rights, only directly represent their own members and function as independent trade union bodies with no obligation to co-operate with managements. In addition, the law provides for a complex system of representative bodies, such as health and safety committees, and committees responsible for working conditions, which function alongside these two sets of institutions.

This complex system of representation is a product of the diverse currents within the French labour movement, in which syndicalism and council communism, corporatism and militant oppositionism, have all exercised varying degrees of influence. The oldest form of representation is that of staff representatives, whose role has not fundamentally changed since their initial conception as shop floor representatives within a broader works council structure. Originally an institution of control in the munitions industry during the First World War, they were legally recognised during the Popular Front Government of 1936. Elected annually by secret ballot, they now function as an institution for monitoring compliance with the law and collective agreements, and can raise grievances on a wide range of issues related to pay, working conditions and staffing arrangements for the entire workforce or for individual employees. However, their scope is comparatively limited in that they have no powers to influence managerial decisions or overall negotiating rights.

Works committees, which have been incorrectly compared with the German system of works councils, are unique in many respects and only distantly related to the German model. Their origins lie partly in the Social Committees of the 1941 Vichy Labour Charter and partly in production committees operated in Britain and Canada during the Second World War. Initially legislated for in 1946, they were legally defined and recognised in 1975 (amended in 1982) as bi-partite company level bodies with rights to information and consultation on economic and technical issues. The obligation to co-operate is reinforced by the fact that works committees are chaired by employers or their representatives. Mandatory in companies of fifty or more employees the committees must be informed of staffing levels, business and production matters and the general situation of the company, and must be consulted before any decision is taken concerning the structure and activities of the company, especially where this affects working conditions, the introduction of new technologies and collective dismissals. But the only field in which works committes have any decision-making powers is in the organisation of company social activities. Works committee members are entitled to limited time-off in order to carry out their duties. Compliance with the law is patchy, both for staff representatives and works committees. Official studies have found, for example, that only a minority of smaller firms (50–99) employees) establish works committees and supply them with the volume and type of information required.

Table 2.2 Results of works committee and industrial tribunal elections

	Works councils			Industrial tribunals		
	1982	1986	1990	1982	1987	1992
CGT	32.3	27.1	24.9	37.0	36.3	33.3
CFDT	22.8	21.2	19.9	23.5	23.0	23.8
FO	11.7	14.4	12.8	17.8	20.5	20.5
CFTC	2.9	3.8	3.6	8.5	8.3	8.6
CGC	7.0	7.5	6.5	9.6	7.4	7.0
Other	4.4	5.0	5.6	3.7	4.5	
Non-union	18.4	21.1	26.6	–	–	

Source: Liaisons Sociales, various issues; *Semaine Sociale Lamy*, No. 627, 14 December. 1992.

Since their inception, the election procedure for works committees has granted unions which are deemed to be representative in a company a monopoly on submitting candidates in the first round of elections; since 1965 they are also entitled to have a non-voting member sit on the company board. As a result, most works committees are dominated by trade union members, at least in large companies.

However, the influence of trade unions within works committees is diminishing, as shown by the growing abstention levels in works committee elections and the fact that non-trade union members gained the largest number of votes – 26.6 per cent (the CGT gained 24.9 per cent in the 1990 elections). Nevertheless, the position of trade unions within works committees is still comparatively strong, especially when set against the low level of direct union membership.

Health and safety committees

Under legislation introduced in December 1982, health and safety committees must be set up in companies with fifty or more employees: their task is both to ensure the health and safety of employees, through monitoring the implementation of regulations, and to improve the working environment. The size of the committee varies according to the number employed in the company. As well as employee representatives, the committees also include the employer, who sits in the chair, an occupational physician and safety engineer if available. Employee members enjoy protection against dismissal and are entitled to time-off to carry out their duties.

Employee's 'right of expression' groups

Under a body of legislation passed in 1982 and known as the 'Auroux laws' after the then Minister of Labour, measures were introduced with the aim of strengthening employee representation at workplace level and encouraging local bargaining (see also below). One of these provisions gave employees the right to express opinions on a broad range of workplace matters, primarily through collectively agreed arrangements. Agreements on the employees' right of expression are negotiated at company level between employers and trade union delegates (or staff representatives where there is no trade union delegation). Where there are neither trade union delegates nor staff representatives, or should negotiations break down, the employer may unilaterally create and run right of expression groups, and is legally required to consult annually on such rights.

Research into the workings of these groups has shown that they have not fulfilled trade union hopes of gaining access to and recruiting non-organised employees. 'Right of expression' groups, which in theory are well placed to put forward ideas on how to improve working conditions and raise quality, have so far not played a significant role in companies. But neither have fears been borne out that they would undermine workplace trade union representation. Nonetheless, there are still concerns that employers might use such groups as part of a human resource management strategy, designed both to bypass trade union representation and inculcate an unchallenged, company-defined set of values and expectations.

Trade union delegates
(délégués syndicaux)

Although the 1936 Popular Front Government outlawed discrimination against employees on grounds of trade union membership, a right subsequently enshrined in the 1946 Constitution, the employers succeeded in preventing the statutory recognition of company trade union sections until the events of May 1968. Legislation passed in November 1968, which met the long-standing demands of employee organisations, granted recognition for trade union representation and bargaining at company level. Its provisions, subsequently amended in the 1982 Auroux laws, form the basis for union workplace representation. In 1987 there was at least one trade union section (*section syndicale*) in around 50 per cent of companies with over fifty staff, and around 95 per cent of companies with over 1,000 staff. Elected or appointed delegates from trade unions represented within the company have the same rights to protection against dismissal as staff representatives and works committee members, and are entitled to a certain amount of time-off (for example, ten hours a month in companies of 50-150 employees and twenty hours a month in companies of over 501 employees). Trade union delegates in companies of more than 200 employees are entitled to their own office. There is one trade union delegate per union in companies of 50-999 employees and up to five in companies of over 1,000 employees. Trade union delegates are responsible for the professional and economic interests of trade union members.

The most important function of these delegates is their role in collective bargaining. Employers are required to bargain annually where a trade union section exists, although there is no obligation to come to agreement. As the only workplace representative institution which can bargain on pay and other matters, trade union sections' rights at this level are becoming increasingly important with the growing trend towards company level bargaining in France.

Employee representation at board level

Under a decree passed in 1986 employee representatives may sit on the board of quoted companies with full voting rights, as long as this number does not exceed five representatives or one third of total board seats. Employees who sit on one of the other representative bodies cited above may not become board-level representatives. In private companies with a board of directors, two members of the works committee may sit on the board, although they do not have voting rights.

In public sector companies, legislation passed in 1983 which aimed to liberalise the public sector, provides for the right of two employees to sit on the board in companies which are at least 50 per cent publicly owned and have 200-1,000 employees. In companies with more than 1,000 employees, the workforce is entitled to one-third representation on the board.

National forms of representation

French trade unions have always regarded state institutions with a high degree of scepticism, extending to outright rejection. Support for, or close co-operation with government, stands in contradiction to their traditional insistence on autonomy and struggle. As a consequence, trade union access to politically influential positions in government and Parliament has remained very limited, and trade unionists are under-represented in Parliament. However, many important changes in bargaining arrangements and working conditions have been legislated for rather than negotiated between employers and unions, both offsetting union weakness but at the same time compounding and perpetuating it. The tripartite National Collective Bargaining Board is a consultative body administered by the Ministries of Labour and Agriculture. Its two functions are to advise the Minister responsible for employment on legislation connected with collective agreements and to oversee increases in the national minimum wage, SMIC.

Despite the ambivalent relations between unions and the state, unions are represented on a large number of advisory councils, bi- and tri-partite committees, and in corporatist institutions such as the national Economic and Social Council and Planning Commissions. They are also represented on the High Council for Modernisation and Supplies, on social organisations such as the High Council for the Prevention of Occupational Hazards (CSPRP), on retirement and unemployment bodies such as the governing bodies of pension funds, the national inter-industry body for employment in industry and trade (Unedic) and on the boards of social security and family allowance funds and regional economic and social councils. However, almost without exception, these institutions have only limited powers. Left-wing trade unions remain equivocal about these institutions, viewing them partly as a public platform for voicing their demands and partly 'as a means of obtaining useful information'.

Germany

The foundation of the German Trade Union Confederation (*Deutscher Gewerkschaftsbund* – DGB) in October 1949, in the wake of the establishment of the Federal German Republic, did not realise the hopes for the creation of an all-German trade union centre which many unions had striven for in the immediate postwar period. Differences between trade unions in the Allied occupation zones in the west and those in the Soviet occupation zone, combined with the onset of the cold war internationally, ultimately made it impossible to fulfil this ambition. The DGB was constituted, and continues to be, a non-party union confederation whose affiliates are organised as industrial unions: that is, aside from any problems of demarcation between industries, there is only one DGB union for each industrial sector. Each union, therefore, consists of employees of all occupations and categories, encompassing manual and non-manual workers (including supervisors and managers).

In addition to the DGB, which organises the vast bulk of trade unionists, there is a white-collar union, the Salaried Employees Union (*Deutsche Angestellten-Gewerkschaft* – DAG), which bargains either independently or at a single table with DGB unions, and a Christian Trade Union Confederation (*Christlicher Gewerkschaftsbund* - CGB). There is also a separate association for established civil servants, the DBB (*Deutscher Beamtenbund*), which does not have bargaining rights, as civil servants' pay and conditions are set by administrative decree, usually in the wake of the main public sector settlement. However, some civil servants do opt to join those DGB-affiliated unions which organise in the public sector.

Compared with the experiences of the Weimar Republic (1918–33), overcoming the political divisions within the trade union movement and bringing the vast majority of the organised labour force into industry unions was a major advance. And despite the failure of efforts to keep the DAG within the DGB, which meant that some white-collar workers remain outside DGB-affiliated unions, the fact that a substantial proportion of civil servants are members of the DBB, and the existence of the small Christian Trade Union Federation, this essentially positive assessment still holds good. However, the comparatively meagre representation of women and young people was, and is, one evident weakness in the postwar confederation.

The decision to adopt a federalist central organisation with autonomous industrial unions as the membership organisations, in contrast to the centralised single union initially favoured by some trade union representatives, has also proved beneficial in terms of internal democracy. The dangers of bureaucratisation, and remoteness between the leadership and membership in a centralised structure would certainly have been greater than in the confederal arrangement chosen.

Following the decision to establish a confederation of autonomous industry unions embracing all employees, and rooted in district – not workplace – organisations, the central issue became the precise regulation of the relationship between the individual unions and the central confederation. The 1949 DGB constitution gave extensive powers to the individual affiliated unions, with the result that the preponderant influence over important policy decisions within the DGB is exercised by the larger unions. Although the DGB's constitution was amended in 1962 to strengthen the position of the Federal Executive Committee, and an Extraordinary Federal Congress examined the controversial issue of the distribution of powers within the DGB, there has been no move towards strengthening the powers of the confederation at the expense of the affiliated unions.

The structure of the DGB and affiliated unions

Both the DGB and its (present) sixteen affiliated individual trade unions share a similar structure. (Several union mergers have been decided or proposed which will decrease the number of DGB affiliates over the next five years or so: these include the merger of the chemicalworkers' union, IG Chemie-Papier-Keramik, with the mining and energy union, IG Bergbau, and the leatherworkers' union, Gewerkschaft Leder, and the building workers' union, IG Bau-Steine-Erden, with the horticulture, agriculture and forestry workers' union, Gewerkschaft Gartenbau, Land- und Forstwirtschaft.) The DGB is financed by dues contributed by the affiliated unions. Presently, each sends 12 per cent of its membership contributions to the DGB. On average, individual members pay around 1 per cent of their gross income. As well as maintaining its administrative structure (again, see below), the DGB runs a publishing house (Bund-Verlag), a research institute (WSI), and a network of training and educational establishments. In addition, the directors' fees payable to employee representatives on company supervisory boards (see below) are used to finance a DGB research foundation (the Hans-

Böckler-Stiftung) which focuses on issues related to industrial democracy and workplace organisation.

With the exception of the education and science union GEW (*Gewerkschaft Erziehung und Wissenschaft*), the unions within the DGB each encompass all the organised employees of a specific industrial branch. In some cases, these definitions are very broad (the DGB has responsibility for resolving any inter-union disputes about industrial boundaries). For example, IG Metall, which represents metalworkers, negotiates on a regional basis a single agreement covering aerospace, the automotive industry, metal fabrication, electrical engineering and electronics. In addition, the union also represents workers in the iron, steel and non-ferrous metal industries.

The basic level of organisation is the local association (*Ortsverein*) whose members (or their delegate or representative meeting) elect lay and full-time members to the local executive committee. The full-time members of the local executive committees exercise a double role. On the one hand, they represent the executive committees to the outside world and vis-à-vis higher trade union bodies. On the other hand, as employees of the central executive committee, they are subject to its instructions and are obliged to implement these among the membership. Nevertheless, the proportion of members' dues which remains at this local level – between 12 and 25 per cent – allows scope for some local initiative.

Whereas the network of local executive bodies in the affiliated industry unions is generally structured according to the location and size of their respective industries, the DGB districts (*Kreise*), the lowest level of organisation of the DGB itself, are usually co-terminous with the administrative sub-divisions of the constituent states or *Länder* of the Federal Republic, also termed *Kreise*. (Prior to unification there were just over 200 DGB districts.) District executive committees may establish local associations or trade councils (*Ortskartell*) with the agreement of the executive committee at *Land* level: in 1986 there were 1262 such local cartels. These have the task of recruitment and of servicing members in the areas in which they live, and are also expected to raise trade union concerns at the lowest tier of local government.

The local executive committees of the individual trade unions are co-ordinated and controlled by regional (*Bezirk*) administrations. These do not coincide with the DGB's regional administrations (*Landesbezirken*). Since collective bargaining is undertaken at regional level by independent collective bargaining committees, usually composed mostly of elected works councillors and full-time union officials from the local executive committees and the region, the regional level is particularly important within the structure of the individual unions. In some unions, the regional executive committee can be directly elected by the regional conference, consisting of delegates elected from local executives, without any involvement by the unions' national executive committee; in others, confirmation by the national executive is required. In the event of conflicts between the heads of a regional and of the national executive committee, the overall interest represented by the central executive takes precedence over any district or local special interest. Within the DGB, the regional administration, consisting of an executive committee and a conference, exercise similar functions to those carried out by the individual unions' regions.

The supreme body of the individual unions is the conference, delegates to which are elected at local level on a quota system for each of the regions. Full-time officials make up a substantial proportion of the delegates. Between conferences, the highest decision-making body is the Advisory Council (*Beirat*), usually dominated by full-time officials. The conference elects the full-time members of the unions' central executive committee and formulates the guidelines and tasks of union policy. The composition of the delegates to union conferences, in so far as it is known, suggests that control over the conduct of union executive committees is rather limited. Real power in the individual unions lies with the central executive committees, which in turn are divided into a full-time administrative committee and a lay committee. The executive committee is required to direct and control all the lower level organisations, conduct collective bargaining, administer unions' publicity and information activities, and organise trade union education and other tasks.

Table 2.3 Membership of German Trade Union confederations (31.12.92)

Confederation		Membership 31.12.92	Change 1991–92
DGB		11,015,612	- 784,801
DBB		1,095,399	+ 42,398
DAG		578,352	- 6,423
CGB		315,550	+ 4,719
Total	1992	13,004,913	
	1991	13,749,019	
	1990*	9,534,170	

Note: * former West Germany.
Source: WSI

Table 2.4 Membership of DGB affiliated unions, (31 December 1992)

Union	Sector	Total membership	% in W. Germany	% female members
IG Bau, Steine, Erden	Construction	695,712	64	11
IG Bergbau und Energie	Mining and energy	457,240	66	8
IG Chemie, Papier, Keramik	Chemicals, paper	818,840	81	25
Gew. der Eisenbahner	Railways	474,530	64	19
Gew. Erziehung und Wissenschaft	Education and science	346,040	49	68
Gew. Gartenbau, Land- und Forstwirtschaft	Horticulture, agriculture, farming	120,190	34	30
Handel, Banken u. Versicherungen	Financial services	629,730	61	68
Gew. Holz und Kunstoff	Wood and plastic	204,760	78	20
Gew. Leder	Leather	31,890	80	48
IG Medien	Media, printing	236,300	76	34
IG Metall	Metalworking	3,394,280	76	20
Gew. Nahrung-Genuss-Gaststätten	Food, catering, leisure	394,680	68	41
Gew. Öffentliche Dienste, Transport und Verkehr	Public services and transport	2,114,520	59	47
Gew. der Polizei	Police	197,000	75	12
Deutsche Postgewerkschaft	Postal service	611,240	76	43
Gew. Textil-Bekleidung	Textiles, clothing	288,000	79	61
TOTAL DGB		11,013,612	69	32

Notes: IG = *Industriegewerkschaft* (Industry trade union); Gew. = *Gewerkschaft* (trade union). Some 66 per cent of all DGB-affiliated union members are manual workers, 24 per cent white-collar and 10 per cent established civil servants.

The DGB's Federal Congress, which initially met every two years following the DGB's foundation in 1949 and has convened every four years since 1978, is dominated by the large affiliated unions (IG Metall; ÖTV, the public sector union; and IG Chemie-Papier-Keramik). A high proportion of delegates are full-time officials: that is, 'the Parliament of Labour' is largely controlled by the representatives of union executives. This applies in particular to the DGB's Federal Executive Council (*Bundesausschuß*), the highest DGB body between Federal Congresses.

Internal trade union democracy has exhibited a rather disappointing trend over the years, compared with the immediate post 1945 period. The proportion of trade union members participating in union affairs has fallen considerably, and the influence of central bodies and full-time officials has grown. Local bodies have lost rights, for example to submit motions to Federal Congresses; and elected officials have had their periods of office lengthened.

In 1992, overall tade union density in Germany stood at some 40 per cent. Unions affiliated to the DGB accounted for 85 per cent of all trade union members and 34 per cent of the dependent labour force. Prior to unification, trade union density in West Germany was some 37 per cent. Unification initially both boosted membership of trade unions (see below), raised the overall level of union density, and increased the proportion of women members – reflecting almost universal trade union membership and the very high female participation rate in the ex-GDR.

Following social and economic unity in July 1990, the former East German trade union confederation, the FDGB, entered into a phase of rapid collapse. Unable to adjust to the new political and legal realities of economic union and the importation of West German industrial relations and collective bargaining, it was also overtaken by its past as a mere 'transmission belt' for the policies of the East German Communist Party, the SED. During the autumn of 1990, West German unions began to prepare for a formal extension of their activities into the Five New *Länder*. The FDGB was formally dissolved on 30 September 1990, and its individual constituent unions made arrangements to transfer their members, either individually or less often en bloc, to the corresponding West German industrial union.

After the initial boost in membership of some 4,000,000, the accelerating pace of de-industrialisation in 1991/2 was accompanied by substantial membership losses. The DGB as a whole lost 766,000 members in East Germany in 1992 – 18 per cent of the East German total. In some cases, trade unions whch had expanded their offices and number of full-time officials to deal with the influx of members have found themselves financially overstretched. Whereas the onset of recession led to membership losses of 1–2 per cent in the main industry-based unions in West Germany in 1992 (no doubt greater in 1993), manufacturing unions lost over 40 per cent of their members in some cases in East Germany. In other instances, most notably the banking and commerce union HBV, the loss of some 30 per cent of its members may be attributable as much to individual white-collar employees exercising a genuinely free choice over union membership for the first time in their working lives.

Although manual workers have accounted for a steadily shrinking proportion of the overall labour force in the past two decades, they continued to make up 63 per cent of trade union members in 1992. The critical recruitment issue for the future is the need to attract white-collar workers. The proportion of the dependent workforce accounted for by white-collar workers rose from 29 per cent in 1960 to over 50 per cent by the late 1980s (excluding civil servants). And although the share of white-collar members in the DGB's overall membership has also progressively increased, they still only accounted for 29 per cent of DGB union membership in 1990. Union membership among this category of employees remains well below that for other workers. However, over the past thirty years DGB-affiliated unions have performed better at white-collar recruitment than the non-DGB white-collar union, the DAG: between 1960 and 1985 the proportion of organised white-collar employees represented by the DAG fell from 38 to 21.5 per cent.

Membership growth among women – previously another critical target group – has also been above average in recent years. Their share of total DGB membership exceeded the 20 per cent mark for the first time in 1980, and by 1992 they accounted for 32 per cent. The effects of unification on the gender composition of the DGB's membership can be seen in the fact that in 1990, women made up only 24 per cent of union membership in West Germany. This positive development has been offset by a steady decline in male membership, with overall membership remaining broadly constant over the decade (see also the chapter on Germany in Part I). In contrast, the share of young members has been falling, possibly reflecting the general rejection by young people of 'establishment' organisations.

Trade unions and workplace employee representation

The German system of industrial relations – the product of several decades of struggle by trade unions and employees for rights of representation at the workplace – is characterised by a dual structure in which works councils, established and organised under statutory provisions, exist alongside workplace union representation in a relationship which, if co-operative, is not without its tensions and conflicts. Fundamental to the relationship is the fact that trade unions as institutions, that is, the actual organisations staffed by full-time officials, have never been rooted in the workplace but have located their basic unit of organisation in geographical bodies (local, regional and national).

The works council system

Works councils are employee-only bodies, directly elected by the whole workforce, initially at 'establishment' level, where there are at least five eligible employees: an 'establishment' (*Betrieb*) may be a single company, but in larger organisations might be an individual plant, administrative unit, or retail outlet. In turn, individual works councils can establish corporate-level works councils by delegation, or group works councils in conglomerates. In contrast to the employee representation in some other EU member states, there is no obligation on the employer to set up a works council. It is a matter entirely for the workforce. However, once established, the employer must recognise it, provide appropriate facilities, and comply with the various statutory obligations on information disclosure, consultation, and codetermination (see below). The rights enjoyed by works councils vary according to workforce size, and on certain issues (such as rights to redundancy compensation) to how long the business has been in operation.

There have been three laws regulating works councils: the 1920 Works Councils Act, introduced following the 1918 revolution and the subsequent establishment of the Weimar Republic; the 1952 Works Constitution Act; and the 1972 Works Constitution Act, which introduced substantial improvements to the 1952 law, and which, amended in the late 1980s, provides the current legal basis for workplace employee representation.

The organisational provisions of the 1952 Works Constitution Act (*Betriebsverfassungsgestz*), introduced under the Christian Democrat administration led by Chancellor Adenauer, harked back in many fundamentals to the 1920 Works Councils Act of the Weimar period. However, the 1952 law contained a number of important qualifications. On the one hand, it included a number of limitations, such as political neutrality, an absolute 'peace obligation' obliging works councils to refrain from all forms of industrial action, and an injunction to co-operate with the employer in a spirit of 'mutual trust'. The law, which was opposed by the trade unions and the Social Democrats, ran directly counter to the broad subordination of works councils to the trade unions – a policy which had been pursued by the unions after 1945 and which had been supported by the occupying military governments. On the other hand, the law established clearly defined rights of co-determination (*Mitbestimmung*) which could be enforced through conciliation machinery established under the Act and empowered to issue binding rulings. 'True' codetermination, however, was only conceded on such 'second order' social matters as the company rule-book, the administration of working-time and holidays, and payments systems, where these had not already been adequately regulated by an industry (or, more rarely, a company) collective agreement. On personnel questions, and more particularly on matters directly related to the conduct of the business, works councils had, and have, only rights of consultation, not codetermination.

The trade union response to the neutrality of works councils sought by the 1952 legislation was the establishment of a system of workplace-based union representatives – that is, of shop-stewards (*Vertrauensleute*). This was prompted, in particular, by the fact that the statutory limits on the scope and powers of works councils, together with their duty to represent both union and non-union employees, prevented them from functioning as an adequate vehicle for representing union policies and interests at the workplace. Compared with the 1952 Act, the 1972 Works Constitution Act – introduced by the Social Democrat government under Willy Brandt – extended codetermination rights on 'social matters' and strengthened the participation of the works councils on dismissals. For example, works council agreement must be sought over the pattern of working hours (but not their overall duration, which is set by industry agreement), the introduction of overtime and short time, devices designed to monitor employees' performance, and health and safety. Where no agreement is reached, either party can seek a binding ruling from a conciliation committee. All dismissals must be notified to a works council, with appropriate justification. Although a works council cannot prevent a dismissal, its opinion will be taken into account in any labour court proceedings.

A new right of codetermination was created on issues of work organisation and job design to ensure that any changes were not 'in obvious contradiction to the established findings of ergonomics', although this was hedged in a number of respects. An enforceable right to negotiate a 'social compensation plan' (*Sozialplan*) to provide payments for redundancy, retraining or other support to employees was also granted to works councils in the event of changes in the running or organisation of the establishment impinging on the workforce. Major improvements were also made in the conditions under which trade union officials had access to workplaces and works meetings. Under the 1952 Act, employers had effectively been able to deny union officials access to plants.

These rights enable works councils to conduct negotiations with managements on a broad range of issues, although any formal agreements they might make lack the legal force of collective agreements and may not supersede them.

The relatively high share of non-union works council members compared with the Weimar period, especially in small and medium-sized establishments, illustrates that the anti-union 'integrationist' policies pursued by countless employers have not been without success. Amendments to the 1972 Act, pushed through by the Conservative-Liberal coalition in 1988–89, extended the period of office of works council members from three to four years, bolstered the position of minority organisations (such as smaller non-DGB unions) in works council elections, and established representative bodies for executives. They may make it more difficult in future for works councils to present a unitary standpoint to the employer. However, the 1990 works council elections (see below) did not show any marked trend in this direction.

Table 2.5 Works council election results from 1978–90

		1978	1981	1984	1987	1990
Participation:						
All employees		81.3	79.9	83.7	83.3	78.14
Manual		81.9	79.9	82.6	82.5	79.14
White-collar		80.8	79.3	82.5	83.6	75.85
No. of establishments		35,294	36,307	35,343	34,807	33,012
No. of councillors		194,455	199,125	190,193	189,292	183,680
Percentage:						
in DGB:	WC Members	58.6	63.2	63.9	65.4	69.3
	WC Chairs	71.4	79.9	75.1	74.8	78.4
in DAG and other unions:						
	WC Members	18.1	13.5	10.7	7.1	5.6
	WC Chairs	15.2	9.6	7.9	5.1	5.2
Non-union:	WC Members	23.3	23.3	25.4	27.5	25.2
	WC Chairs	13.1	10.5	17.04	20.1	16.45
Women:	Members/ chairs	20/13	15/6	19/11	19/9	19/11

Source: *Gewerkschaftsreport* (September 1990), DGB.

Of the 75-80 per cent of works councillors who are trade union members, those given time-off for works council duties also serve in an active way in the internal democracy of the trade unions, often as lay officials. A study carried out by IG Chemie-Papier-Keramik found, for example, that the executive committees of their local administrations were largely staffed by works council members from large firms who had been given time-off under the works council legislation.

Trade union organisation at the workplace: shop stewards

The anti-union thrust of the 1952 Works Constitution Act, which denied trade unions any possibility of developing works councils into trade union bodies for workplace employee representation, combined with economic crises, especially in 1966–67 and after 1974, led to the reinvention of a type of workplace representative which had first emerged in the late nineteenth century – the shop steward (*Vertrauensmann* or *Vertrauensfrau*, literally 'man/woman of trust').

Whereas some unions, such as IG Metall, made intense efforts to set up shop stewards' organisations during the consultation period for the 1952 law, other unions, such as the railway workers' union (GdEB) and the postal workers' union (DPG) did not create their own networks of shop stewards until some decades later. Several trade unions, such as the construction union, IG Bau-Steine-Erden, and Gewerkschaft Gartenbau, Land- und Forstwirtschaft, still rely almost exclusively on their representatives on works councils. Shop stewards are elected by trade union members in a work unit or area at the workplace. If this does not function, they are often elected by the local trade union organisation for various departments at a workplace. Shop stewards at a workplace will constitute a shop stewards' committee (*Vertrauenskörper*), headed by a convenor (*Vertrauenskörperleitung*). Large establishments may have intermediate departmental committees.

Although delegates at trade union conferences frequently seek to obtain greater powers for shop stewards within unions, most trade union organisations in Germany have so far continued with their policy of not conceding shop stewards any autonomous scope for negotiation or action. They cannot initiate industrial action, for example, and do not play a part in union bargaining machinery. And, in contrast to works councils, they have no legal rights at the workplace itself. Rather, shop stewards serve as an extended arm of local and regional trade union organisations, and transmit workplace interests, opinions and demands back to the organisation.

Progress towards the goal of having shop stewards acknowledged by employers, as a legitimate trade union presence and as a valid voice on corporate policies, has been very slow. Nonetheless, there are some collective agreements providing for the recognition of shop stewards' organisations, and under German law there is no formal difficulty in concluding binding arrangements for shop stewards on temporary release from work or for additional protection against dismissal.

In contrast to the position of shop stewards in Great Britain or *delegati* in Italy, the position of works councils in Germany is much more protected and legally secure than that of union workplace representatives.

Moreover, central union organisations have been very reluctant to cede powers to their shop stewards. As a result, stewards' organisations play an active role only in a small number of large companies. In most companies, or in public administration, finding suitable union members to take on the task remains a major problem. At best, shop stewards' committees function as auxiliaries of the works councils and as important agents in the shaping of opinion and in inner-union democracy.

Employee representation at enterprise level

Employee representation on the supervisory boards of German companies is provided for under three separate statutory provisions, dating back initially to the immediate postwar period. German companies above a certain size threshold must establish a two-tier board structure. The supervisory board (*Aufsichtsrat*), on which employee and union representatives sit, oversees the general policy of the company, appoints managers, and has a right to information on the company's business activities. The management board (*Vorstand*) or managing directors, responsible for day-to-day management, are appointed by the supervisory board. In contrast to representation via works councils, which has considerable day-to-day practical impact, board level representation is primarily concerned with access to corporate information.

In 1950–51 the Federal German Government, which needed trade union support for the implementation of the Schumann Plan for the restructuring of the coal, iron and steel industries, declared itself willing to grant a measure of employee codetermination in the running of these industries, albeit under the threat of a strike by the engineering and mineworkers' unions. Under the 1951 Act on codetermination in the coal, iron and steel industries (*Montanmitbestimmungsgesetz*) employees are entitled to complete parity with shareholder representation on the supervisory boards of companies engaged in these industries, with a neutral member in the chair (with a casting vote). One member of companies' management boards, the Labour Director, who has special responsibility for personnel matters, may not be appointed against the wishes of the majority of employee representatives. In contrast, under the 1952 Works Constitution Act, employee representatives were granted only one-third representation on the supervisory board of companies with more than 500 employees, and despite trade union efforts, this situation was not revised in the 1972 Amendment.

The 1976 Codetermination Act, which the unions hoped would extend equal employee/shareholder representation into all large companies with 2000 or more employees, did not fulfil all the ambitions of the trade union movement. Although there is nominal parity of representation between employee and shareholder members on the supervisory board, the chair, who has a casting vote, is always a shareholder representative. (The deputy chair is an employee representative.) Moreover, managerial employees have separate representation on the employees' side, and can often be relied on to support shareholders in the event of a conflict. The 1976 law also allows the employer to appoint a Labour Director of their choice.

Although most employee board members will be employees of the enterprise, with separate representation for manual, non-manual and managerial staffs, some seats are set aside for trade union representatives. Senior trade union figures, such as the general secretaries of unions, often sit as deputy chairs of the largest companies. Their fees are used to finance the Hans Böckler Foundation, which carries out research into industrial democracy and work organisation.

Trade union influence at regional and national level

German trade unions are not formally political, although there are close ties between the DGB and the Social Democratic Party. In 1986 some 80 per cent of the top officials of the DGB were members of the the SPD; the remainder were members of the Christian Democrats, the CDU. The national executive of the Christian Trade Union Confederation, the CGB, was made up solely of members of the Christian Democrats and the Bavarian-based Christian Socialists (CSU). In the white-collar union DAG, the national executive was made up of six SPD members and three CDU members. The only union in which a top official was a member of the Liberals (FDP) was the German Civil Servants Confederation, the DBB. The close personal links between the SPD and DGB are illustrated by the table below, showing the composition of the Lower House of the Federal German Parliament, the Bundestag.

In the past, the fact that trade unionists have accounted for a majority of members of the Bundestag (in 1981, 304 out of 519; in 1987, 275 out of 519; but in 1990, 265 out of 662) has been used by critics of the trade union movement to allege that Germany had become, or was in danger of becoming, a 'trade union state'. To some extent, this criticism would have to be modified in the face of the lower percentage of Bundestag members who reported themselves as trade union members following the post-unification elections in 1990. Disillusion with the trade union movement of the former GDR, which was widely perceived as too integrated into the structure of the state, may well have led to a disproportionately high percentage of eastern German candidates not being trade union members shortly after unification. Moreover, voting by trade union MPs is overwhelmingly in line with their party allegiances, or in the interest of sustaining coalitions, rather than following

Table 2.6 Trade unionists in the XII German Parliament (elected December 1990)

Parties	CDU/CSU		SPD		FDP		Bündnis '90/ Greens		PDS		Total	
	Seats	%	Seats	%	Seats	%	Seats	%	Seats	%	Seats	%
	319	48.2	239	36.1	79	11.9	8	1.8	17	2.6	662	100
Of which trade union members:												
DGB	11	3.4	176	73.6	1	1.3	–	0.0	6	35.3	194	29.3
DAG	3	0.9	–	0.0	1	1.3	–	0.0	–	0.0	4	0.6
CGB	6	1.9	–	0.0	–	0.0	–	0.0	–	0.0	6	0.9
DBB	47	14.7	2	0.8	5	6.3	–	0.0	–	0.0	54	8.2
DJV	2	0.6	–	0.0	1	1.3	–	0.0	–	0.0	3	0.5
ULA	2	0.6	–	0.0	2	2.5	–	0.0	–	0.0	4	0.6
Total*	71	22.3	178	74.5	10	12.7	–	0.0	6	35.3	265	40.0

Notes: DGB = *Deutscher Gewerkschaftsbund*; DBB = *Deutscher Beamtenbund* (civil servants); DAG = *Deutsche Angestellten-Gewerkschaft* (white-collar employees); DJV = *Deutscher Journalistenverband* (journalists); ULA = *Union Leitenden Angestellten* (managers); CGB = *Christlicher Gewerkschaftsbund* (Christian).

* Double counting in some cases.

Source: Emil-Peter Müller, *Strukturen des XII Deutschen Bundestages*, DIV, (Cologne, 1992).

trade union interests. Active trade unionists, that is, former and current full-time or lay officials, make up a much smaller percentage. For example, in the VII parliamentary period during the early 1970s, such activists accounted for only 16 per cent of MPs compared with 54 per cent for all trade unionists. Moreover, the share of active officials has been falling for some time, as has the share of all unionists since 1980. This may well reflect the view that the bias towards the Social Democrats was too strong, choking off independent criticism of the policies of governing coalitions in which the SPD had been involved.

Although a matter for concern, the view – advanced by some left-wing commentators – that German trade unions have been swallowed up into governing institutions and policies is both over-simplistic and far from proven. German unions were indeed drawn into tripartite economic management, following the 1967 Economic Stability Act introduced during the 1966–69 'Grand Coalition' of Social Democrats, Liberals and Conservatives. These so-called 'Concerted Action' discussions on pay and employment continued through the early 1970s. However, the DGB withdrew from this forum in 1977, ostensibly because of a decision by the employers to challenge the 1976 Codetermination Act in the courts. But the unions were also concerned that tripartite discussions on pay were edging towards pay norms or guidelines of a more formal and binding character, weakening free collective bargaining.

Although there is no formal national structure of tripartism in Germany comparable with the Benelux countries, trade union representation is spread throughout the broader network of civil institutions. In addition to the possibilities for influencing Parliament, legislatures at *Land* level and their committees, as well as the Federal and *Land* governments, trade union representatives are active in thousands of advisory committees in Federal and *Land* ministries, in the directorates of the public broadcasting institutions, on the benches of labour tribunals and not least in the numerous organisations which administer the social security system. All in all, these bodies offer the trade unions substantial scope to present their policies, seek support for their positions or register their objections. But in contrast to the view that Germany has become a 'trade union state', none of these institutions is in any way dominated by unions.

Great Britain

As the vanguard of the Industrial Revolution, Britain has provided the home for the oldest trade union movement in the world. Following in the wake of industrialisation, numerous, often locally based, craft unions developed during the first half of the nineteenth century. The organisational structures which characterised these craft-based organisations have continued to contribute to the highly heterogeneous make-up of British trade unionism. Efforts to establish general trade unions, often in conjunction with ambitious political objectives, during the 1820s and 1830s largely failed to consolidate themselves into enduring organisations. From the mid nineteenth century onwards, trade union organisation began to take root amongst non traditional craftworkers, though still overwhelmingly skilled, often corresponding to specific industrial occupations, especially in the cotton and coal industries. As a result, semi-skilled and unskilled workers were, in the main, excluded from effective trade union organisation until the final decades of the century.

The displacement of craft skills by the advance of machine-based production, and the creation and concentration of new occupations through urbanisation and technical development (such as the provision of town gas), led to the emergence of an expanding number of un-skilled and semi-skilled workers whose exclusion from the craft unions prompted the creation of new forms of union organisation. These developed in parallel with a different political conception of the role of working-class organisation – the 'New Unionism'. The decisive period was the 1880s, and in particular the immediate wake of a bout of intense industrial struggle in 1889. That year saw the foundation of the gasworkers' union (led by Will Thorne, a member of the Marxist Social Democratic Federation) which won a number of decisive victories for the eight-hour day, and the dockers' union (led by Ben Tillet). Each served as the nucleus of the great general unions of the twentieth century, the gasworkers' union becoming the General Municipal and Boilermakers' Union (GMBU) and the dockers' union growing into the Transport and General Workers' Union (TGWU).

The pressure from such generally more combative unions, combined with a desire to maintain or expand the size of their organisations, led to many craft unions widening their memberships to admit semi- and unskilled workers. This, for example, characterised the policy of the Amalgamated Society of Engineers, founded in 1851, after 1912. As a result, the union (as the AEU) developed into a general union for large areas of the engineering industry. The process continues today; the 1992 merger of the AEU with the electricians' and plumbers' union (EETPU) (itself a conglomerate extending beyond its initial occupational scope) to form the AEEU has, in turn, created a union of skilled and semi-skilled workers, including white-collar employees, organising throughout manufacturing industry. Broadening the criteria for membership has also gone hand-in-hand with an accelerating process of union merger, by which larger unions have absorbed smaller and more specialist unions. This has culminated in a trend towards the creation of 'super unions' through the amalgamation of more or less equally large organisations (see below).

Despite the great variation and constant change in the organising bases of British unions, the following main forms can be identified. In reality, these organisational types are rarely encountered in their pure form, and most trade unions exist as deviations or as mixtures of these types.

— *Industrial unions*, which organise all employees in a particular branch of industry, irrespective of their type of activity or skill level. These barely exist in Great Britain in a form comparable with German industrial unions. Even organisations which most closely resembled a true industrial union, such as the National Union of Mineworkers up until the mid 1980s, often co-existed with separate unions for some specialist occupations. Moreover, the rapid abandonment of industry-bargaining by employers since the early 1980s means that such organisations would not have a comparable employers' organisation to negotiate with at industry level. Some occupational unions, such as the Fire Brigades Union, function virtually as industrial unions as they embrace such a high proportion of the relevant membership within an area of activity. Although, in the past, the TUC supported initiatives to establish industrial unions, facilitating the necessary mergers has proved more difficult. Organisations representing the employees of an individual company – staff associations – are also accepted as trade unions in the United Kingdom. The main examples can be found in banking and finance. Many staff organisations have joined broader trade unions in recent years.
— *Craft unions*, which recruit their members solely on the basis of a completed apprenticeship in a recognised trade or narrowly defined

area of skilled work. As well as craft manual unions, this category would also include some professional associations which engage in negotiation and representation, as well as the traditional activities of professional regulation. There are numerous examples embracing such occupations as airline pilots, radiographers, hospital consultants and many other health service occupations. Many larger craft unions, as noted above, have extended their scope either to include a greater number of skilled occupations or to recruit semi-skilled and unskilled workers. Many smaller craft unions have been absorbed by merger in recent years.

— *General unions*, which in principle organise members of all industrial branches and trade unions without any occupational demarcation. General unions with a bias towards one sector, a grouping of sectors or a set of broadly related occupations, have become the dominant form of trade unionism in Great Britain. Even within general unionism there are distinctive types. The GMB and TGWU, both of which date from the late nineteenth century, provide examples of organisation across sectors, occupations and categories. There are also unions which organise across occupation and category but which remain confined to the public sector, while others have arisen as general organisations for white-collar employees only. As a result of privatisation in the 1980s, a number of public sector unions now represent workers in private sector organisations. Many general unions are the product of specific histories and organisational ambitions: MSF (Manufacturing, Science, Finance), for example, with 668,000 members, emerged in 1988 out of an amalgamation between the union ASTMS, which was rooted in supervisory staffs but which represented a vanguard of white-collar organisation in many service industries in the 1970s, and TASS, the white-collar and technical section of the engineering union AEU. As such, MSF is now a multi-industry union primarily for skilled white-collar employees, but also encompassing some manual workers. Up until the 1980s, the manual/non-manual divide was an important one within the British trade union movement, despite the existence of white-collar sections within both general and industrial unions. Union mergers and the erosion of status differences have substantially weakened the rigidity of the divide and there are now few pure status-based trade unions.

The proliferation of different types of union means that the scope for a collision of interests is very high. Several unions, either by virtue of their history, occupational focus or organisational logic, may lay claim to be the appropriate representative for any given group of workers or any given workplace. Potential inter-union conflicts over representation are dealt with by the single central confederation, the Trades Union

Congress (TUC), for affiliated unions, through an agreement (the 'Bridlington Agreement' of 1939) which sets out principles for resolving contested areas of recruitment. During the 1980s, there were a series of high-profile conflicts over the issue of single-union representation, principally on new, greenfield sites where unions engaged in so-called 'beauty contests' to win managerial recognition.

In a small, but symbolically significant, number of cases, these involved unions, most notably the electricians' and plumbers' union (EETPU), offering a package of industrial relations innovations, such as 'no strike' clauses and final offer arbitration ('pendulum arbitration'), in return for sole bargaining rights. These conflicts between unions were an expression both of immediate organisational ambitions, as unions sought to preserve themselves during a period of rapid membership decline, as well as broader political disagreements on the character of trade unionism and its role in the United Kingdom's protracted economic problems. Unions such as the AEU and EETPU represented the 'New Realism' of abandoning class warfare, adapting to Conservative Party legislation, and welcoming inward foreign direct investment. The problems came to a head with the expulsion of the EETPU from the TUC in 1988, but have been mitigated through its subsequent merger with the AEU, and the acceptance of the new organisation back into the TUC.

In general, the continuing pace of union merger in the early 1990s has eased the problem of inter-union conflict over representation. Moreover, a change in the law could also throw the entire system into disarray. Under the 1993 Trade Union Reform and Employment Rights Act, employees will have a statutory right to join any trade union they wish, irrespective of any action taken by the TUC to regulate a dispute over recognition between unions.

The number of trade unions has fallen steadily. In 1865 there were some 1340, and still over 1000 in 1940. The decline in the number of unions, primarily through amalgamation and the incorporation of small unions into larger ones, but also through outright disappearance, accelerated after 1945. By 1991, the number had fallen to 302, with a total membership of 9.5 million. In that year, just over 80 per cent of all union members were in unions affiliated to the TUC – a fall from the approximate figure of 90 per cent in TUC-affiliated unions at the start of the 1980s. In all, there are some 70 unions in the TUC.

Overall trade union density rose from around 25 per cent in the interwar years, to about 45 per cent in the immediate post-war period and remained at this level between 1950 and 1968. It then rose steadily through the 1970s to peak at 53 per cent in 1979, aided by a supportive legal framework after 1974 but also boosted by the prevalence of high inflation in the 1970s. Employer policies during the 1970s also favoured union representation, especially within the public sector. By 1988 it had fallen to 41 per cent, and by the early 1990s was down to between 35 and 37 per cent.

Table 2.7 Total union membership and TUC membership 1980–91

Year	Total union membership*	TUC membership
1980	12,900,000	12,172,000
1985	10,818,000	9,855,000
1990	9,810,000	8,405,000
1991	9,489,000	8,192,000

* rounded to nearest 1000
Sources: Annual Report of the Certification Officer, TUC.

TUC membership has fallen markedly since its 1979 peak of over 12 million. By 1993 membership was down to 7,786,890. Hopes for a stabilisation in the rate of decline, after the precipitate drop of the early 1980s, were dashed by the recession which began in 1990, and which led to further large-scale losses in the more strongly unionised fields of manufacturing employment, as well as in many of the previous white-collar gains in fields such as banking and financial services, also seriously affected by the downturn.

There is continuing controversy over the explanation for the fall, and, in particular, the extent attributable to new industrial relations practices and the introduction of human resource management, with their associated non-recognition of unions, and the extent attributable to industrial (and thus regional and demographic) shifts in employment. The most severe drops in union membership have taken place during the two periods of recession (1980–82, and since 1990), lending weight to the view that the economic cycle and associated impact on the composition of the workforce have been paramount. However, non-recognition of unions at new sites, together with derecognition and the shift towards greater individualisation of pay setting continued throughout the 1980s. De-recognition, though limited, has had a marked effect in smaller firms and particular sectors, such as printing and publishing.

The Trades Union Congress (TUC)

In contrast to trade union movements in many other EU member-states, the British movement has only one central confederation, the Trades Union Congress (TUC). The TUC was founded in 1868, primarily as a lobbying organisation to influence existing and prospective legislation on union matters, and, in particular, to free workers from the threat of criminal prosecution for organising and taking industrial action. Initially, the TUC's activities were channelled through its Parliamentary Committee, which consisted of the leaders of the main affiliated unions. As such, the TUC did not possess an administrative apparatus of its own until after 1900, and did not begin to function in its current form until the 1920s.

Although the Labour Party, established in 1918, was founded by TUC-affiliated unions, the TUC itself is neither formally nor organisationally linked to the British Labour Party. Nevertheless, during the 1970s, the TUC-Labour Party Liaison Committee, which comprised key senior TUC General Council members, played a crucial part in the shaping of policy during the 1974–79 Labour Government. This body has now been replaced by less formal, though nonetheless close, links – paralleling the changing institutional relationship between individual unions and the Labour Party (see below). Not all member unions of the TUC are affiliated to the Labour Party. For example, a number of unions which organise within the civil service do not affiliate. In all, some 30 unions affiliate to the Labour Party. A larger number, 52 in 1991, operate a political fund which may be used for campaigning purposes as well as for Labour Party affiliation and the sponsorship of MPs (see too, section on Great Britain in Part I).

In contrast to many other EU union centres, but like the German DGB, the TUC does not bargain directly with employers. However, from the Second World War until the election of the Conservative Government in 1979, the TUC played a major role in national economic and industrial affairs, and from the early 1960s was deeply involved both in the growing number of tripartite institutions and accords, mostly taking the form of incomes policies, which characterised that period. This involvement was most intense during the later periods of Labour Government (1964–70 and 1974–79).

The supreme policy-making body of the TUC is the annual congress, which consists of 800 delegates from its affiliated unions, represented in proportion to membership on the basis of one delegate for each 5000 members – or fraction of that number. The congress's task is to debate and vote on motions submitted by affiliated unions, set the organisation's policy, elect the General Council and scrutinise the annual report produced by the General Council.

Between congresses the key policy and executive body is the General Council, which meets monthly, and consists of fifty members. Elections to the General Council are on the basis of union size, with four separate sections. Section A is made up of unions with at least 200,000 members: such unions are automatically entitled to at least two members of the General Council, rising to six for unions with more than 1.2 million members. All unions with a female membership of more than 100,000 must also nominate at least one woman. Section B consists of members from organisations with between 100,000 and 199,999 members: such unions can nominate one member each. Section C embraces unions with fewer than 100,000 members: these are elected, with the total number of seats available depending on the total membership of the smaller unions. Section D consists of four women members elected from unions with fewer than 200,000 members each.

The General Council also operates through, and is serviced by, a number of committees handling administrative and financial questions, and specific policy areas such as education and training, equal rights, European strategy, social, health and environmental matters, and women's interests. Since the early 1970s, a number of industry committees have also been established, with representatives from all the relevant TUC-affiliates in each industry. In 1992 there were seven such committees, covering both the private and public sectors. During 1993, the TUC embarked on a major review of its role, function and methods of operation. Particular concern was expressed over the fact that a disproportionate amount of the TUC's activity was directed towards servicing its committees rather than pursuing clearly defined policy objectives of external relevance. As a result, a major re-shaping is in train, with a suspension and/or concentration of committees, less frequent meetings of the General Council, and the redeployment of staff and resources to projects identified as important to the TUC's broader objectives. For example, a major study was commissioned on trade union responses to human resource management techniques.

The TUC is organised on a regional basis into Regional Councils for the main regions of England, together with a Wales TUC which is part of the British TUC. There is a separate Scottish TUC and a Northern Ireland Committee of the Irish Congress of Trade Unions: both are invited to attend meetings of the TUC's regional councils' consultative committee. The TUC's regional organisations are to be alloted an enlarged role following the TUC relaunch in 1994.

The TUC does not have a local organisation as such. Rather, there are around 340 local trades councils consisting of representatives of local trade union branches. Trades councils are grouped on a county basis into county associations. Compared with their constituent unions, the councils have few rights and powers, with only a consultative role within the TUC itself. Their relatively minor importance is testified to by the fact that only a third of total trade union membership is affiliated to trades councils.

Despite a proliferation of sometimes competing unions and an organisational heterogeneity, the distribution of members between the TUC-affiliated unions reveals a marked concentration within a small number of organisations. The eight largest TUC unions account for some 60 per cent of total TUC membership. This phenomenon is likely to become more pronounced with the creation in July 1993 of the 1.4 million strong 'super union' UNISON, in the public sector, and the possible merger between the TGWU and GMB.

The process of concentration has been fostered by the TUC, although it carries risks for the importance and role of the TUC itself which have been the subject of recent debate. Union merger and rationalisation have also been a response to the frontal attacks mounted on the trade union movement by Conservative Governments since 1979 and the associated decline in membership. The increase in 'atypical' forms of employment during the 1980s has also created further recruitment difficulties for unions, and unions are still grappling with the need to develop strategies to recruit more effectively among groups such as part-time workers.

Internal union organisation

Given the continuing diversity of organisational principles among TUC unions, there is also considerable variation in their internal arrangements. The trade union legislation introduced by the Conservative Governments during the 1980s has had a major effect both on the formal democracy of trade unions and on the relative power and scope of union executives, full-time and lay officials, and members. In addition, by creating a common statutory framework for many aspects of internal union government, it has led to some convergence of arrangements between formerly very different union structures, in particular in the procedures for electing senior officials.

The basic unit of trade union organisation is the branch. However, the composition and organisation of branches varies considerably between unions. Whereas some unions constitute branches on a trade or single employer basis, others – most notably the Amalgamated Engineering and Electrical Union (AEEU) – have a geographical structure. The Transport and General Workers Union (TGWU) has over 5000 branches with members organised in terms both of their place of residence and of their place of work.

At local level, branches are customarily run by lay officials directly elected by the membership (see also workplace representation below). Most union branches also have a right to elect delegates to their national union conference, the supreme decision-making body. Compared, for example, with German trade unions, the scope for local bodies, such as branches, to influence national union policy is much greater, with more say by rank-and-file members in the running of the union.

In some unions, branches frequently demonstrate a considerable degree of autonomy over policy matters.

As with the TUC, the individual unions also have regional or district structures, although the precise pattern is highly variable (the TGWU has eleven geographical regions; the AUEW twenty-six regions and 244 districts). Most of these bodies are headed by full-time officials who answer directly to the national executives, although district committees may also consist of lay officials.

Before the 1980s, unions exhibited a variety of mechanisms for the election of principal officials and union executives. Some positions were directly elected, others appointed, increasingly following a conventional external recruitment exercise. In some cases, election or appointment was for a fixed period; in others, it was for life. The 1984 Employment Act introduced the requirement that all voting members of a union's principal executive committee had to be elected by a ballot of the whole membership every five years. The 1988 Employment Act required that all such elections be by postal ballot. A further change introduced by the 1988 legislation was the additional requirement that non-voting members of national executives, which in some unions included general secretaries, also had to be elected to office every five years.

Some unions also have executive committees composed of full-time officials whilst others consist of lay representatives. Together with a secretariat, it is these national executive committees which determine union policy.

Contribution levels are low by international comparison. In 1988 they stood at 0.36 per cent of average earnings, against 1 per cent in Germany and up to 1.8 per cent in some Scandinavian unions. However, there are wide differences in contribution levels and the wealth of individual unions. Benefits, especially strike pay, are commensurably lower. The share of income devoted to the provision of social benefits, which formed an important component of unions' activities until the 1960s, declined from over 44 per cent as recently as the 1930s, to around 12 per cent by the late 1980s. At the same time, in an effort to enhance their attractiveness as organisations, some unions and the TUC have introduced schemes to give members discounts on the purchase of a wide range of goods and services, free or cheap access to legal services, and preferential terms for house purchase or other financial services.

In contrast to the TUC, which does not have a formally institutional relationship with the Labour Party, the individual unions are directly represented in the organisation of the Labour Party and account for the bulk of its income via their 'political funds', which can be established subject to a membership ballot. The role of the unions in the Labour Party is in a state of flux, and the future is likely to see a growing formal separation, although unions will continue to exercise considerable institutional power in the Party (in particular, through votes at the Party's annual conference) for some time to come. For the trade unions, separation has been sought first on the grounds of needing to recruit beyond a traditional Labour-aligned working class, second because of the unprecedentedly long period of Conservative government since 1979, and third because of the observation that, in general, non-political union movements in Europe have been more successful at retaining members than highly politicised ones. For the Labour Party, a position more closely resembling that of continental social democracy, though with a commitment to support trade unionism, is felt to offer better electoral prospects than the perception that 'the unions control the Labour Party', despite the arguable nature of this proposition on important policy matters since the late 1970s. Irrespective of the need which both the trade unions and the Labour Party see in reducing their constitutional entanglement, there will be continuing contact, negotiation and exchange around mutual objectives.

Inter-union co-operation – the federations

One set of institutions designed to offset the disadvantages of multi-unionism and foster union co-operation are the trade union confederations and federations. These consist of individual unions, not all affiliated to the TUC, either in specific sectors or representing broad occupational groupings (insurance, the entertainment industry, seafarers, civil servants). The most developed is the Confederation of Shipbuilding and Engineering Unions (CSEU), which consists of some twenty-two unions representing around 2 million workers. The aim of the confederation is to facilitate common action by the affiliated unions on negotiations, and the CSEU played a prominent role in the campaign for a 35-hour week in 1989–90.

Workplace employee representation

There are no individual statutory rights to representation at the workplace. Individual employees only have rights to representation if they are members of a trade union which has obtained recognition from the employer. Typically, recognition will be for the purposes of collective bargaining. However, it is possible for an employer to recognise a trade union for the purpose of representing individual employees, or for discussing matters other than pay and conditions. Officials, including lay officers, of recognised unions have rights to time-off for the exercise of union duties, including training. Employers are also required to provide a recognised trade union with sufficient information for them to bargain effectively.

Workplace union representatives (shop stewards)

Compared with employee representatives in many European Community countries, British lay union workplace representatives (shop stewards) lack the legally anchored rights of German works councillors, but usually enjoy negotiating rights, a power denied their German counterparts. As directly elected employee representatives, who can usually be recalled at any time, shop stewards represent the organised workforce in both their place of work and their trade union. On average, each steward represents around twenty-two employees. Although most union constitutions do not grant workplace representatives a formal voice in local union organisations, and rank-and-file membership at workplace level is only rarely engaged closely with the geographically based, official local bodies of the individual unions, most shop stewards see themselves and are seen by unions as an integral part of the overall trade union organisation. For instance, it is lay bodies, such as combine committees bringing together stewards from different plants within a single employer, which provide key institutions for co-ordinating bargaining and disseminating information.

Since the election of the Conservative Government in 1979, industrial relations in Britain have returned to a system characterised by free collective bargaining, with negotiations conducted without state intervention and largely free of legal regulation on the determination of terms and conditions of employment (though not on trade union organisation). This is a principle which continues to find support among both employers and British trade unions, though with a number of qualifications. (Moreover, despite the principles of both free collective bargaining and 'voluntarism', the UK probably witnessed more incomes policies between 1962 and 1979 than any other EC member-state.) Bargaining has shifted significantly to company and site level, with multi-employer bargaining in only a small, and diminishing, number of sectors. In 1990, 49 per cent of all manual workers in manufacturing were covered by employer/workplace negotiating arrangements, compared with 19 per cent by multi-employer bargaining. Privatisation and the ending of industry bargaining in a number of sectors will undoubtedly have added to the proportion of employees covered by single employer bargaining since 1990. Overall, the proportion of manual workers in manufacturing covered by collective bargaining fell from 79 per cent in 1984 to 70 per cent in 1990; the comparable figures for non-manuals were 59 per cent and 50 per cent respectively. In all, 54 per cent of employees included in the 1990 Workplace Industrial Relations

Survey (WIRS) were covered by collective bargaining – allowing for the composition of the sample, probably a minority of the total working popoulation.

There is no legal obligation on an employer to negotiate with shop stewards or, at branch level, with a trade union, even if their establishment is 100 per cent trade union organised. Negotiating rights are solely dependent on the balance of power – in contrast to the legal rights of German works councils – and this in turn is a function of the level of union organisation, and ultimately the readiness of the workforce to back their demands with strike action. Historically, this has led to a heavy emphasis on workplace recruitment and organisation, and in the past to the pursuit of a closed shop (although, in the narrow sense, this has been illegal since 1988). Nevertheless, effective 100 per cent trade union membership does continue in some workplaces. Formal closed shops declined dramatically in the 1980s as a result of Conservative legislation (as well as the economic decline of sectors of traditional high union membership). According to the 1990 WIRS, they fell from 17 per cent of workplaces in 1984 to 3 per cent by 1990. Between 1980 and 1990, the number of workers covered by closed shop arrangements fell from nearly five million to half a million. Effective workplace representation, and often the persistence of de facto closed shops, has customarily depended on employer support and facilities, either granted in the face of union power or in order to formalise company level bargaining arrangements to meet business objectives. Indeed, one argument advanced for the fall-off in average union density over the 1980s is based on the withdrawal of employer support or endorsement for union membership.

There is considerable variation in the role and effectiveness of the 300,000 odd shop stewards. In well-organised establishments where collective bargaining has been retained, their actual powers may be substantially greater than those of German statutory workplace representatives, and the accelerated shift to workplace level bargaining during the 1980s may have served to formalise and strengthen their position.Their field of activity is not usually confined to negotiating on pay and conditions: they are also often responsible for grievances and disciplinary matters, and for concluding numerous local agreements. In workplaces with a high level of organisation and a combative workforce, they may be engaged in direct negotiations with managements on issues related to production, the allocation of work, and distribution of overtime, as well as pay. Whether they have a right to information or consultation, or even effective codetermination, depends purely on local agreement or custom and practice.

The absence of statutory recognition rights has contributed to an enormous degree of variation of workplace union representation. For example, according to the 1990 WIRS, the percentage of establishments with lay union representatives ranged from 80–85 per cent in central and local government, to 9 per cent in business services and 5 per cent in hotels and catering. The average level overall was 38 per cent, down from 54 per cent in 1984. Whereas there was a degree of stability in union representation in larger and well-organised workplaces, which also largely maintained the lay officials engaged full-time on trade union representation, the number of representatives had declined in workplaces with low union densities.

Forces which might have fostered the status of lay representatives, to some degree at the expense of national union organisations, must be set against the numerous counteracting forces of the period of Conservative Government since 1979. In particular, the ability of lay officials to initiate industrial action has been severely circumscribed through the legislation of the 1980s (see Part I), although balloting procedures may have raised both the effectiveness and legitimacy of negotiating strategies.

Works councils

There is no statutory form of employee representation at establishment level. In the past, it would have been correct to say that neither trade unions nor employers wished to see the introduction of institutions with statutory rights comparable with German works councils. This no longer applies unreservedly to the trade union position, although both the Government and employers remain opposed to statutory forms of representation at either national or European level. The experience of the 1980s, in which the principle of voluntarism combined with a general assault on membership levels seriously dented union representation, has produced a greater interest on the part of some unions and the TUC in statutory forms of representation, provided the position of the trade unions is safeguarded. For example, the 1990 TUC Congress approved a motion which called on the General Council to 'examine how features of the Franco-German approach to industrial relations, such as works councils and greater rights to information and consultation', might be adapted to British circumstances.

According to the 1990 WIRS, 29 per cent of workplaces had a joint consultative committee – a body established on the initiative of particular managements and unions – for facilitating employee consultation and communication (though with no statutory rights); and many of their functions overlapped with bargaining procedures and with the establishment of regulations on working practices, production and employment issues. This compared with 34 per cent of workplaces in 1984. The number of joint committees tends to be higher in unionised workplaces, and the incidence of such committees in unionised workplaces did not fall during the 1980s (suggesting that the drop in the number of committees was related to the fall in the number of large, well-unionised plants).

The mid to late 1980s also saw the growth of institutions for employee communication and involvement (team briefings, quality circles, etc.) which were introduced and operated solely by managements, especially in the service sector. In all, a third of workplaces reported such initiatives in 1990, with a higher incidence in foreign-owned workplaces than in UK-owned businesses.

Health and safety committees

The 1974 Health and Safety at Work Act gives recognised trade unions the right to nominate employee safety representatives. These have the task of representing employees in consultations on health and safety issues, and can initiate investigations into hazards and pursue complaints from employees. Safety representatives are entitled to paid time-off for carrying out their functions, and for appropriate training. When requested to do so by trade union safety representatives, the employer is required to set up a safety committee. Disputes on safety matters are normally dealt with through the machinery available for resolving differences arising during collective bargaining.

However, the fact that nominating safety representatives is a right reserved for recognised trade unions means that many trade unions have found it difficult to exercise their rights where recognition is withdrawn. Around a quarter of all establishments had a joint health and safety committee in 1990, compared with the 37 per cent of establishments in which management dealt with health and safety issues without any form of employee consultation. This category increased substantially during the course of the 1980s.

Board level representation

There is no statutory system for board level representation. Proposals made in the 1977 Committee of Enquiry into Industrial Democracy (Bullock Report), according to which shareholders and employees should have equal representation on an administrative board with a number of independent neutral members, were never adopted. Resistance came not only from the employer side, but also from some trade unions who regarded such representative bodies as a threat to their own freedom of action. Some experiments with employee board representation in formerly nationalised organisations as British Steel and the Post Office were initiated, but subsequently abandoned by the Thatcher Government.

Trade unions at national level

The relationship between trade unions and governments, both Labour and Conservative, after the Second World War, was initially characterised by a fairly high degree of 'social democratic' consensus. For example, it was a Conservative administration which established the tripartite National Economic Development Council in 1962. The 1964–70 Labour Government, led by Harold Wilson, succeeded for a period in obtaining support from both employers and unions for a prices and incomes policy with statutory backing. However, industrial relations – especially the regulation of industrial conflict – emerged as a central element in diagnoses of British economic failures. Attempts to legislate on industrial disputes by the Labour Government in 1969, and by the Conservatives during 1971–74, generated major tensions between unions and government. Neither initiative succeeded, partly because of union resistance and partly because of a lack of serious employer enthusiasm, and following the election of a Labour government in 1974 in the wake of the miners' strike, a new phase of union–government cooperation took place. The 'Social Contract' (1975–79), which was in essence a voluntary incomes policy negotiated between the TUC and Labour Government in return for sympathetic labour legislation and commitments on public spending, coincided with a high point of union organisation and influence. The breakdown of the policy, occasioned by a failure of private sector compliance and disputes in the public sector, created the backdrop to the election of the Conservative Government under Margaret Thatcher in 1979.

Thatcherism, which had emerged as an ideological tendency in the Conservative Party following the 1974 industrial and electoral defeat, was a built on a neo-liberal commitment to minimise intervention in market processes, with an implied rejection of formal and informal tripartism. Moreover, the 1979 and 1983 Governments were prepared to engage in industrial conflict, if needed, to push through its economic aims (cutting subsidies, privatisation, etc.). As a consequence, during the 1980s, and into the early 1990s, the trade unions were deprived of participation in the making of economic and social policy, and a number of institutions with union involvement were abolished (such as the Wages Councils, which set pay levels in industries with low pay and undeveloped collective bargaining; and the National Economic Development Council). New bodies, like the TECS (Training and Enterprise Councils), which administer training schemes in localities, have been established without a guarantee of union involvement and are deliberately employer-led. Nonetheless, trade union representatives continue to sit on a number of public bodies, and the TUC's General Council is represented on the Health and Safety Commission, the Advisory,

Conciliation and Arbitration Service, the National Council for Vocational Qualifications, the Equal Opportunities Commission and other organisations. The TUC also makes submissions to Royal Commissions and Commissions of Enquiry, which have a more limited lifespan.

Greece

The foundations of the trade union movement in Greece were established in the nineteenth century and the present-day central union confederation, the GSEE (*Geniki Synomospondia Ergaton Ellados*), was formed in 1918. However, periods of dictatorship, splits and political divisions within the union movement, party political influence and, finally, the manipulation of the unions by the state – all accompanied by a high degree of organisational fragmentation which is still not entirely overcome – have both weakened unions as effective instruments for representing employee interests and continued to compromise their autonomy.

Even after the period of the most recent military dictatorship (1967–74) the trade unions were not able to develop independently. The continued presence of former leaderships, often propped up by dubious electoral procedures and the existence of paper unions, and past dependence on funds channelled via the state, all contributed to the lack of progress in consolidating the trade union movement and developing truly autonomous institutions. Political groupings within the GSEE executive – with differences sometimes ending up before the courts and on occasion culminating in boycott actions at union congresses – and the restrictions on free collective bargaining imposed by the state during the 1970s and 1980s, including by the socialist PASOK government, have exacerbated the problem.

However, legislation passed in 1990 during a brief period of Socialist-Liberal coalition government, set out to create a new framework for collective bargaining, with greater emphasis on direct negotiation and conflict resolution between the employers and unions, and an end to compulsory arbitration and intervention by the state in private sector bargaining. The coming into force of the new law in 1991–92 also coincided with attempts to negotiate over a broader agenda at national level, with initiatives agreed on training and other issues. As yet, the new machinery for arbitration and mediation, which did not come into existence until early 1992, has not been operating for sufficiently long to assess whether the industrial culture in Greece has been decisively changed. For example, serious conflicts continued in the public sector in the face of

government efforts to cut public employees' real pay and privatise large
numbers of nationalised undertakings, many of which were firms in economic difficulty taken into state ownership during the early 1980s.

Organisational structure

Although there are other trade union confederations alongside GSEE
and its constituent organisations in the private sector, GSEE is deemed
to be the most representative centre and it alone has the power to sign
national level, private sector, general collective agreements with the
main national employers' associations. There are a number of independent confederations in the public sector, the most important of which
is the ADEDY which brings together several civil service unions.

There are three levels of organisation within the Greek trade union
movement. The lowest level, termed 'primary trade unions', consists of
local craft and branch trade unions, or enterprise or factory unions.
The latter grew markedly from the mid 1970s and appear to have both
led to some degree of consolidation of the highly fragmented structure
of Greek trade unions at this level and encouraged the development of
industrial unions.

The establishment of enterprise unions was one response to weaknesses in union representation following the end of the dictatorship and
was also a form of protest against the political ties which played a major
role in the older craft unions. It also reflected the wider process of economic concentration in the Greek economy. Their role was formally
acknowledged in the 1982 trade union legislation, introduced by the
PASOK Government, which still regulates the present structure. Although they have not become the dominant form of trade union, and are
unable to develop sufficiently extensively to supplant the craft-based fragmentation of the Greek trade union movement, enterprise unions have
taken root in many large companies and made a considerable contribution to the growth in GSEE membership in the first half of the 1980s.

However, attempts to reform the overall structure of trade union
organisation initiated by the enterprise unions foundered for several
reasons, primarily connected with the organisational constraints imposed by the existing pattern of unionism and the make-up of Greek
industry. In the first place, enterprise unions have tended to be confined to large companies which account for only a minority of the
workforce: most employees work in establishments with fewer than fifty
employees. No functional inter-company structure able to bring together
enterprise unions has been established: attempts to set up a federation
outside the traditional structure simply provoked a counter-response
from the existing craft and branch federations, and were ultimately
doomed to failure because of the neglect of an industry-specific form

of union representation. Finally, the fact that, as they formed, most enterprise unions affiliated to existing craft and branch federations also served to strengthen the latter.

Above the primary level of enterprise or local unions, primary unions can join together into secondary level organisations, either as national federations or regional labour centres. National federations can be organised along occupational or industry lines, represent specific groups of employees working in the same undertaking (for example, white-collar unions in the telecommunications organisation), or bring together employees from one type of enterprise or specific branch of the economy (for example, the banks, the cement industry, or dockworkers).

The predominantly craft-based structure combined with the legal provision that two primary unions can establish a federation has contributed to a high, and generally unchecked, degree of organisational fragmentation of the union movement. Although the need to meet certain criteria of representativeness for bargaining purposes, in theory, imposes some limitations on this proliferation of organisations and should favour the formation of larger unions, as yet there has been little discernible movement in this direction. Whereas the number of primary unions fell from over 5000 in the late 1970s to around 2400 active organisations by the early 1990s (especially with the elimination of paper unions that had been kept in existence largely for political reasons), the number of secondary federations doubled in the decade following the end of the dictatorship. As with primary unions, some of the federations consist of unions whose main purpose is to facilitate the representation of political groupings within the GSEE rather than represent employees industrially.

In addition to federations of primary unions, 'secondary trade union organisations' also include labour centres which are general associations of unions at local or regional level. 'The labour centres are the product of the isolation of various economic regions. Their composition reflects the locally dominant sector.' (Katsoulis, 'Griechenland', in S. Mielke (ed.) *Internationales Gewerkschaftshandbuch* (Opladen, 1983)). Their task is to administer and co-ordinate local union matters, and in addition to supporting primary unions they also attend to social problems and concerns at local and regional level and press union concerns on the local authorities. The development of the labour centres, which are recognised by the GSEE, has been less dramatic than in the case of the federations: they increased in number from seventy-seven in 1976 to eighty-six by the mid 1980s. Their membership is dependent on the local and regional economic structure and the level of corresponding trade union organisation. In the economic centres of Athens, Piraeus, Salonika and Patras, they represent, based on their own figures, some 400,000 members.

The tertiary level of organisation consists of the national confederations to which secondary federations and labour centres can affiliate: in practice, the only relevant organisation at this level is GSEE, together with the civil servants' organisations which, by law, are organised separately from the private sector. The (approximately) 2,300 primary unions in the public sector, which are formed into forty-eight federations, are subsumed under the national confederation, ADEDY.

The 1982 trade union law represented an attempt to democratise the internal operation of the trade unions, especially as regards their representational structures and electoral procedures for representative bodies. At the same time, the law sought to create the preconditions for limiting trade union fragmentation and developing a greater degree of centralisation, not least with the aim of reducing the number of paper unions established for political reasons. For example, primary unions were deprived of direct representation at the GSEE's congress, which meets every four years and is the supreme decision-making body within the confederation. Instead, they are now represented indirectly through the secondary level federations and labour centres, preventing the previously common practice of dual representation. The law also prescribed proportional representation for elections to union bodies and thus removed one contentious issue created by competition between political groupings within a simple majority system (at least as far those organisations which felt themselves to be consistently underrepresented were concerned).

In addition to its congress, GSEE has a number of decision-making and executive bodies which determine policy between congresses. The General Council, on which union federations and regional labour centres are represented, meets between congresses when important issues need to be resolved. The Board of Directors, which consists of forty-five delegates elected by secret ballot from the congress, implements congress decisions. Its composition is decisive for the overall political direction of GSEE as it elects the members of the National Secretariat and the Executive Committee, which meets regularly and is responsible for GSEE's administration.

The organisational structure of the unions throws up several major problems which impede their organisational effectiveness, have provided the state with opportunities to wield influence, and which favour the formation of party political groupings. Elections from the congress to the Board of Directors, for example, are conducted on a political-factional basis, with PASOK, New Democracy, orthodox Communist and Eurocommunist tendencies all represented in varying proportions. GSEE also lacks its own organisation at all levels, hampering its ability to exercise direction vis-à-vis the individual unions and labour centres, a situation which is only compensated artificially through GSEE's national competence to bargain with the employers. The legally regulated, but meagre, requirements on the formation of primary trade unions and federations serve to encourage union fragmentation, the setting-up of paper organisations and their exploitation for party political purposes. Finally, there is a high degree of legal regulation of unions, on the back of years of direct intervention in bargaining via compulsory state arbitration.

As well as requiring independence from the employer, and banning external employer or party financing of unions, the 1982 trade union legislation also sought to establish guidelines for the financing of trade unions by membership contributions. This was intended to replace the previous system of financing based on compulsory deduction of dues from all employees, supplemented by an employer's contribution, and paid via the state social insurance system and its distribution to union organisations through a specific state institution. However, despite the legislation, state-funding of unions effectively continued through the 1980s as unions were reluctant to increase dues to realistic levels and successive governments postponed reform of the old system. Only a few organisations, such as the bank workers' union and the sailors' union, introduced compulsory membership dues which enabled them to maintain their organisation free of state support and to accumulate strike funds. Finally, legislation passed in December 1990 by the New Democracy Government provided for the removal of state subsidies from 1 January 1992.

Membership structure

Figures for GSEE membership, and that of its affiliates, are somewhat imprecise. Estimates put the membership at about 500,000, equivalent to an overall union density of some 20 per cent (but nearer 35 per cent of dependent employees). Union density in the private sector is estimated at 15–29 per cent. Of the total of 3–4,000 primary unions, not all of which are affiliated to GSEE, about 2000 are active. The diverse criteria on which primary organisations recruit make it virtually impossible to estimate their membership. The potential and actual number of members in the eighty-four federations ranges from several hundred up to 50,000 members (as in construction, engineering and the banks). This plethora of organisations has only been sustainable in the past because of the small number of unions which have been forced to demonstrate their true viability in terms of ability to finance themselves independently through membership dues.

Workplace employee representation

Up until 1988, there was a single form of employee representation at establishment level undertaken by the primary trade unions. Since 1988, trade union representation has been supplemented in the private sector by works councils which must be instituted should a majority of employees wish it (see below).

The basis for trade union representation at the workplace is the legal right to establish a primary trade union if at least twenty-one employees wish it. Workplace trade union representatives, who are elected by union members in an enterprise, are protected from most forms of dismissal and also enjoy limited rights to time-off to carry out their tasks and for union education. Primary trade unions have a right to meet within the workplace and, where there are more than 100 employees, a right to office space. Employers must consult with primary trade unions on current problems and union demands. Since the 1990 legislation, enterprise unions can now conclude fully valid collective agreements in contrast to the previous situation in which company level agreements had to be concluded as a private treaty under civil law, with no resort to arbitration in the event of a dispute.

In the private sector, there is also the possibility of establishing works councils in establishments with more than fifty employees, or twenty to fifty employees where there is no recognised trade union, should the workforce request it. The number of employee representatives varies between three and seven depending on the size of the establishment, with no separate representation for specific employee categories. They have limited rights to time-off and, as with trade union representatives, are protected against dismissal. Works councils are independent of the employer, with whom they meet at regular intervals (at least every two months). They have rights to be consulted and to receive information, primarily on the economic and financial situation of the company, changes in working conditions, ownership and the legal form of the enterprise, together with the introduction of new technology. In enterprises without any trade union representation, works councils also have rights to consultation and negotiation, and enjoy consultative rights (provided for in European Community law) on collective dismissals. Implementation of the 1988 law has been very patchy, however, and unions have remained suspicious about works councils' potential for rivalling union representation at workplace level.

As well as these structures of representation, the workforce in companies with more than fifty employees has a legal right to elect health and safety committees, which have consultative rights.

Board level representation

More elaborate participation arrangements for trade unions exist in nationalised undertakings, which still account for some 50 per cent of Gross Domestic Product, although many now face privatisation. Trade unions have a right to elect delegates to a special 'social supervisory board' and a conventional supervisory board, are entitled to elect a central works council, and can influence appointments to boards of management.

Social supervisory boards have consultative and directing powers, and are involved in long-term planning. They comprise trade union delegates, as representatives of the workforce, and representatives of government, local authorities, social and cultural organisations, and consumers' associations.

The administrative board, which appoints the management board and which has general decision-making competence on all matters affecting the administration and representation of the undertaking, consists of nine members, of which three are elected by employees. The central works council, which consists of nine members, has a consultative role on working conditions and health and safety issues.

Practical experience with participation in the public sector has been mixed, and has become the focus of political conflict both between unions and government and within the union movement itself.

Representation on public authorities

Representation vis-à-vis public authorities takes place, in the first place, through the links between the political factions within GSEE and the political parties. However, in the past the various mechanisms which allow the state to influence trade unions have led to a situation in which the majority of GSEE's Executive Board has consisted of party groupings which support the government – a situation which generated serious conflicts within the movement, extending to a threatened split in GSEE itself.

Secondly, GSEE has some limited scope for participation and influence in social policy, through its representation in the Social Security Agency (IKA), which is responsible for providing statutory social insurance in the areas of sickness, workers' compensation, occupational illness, disability and old-age pensions. There is also union representation in the National Employment Authority (OAED), which is responsible for running the job placement system and for vocational training, in the Social Housing Agency (OEKA), and in the Worker's Hearth organisation (*Ergatiki Estia*), a housing trust which also formerly served to collect and distribute compulsory union dues to the individual organisations.

The Republic of Ireland

The Irish trade union movement originated in the nineteenth century in close association with the development of the movement in Britain, and a number of British-based unions continue to operate in the Republic. The Irish movement has managed to avoid political divisions, except for a short period during the 1940s when a split occurred over the presence of British unions, a situation since resolved. The single union centre, the Irish Congress of Trade Unions (ICTU), is composed of a large number of individual unions organised along craft, general and industry lines. The voluntarist tradition remains strong and there is little prescriptive legislation on terms and conditions, but greater legal regulation on the structure and conduct of unions and other industrial relations bodies, such as the Labour Relations Commission. The ICTU retains close links with the Irish Labour Party, a minority party compared with the traditional main governing parties (Fianna Fail, Fine Gael) but with growing influence following the election of a Fianna Fail–Labour coalition in 1992. These features are characteristic of Irish trade unionism and also explain its limitations and difficulties.

Structure

The ICTU currently has around fifty-five affiliated member unions of varying type. As in Great Britain, the co-existence of craft unions and large general unions – originally for the unskilled, but now open to broader categories of employee – has hampered the development of industrial unionism. By far the largest union is the Services Industrial Professional Technical Union (SIPTU), which was formed in 1990 through a merger of the two biggest general unions, the ITGWU and FWUI. There are also a number of unions representing a particular category of worker, such as white-collar or civil servant. The 1980s generally saw a process of union merger, with many of the very small unions being absorbed.

The geographical organisation of Irish trade unions is also distinctive.

The ICTU serves as a national confederation in both the Republic and Northern Ireland. Its affiliated unions, therefore, consist variously of unions operating in both parts of Ireland, unions operating either in the North or the South, and unions with their headquarters in the UK. (In 1959, Northern Irish trade unions set up their own representative and co-ordinating body, the Northern Ireland Committee. It has twelve member unions and is elected by a Northern Irish trade union conference.)

The large number of individual unions and the jealous protection of their independence, reinforced by mutual competition for members within a framework in which unions often sort out demarcation problems directly between themselves, have all conspired to limit the ICTU to a mainly co-ordinating, representative and support role. The ICTU thus represents trade unions in negotiations with state institutions and employer organisations, and plays a particular role in helping smaller affiliated unions in areas such as training and legal advice and representation. These tasks and others (such as resolving demarcation problems between unions, drawing up policy positions and resolving strikes and collective bargaining issues), are dealt with by a network of the ICTU committees which try to co-ordinate individual union activity. The central ruling body of ICTU is the Executive Committee, elected at the annual congress. The ICTU also has a local structure of trades councils.

The prevalence of tripartite agreements on pay and economic policy since the 1970s has enhanced the role of the ICTU as a national representative organisation. Indeed, the ICTU itself has on occasions been an advocate of tripartite package deals, involving pay limitation in exchange for commitments in the area of social policy, taxation and employment. Pay has been subject to a national voluntary pay policy agreed between the government, the ICTU and the main employers' organisation, the FIE, since 1987: the first policy, the Programme of National Recovery, ran from 1987 to 1990, and the second, the Programme for Economic and Social Progress, ran from 1990 to 1993 and was renewed, after some internal union debate, on expiry. However, ICTU's role in these corporatist arrangements has done little to alter the balance of power between the national confederation and individual unions. Similarly, efforts to create a structure based more on sectoral unions have as yet yielded only a small number of mergers, with little impact on the basic structure.

Individual unions are structured in a variety of ways but, like British trade unions, all have representative structures at company level. Members belong to shop-floor organisations which are grouped into branches at regional or industry level, which in turn have their own representative bodies. Depending on the structure and constitution of the union, shop stewards elected by the members at workplace level will either serve simply as a link between individual members and the union organisation or will also have powers to negotiate and conclude company level agreements.

Membership

Trade union membership has not suffered any dramatic decline despite persistently high general unemployment (18 per cent), and youth unemployment (28 per cent) in particular. Efforts to rectify the performance of the Irish economy, for example through the promotion of export-oriented high-tech industry, have only succeeded in increasing its dependence on world trade. Although union density fell from over 50 per cent in the late 1970s to around 44 per cent in the late 1980s, ICTU unions still organise some 430,000 employees – around 95 per cent of all union members. The decline in union membership is only partly due to overall high levels of unemployment; recruitment is also a problem, compounded by disproportionately high youth unemployment.

In spite of the large number of individual unions based on various organising criteria, the majority of members are concentrated in a small number of unions. The SIPTU accounts for virtually half of the membership, with four other unions (IMPACT, IDATU, the UK-based MSF, and CWU) accounting for a further 100,000 members between them. Their concern to defend their organisations' interest tends to act as an obstacle to reform of the ICTU's basic structure.

Company level representation

There is no statutory form of employee representation. The basic, and most effective, form of workplace representation from shop-floor to company level is the organisation of shop stewards. These have no statutory rights, and generally operate according to custom and practice or specific company agreement.

In some companies consultative bodies have been established through which the employer and unions can discuss working conditions and personnel matters. These bodies may be involved in pay bargaining, especially in highly unionised companies. Under the 1990–93 PESP incomes and employment policy, the central employers' confederation (IBEC, formerly FIE) and ICTU agreed a joint declaration on employee involvement in the private sector. The declaration supports the development of strategies to encourage employee involvement both through mechanisms typically associated with human resource management techniques (team briefings, attitude surveys), formal consultation through representative mechanisms, and the establishment of task forces and quality circles. However, there is little evidence to suggest that the declaration has led to any major new initiatives, above and beyond those innovations in personnel management already in train.

Under legislation passed in 1980, augmented by a number of company agreements, employees in companies with fewer than twenty staff may elect a health and safety representative, with a full health and safety committee in companies with more than twenty employees. These can make recommendations to management and have the right to call directly on the Factory Inspectorate. The employer is obliged to facilitate their activity and must supply them with appropriate information.

In public and state-owned companies, employee representatives may occupy up to a third of seats on the company board. They are elected every four years on the basis of trade union recommendations.

National representation

Since the early 1970s, a number of national tripartite understandings have been agreed between the ICTU, the government and the employers. During the 1970s and early 1980s, the main institutional focus was the Employer-Labour conference, established in 1970. Its delegates include representatives from the ICTU, the central employers' federation, and the government (as representative of the public sector). Although the Employer-Labour conference still operates as a general bilateral forum, more recent national pay policies (PNR, PESP) have been negotiated separately.

Unions are also represented on two types of institution intended to set minimum pay levels in branches with a traditionally low level of unionisation. Joint Labour Committees (JLCs) set minimum wages in low-paying sectors, such as hairdressing, hotels and catering and textiles. Joint Industrial Councils (JICs) operate in sectors with higher levels of union organisation: they may apply to the Labour Court for a Registered Employment Agreement, which specifies pay and conditions.

Four employee representatives sit on the tripartite Labour Court, alongside four employer representatives and a four-person neutral executive. The Labour Court was established in 1946 and has functioned for most of its history not as a judicial body, but as an agency for resolving industrial disputes. Under the 1990 Industrial Relations Act, a new institution was created, the Labour Relations Commission, which serves as a first resort for conciliation, leaving the Labour Court with its existing tasks (adjudicating cases of sex discrimination, for instance, and confirming minimum pay orders). Disputes may now only be referred to the Labour Court after conciliation before the Labour Relations Commission, unless there are exceptional circumstances or the public interest warrants the Court's direct intervention.

Italy

The course of trade union development in Italy in the mid-century decades parallels that seen elsewhere in Western Europe: a politically divided union movement of the 1920s, united in an anti-fascist coalition during the 1940s to form a unitary trade union centre sufficiently durable to stabilise itself under the conditions of the 'growth pact' of the immediate post-war period, but destined to disintegrate once latent political differences re-emerged with the struggle for power domestically, spurred on by the Cold War. The main trade union confederations in Italy – the (former) Communist/Socialist CGIL, the Christian CISL and the Social Democratic/Socialist UIL – were established in the late 1940s and early 1950s out of the dismemberment of this post-war coalition.

After a phase of strict separation during the most intense period of the Cold War, the three trade union centres developed fairly close co-operation on collective bargaining issues in the 1960s. The strike wave which swept through Italy in the late 1960s favoured the creation of a unified organisation, an objective which the individual confederations had always formally adhered to. In 1972 a 'unified federation' was established which, while guaranteeing the autonomy of the individual organisations, allowed co-ordination at national, regional and local level, and led to close association between the industrial affiliates of the confederation. At confederation level, the unified organisation had its own central body on which all the confederations had equal representation. This was allocated various tasks including collective bargaining, reform, economic and social policy, planning and development as well as a form of qualified majority voting. This intermediate step to a fully unified union organisation was supported by parallel developments at industry level in a number of important sectors, including metalworking, chemicals, textiles and clothing, and also by a rule which forbade leading trade union officials from exercising political functions, thus reinforcing union claims to political independence.

Despite such co-operation, the changes to the system of pay indexation, the *scala mobile*, introduced in 1984–85 (see above, Part I, p. 57) exposed the growing differences between the confederations. The reform in the system was not agreed between the unions, employers and government but imposed via government decree in the teeth of opposition from the majority Communist wing of the CGIL and the then Italian Communist Party (PCI), but with the support of the CISL and UIL. When the changes to the *scala mobile* were submitted to a referendum called by the PCI, the CGIL supported the PCI's rejection of the weakening of the system, but the other confederations stood behind the position of their corresponding political parties in the Christian Democrat-Socialist Party coalition Government, undermining the impression of political independence built up during the 1970s.

These differences, combined with growing competition between the confederations, led to the virtual dissolution of the unified structures during the mid 1980s, though not to an abandonment of practical cooperation and unified action between the different centres and industrial unions. For example, immediately after the referendum on the *scala mobile*, the confederations were able to agree a new policy on pay indexation and win its acceptance by the central employers' association, *Confindustria*.

The break-up of the unified federation was to some degree a product of the process of political differentiation in which the PCI returned to a policy of opposition in the early 1980s following a period of 'national unity' (1976-79), and which contributed to efforts by the political parties to re-assert their influence over their respective union movements. More important than this, however, were the major underlying social and economic changes which had profoundly altered the conditions under which Italian unions were obliged to operate. The structural transformation triggered by the modernisation of the Italian economy (a strategy more recently supported by the trade unions) undermined the egalitarian incomes policy of the 1970s which all the confederations had supported. Of particular importance in this context were the differentiation of patterns of employment and its associated effects on union membership (including a growing proportion of white-collar workers and technicians), sectoral changes (the shift from manufacturing to private services and from large-scale industry to small and medium-sized undertakings), and the changed composition of the workforce (marked, for example, by growing numbers of women, young people and higher educational levels).These changes in the economic and employment environment all served to weaken and diminish the status and numbers of blue-collar workers in industry, traditionally the basis and reference point for Italian trade union strategies, especially the CGIL.

The growth of organisations such as the autonomous trade unions and the organisations representing middle managers and specialists (the 'quadri'), which compete with the main union centres, have exposed the gaps in workforce representation now characteristic of the CGIL, CISL and UIL. Whilst much of this is attributable to their bargaining strategy and membership structure, their progressive conversion to a strategy of economic modernisation and a role as a 'force for social reform' has also played a part. Nevertheless, despite losses of membership and competition from the militant autonomous and grass-roots occupational unions, especially in the public sector, the Italian trade union confederations have both avoided marginalisation and serious crisis. As the revival of central tripartite discussions on industrial relations reform in the early 1990s indicated, they remain both established and mass organisations.

Organisational structure

During the period of close co-operation and aspirations for unity in the 1970s, the three confederations created similar organisational structures. At local level these were supplemented by unified structures (councils of delegates and regional councils), which no longer operate.

The individual confederations are combinations of several independent branch or industrial unions which, like the union centres, have their own geographical structure. Guided by efforts to achieve more comparable organisational structures, but also driven by pressures towards union merger, the three confederations currently consist of twenty to thirty industrial unions. Each confederation has twenty-one regional federations and congresses, reflecting the constitutional reforms of the early 1970s which created new regional administrative units.

Up until the break-up of the united federation in the mid 1980s, the basic organisational unit consisted of works and delegate councils (*consigli di fabricca/consigli dei delegati*) which emerged as autonomous workers' organisations in the period of industrial militancy of the late 1960s, and were recognised as representative bodies by the unions in 1972. These delegates were mostly elected according to the rules of the relevant industrial union, but with the entire workforce eligible to vote irrespective of which trade union confederation they belonged to. Works councils represented all the employees at a workplace as well as the individual trade union organisations.

The break-up of the united federation undercut the basis for the delegates' role as union representatives. During the 1980s the individual confederations were concerned to fashion their own workplace organisations alongside the works councils. As a result, a number of different representative bodies emerged in the industrial and private sectors, some appointed, some elected and with varying compositions. This uneven process, with its associated disadvantages for overall union representation, eventually prompted efforts to establish new unified forms of workplace representation. These efforts, which culminated in an inter-confederal agreement in 1991, were spurred on in particular by the need to restore the position of the confederations and maintain a common front in the face of the rise of autonomous unions. Under the newly agreed arrangements, candidates for elections to unified union representative bodies (*rappresentanze sindacali unitarie*) must either be a member of one of the confederations or have the support of at least 5 per cent of those eligible to vote. However, as yet it is difficult to assess how well the new system is functioning. The reconstitution of the Italian Communist Party as the Party of the Democratic Left (PDS), and the shift in emphasis of its associated confederation, the CGIL, away from its traditional politics of class struggle, has also opened the way for greater co-operation between the three confederations – a co-operation increasingly necessitated by the worsening political and economic crisis in the early 1990s.

At national level the three trade union confederations have similar structures of decision-making and management in which both regional organisations and national industrial unions are represented. For example, in the case of the CGIL this includes: the congress, which meets every four years and which establishes the basic direction of trade union policy and elects the Management or Executive Committee; the General Council, the most important decision-making body between Congresses, which is called on an ad hoc basis and includes representation from the CGIL's regional bodies and industrial unions; the Board of Management, which meets every three months, appoints or elects the various bodies which are responsible to it, such as the Executive Committee, the Federal Secretariat and the General Secretariat. With some minor variations, the two other federations have a similar institutional make-up. One area of difference lies in the fact that the UIL and CISL do not have a consultative body akin to the CGIL's General Council, but rather a representative body which corresponds to the CGIL Board of Management. There is a similar structure at regional and local level and within the industrial trade unions.

Internal democracy and mechanisms for implementing policy and bargaining objectives take place through a complex structure which aims to integrate all levels of the organisations. However, the central organisational level plays an especially important role. For example, it was this level which was able to integrate and institutionalise the grass-roots structures which arose spontaneously following the 1968–69 strike wave. And, negatively, the break-up of the united structures in 1984 exposed serious representational problems at company and workplace level, not least because of the absence of any clear and binding rules for employee representation. In addition, the national/industry level has remained the crucial area for collective bargaining, despite local bargaining rights which have been used to supplement the main industry agreements.

The significance of the central level and the confederations is also emphasised by the distribution of members' contributions through which the organisations are almost exclusively financed. In the CGIL 25 per cent of revenue from contributions goes to the confederation, with 30 per cent within the CSIL and 40 per cent in the UIL.

Membership structure

The proportion of the workforce organised by the main confederations fell from almost 50 per cent in the early 1980s to 39–43 per cent (on varying estimates) by 1989. These figures express both the structural transformation of the Italian economy and the organisational and representational weaknesses of the unions themselves. Some, at least, of these problems stem from the transformation of union policy in the 1980s towards participation in the process of modernisation. The fall in the number of trade union members has also been a product of the extremely high level of youth unemployment in Italy which stood at 28 per cent in 1992.

Membership losses and the decline in trade union density have been particularly severe in industry, hitting the CGIL much harder than the other confederations. Marked falls in membership have also been experienced in agriculture, although the fact that trade union membership is a prerequisite for claiming certain social provisions has sustained the level of union organisation at around 90 per cent. Union organisation is over 50 per cent in the public sector, and both the UIL and CSIL have been able to record a growth in membership. However, there has been no expansion of union membership in private sector services, where the level of organisation hovers at around 20 per cent.

The shifts in the relative weights of the main sectors in the economy, and the associated composition of employment and potential for union recruitment, have therefore affected the three confederations to different degrees. The main loser has been the CGIL whose membership has traditionally been composed primarily of industrial workers in large undertakings. In contrast, the CISL, which has roots in both the industrial and public sectors, experienced a relative growth in its public sector membership during the 1980s rather than an overall absolute fall. The growth in the UIL's membership reflects the fact that its organisational focus is among skilled employees in manufacturing industry and in both the private and public service sectors.

The representational weaknesses of the confederations, in part as the result of their bargaining stance up until the mid 1980s, created fertile ground for the formation of independent organisations for particular groups, especially in the public sector, in state undertakings and in private services. These include the autonomous trade unions set up to represent the specific interests of highly qualified employees in the public sector (doctors, teachers, etc.); the emergence of organisations representing the *quadri*, a group encompassing supervisors, technicians and middle managers; and the militant '*Cobas*', grass-roots organisations in public undertakings such as railways and aviation which act in isolation from the confederations. Indeed, their aim of reversing the egalitarian pay policies of the established unions has led to a substantial – though unverifiable – growth in membership. Estimates range from between 600,000 to around 2 million. Some of the organisations which organise in the public sector have been recognised by the employers for collective bargaining.

Workplace employee representation

There are no statutory regulations on workplace or enterprise level structures of representation providing for specific rights to information, consultation or codetermination in the private sector. Procedures for the statutory recognition of trade unions and the establishment of a unitary structure of employee representation, as envisaged by the 1948 constitution, have as yet not been implemented through enabling legislation. Workplace employee representation is, therefore, based on national level agreements between employer and union organisations. These supplement the statutory rights of individual and collective union workplace representation contained in the 1970 Workers' Statute.

Following the Second World War, Italy acquired a dual structure of employee representation. Based on a 1943 agreement between the employers' organisation, *Confindustria*, and the unions, works commissions (*commissione interna*) were established alongside the grass-roots organisations of the trade unions (*sezione sindacale aziendale*) during the 1950s and 1960s, although there were no formal links between the two types of institution. These were elected via trade union lists by all employees in a plant or at a workplace, and had a consultative and monitoring role. However, the trade unions did not concede any collective bargaining powers to the works commissions.

This structure was displaced by the delegates movement which arose spontaneously during the 'Hot Autumn' of 1969. Factory and delegate councils, wholly independent of the employer, were made up of delegates from workplace departments or sections, who in turn were elected by all employees irrespective of trade union membership. In 1972 they were recognised by the three confederations as joint bodies for representing the unions' organisation at grassroots level and as institutions for unitary employee representation. Based on this recognition, unions allowed them to engage in workplace collective bargaining.

However, no detailed statutory regulation of their tasks was undertaken. Their formation and activity are based, on the one hand, on the unions' legal rights of workplace representation set out in the 1970 Workers' Statute and, on the other, in national and industry level collective agreements. The Workers' Statute grants a number of rights to both individual employees and representative trade unions, which allow for a structure of workplace employee representation. However, it applies only to workplaces in the private sector which employ at least fifteen employees and in agriculture with at least five employees. Although the entire public sector is covered, established civil servants are subject to some limitations.

The Statute permits the establishment of trade union representation at the workplace, provides for unhindered trade union activity, including limited rights to time-off for union duties, and allows trade union meetings during working time. Delegates are protected against transfer and dismissal, except for serious misconduct, and unions have a right to office space. These framework provisions are supplemented by national and branch level collective agreements which make detailed provisions on delegates' rights. The tasks of the delegates are primarily concerned with the implementation at the workplace of industry level collective agreements. There are no limits on the bargaining agenda and, in theory, it is possible for a workplace agreement to provide for poorer terms than the relevant industry agreement. Workplace level negotiations may embrace working conditions, the organisation of production, the introduction of new technology and processes, grading and additional pay and salary increases. Union representatives also monitor the application of collective agreements and compliance with regulations on health, safety and accident prevention, as well as elaborating specific workplace regulations.

Rights to information on investment plans, the introduction of new technology, the economic development of the establishment or company, personnel planning and prospects, and various other matters of strategic importance for collective bargaining, were introduced in 1976 through a national level agreement, supplemented by industry level collective agreements. These rights to information, which do not customarily include any obligation to consult, vary substantially, with different rights applicable at different levels (workplace, local district, region, or national trade union organisations). In practice, they are satisfactorily implemented only in a small number of large companies (cf. Treu and Negrelli, 'Workers' Participation and Personnel Management Policies in Italy', in *International Labour Review*, Vol. 126 (1987), pp81–94).

As far as trade union and employee participation in decisions on the introduction of new technology is concerned, the 1984 agreement covering the state holding company IRI (known as the 'IRI Protocol'), modified in 1986, has served as a pioneering model. The Protocol provides for the establishment of a system of information and consultation through joint bodies from workplace to national level. Their task is to reconcile the interests of the two sides prior to the introduction of new technologies or any restructuring of either work organisation or the undertaking itself. Similar agreements have since been agreed for the state chemical company ENI.

The limitations of the Workers' Statute and the fact that implementing workplace representation depends primarily on the strength of the industrial unions have meant that effective delegate systems are mostly confined to highly unionised branches, and in particular to large establishments. According to the European Trade Union Institute only around 5 million employees out of a total workforce of some 23.5 million were covered by such agreed arrangements in the early 1980s.

As already noted above, the differences between the confederations and the dissolution of the unified structures led, in the second half of the 1980s, to a 'crisis of workplace representation' for the trade unions. At workplace level in the industrial and private sector this yielded a 'multiplicity of representative bodies' which 'in part have been appointed by the individual trade union organisations and in part have been elected using procedures giving rise to varying compositions' (Mariucci, 'Gewerkschaftsrechte im Betrieb nach italienischem Recht' in *Arbeitsrecht im Betrieb*, 1989, No. 12, pp. 376–82). These developments also coincided with broader concerns about the functioning of the Italian industrial relations system. Attempts to resolve problems of workplace representation, culminating in the 1991 agreement between the three confederations (see above) and continuing with national tripartite talks on bargaining arrangements, have initially strengthened the national level pattern of bi- and tri-partite arrangements.

National structures of representation and participation

The trade unions are well represented and potentially influential in public institutions and bodies. The tripartite National Economic and Labour Council (CNEL) undertakes research, gives advice to government and can make recommendations, and also has a right to propose legislation. Unions are also represented in the state programme commissions, have a majority on the administrative council of the National Social Insurance Institute (INPS), which administers the social security system, and are a key influence on the special wage support funds, the *Cassa Integrazione Guadagni* (CIG), which make payments to employees laid-off or facing redundancy. There is also trade union representation on various administrative boards in public enterprises such as the postal service and railways.

These representative systems in public bodies and institutions are complemented by joint committees and commissions which have been established by employer and employee organisations on the basis of bipartite agreements. Examples include, at national level, committees to oversee the employment impact of introducing new technology, which have operated in specific sectors since 1978. Formal institutions also operate within a framework of informal bi- and tri-partite arrangements, which provide both channels of communication and opportunities for discussions or negotiations to be taken up on specific subjects at national level.

Luxembourg

Luxembourg's first trade unions, established during the second half of the nineteenth century, were primarily organisations of skilled workers or, in some cases, branches of the free trade unions operating in the German Reich. The formation of the first industrial unions followed around the turn of the century with the development of large-scale industry, especially in the steel sector. Despite the small size of the country, and its correspondingly small workforce, the trade union movement is highly pluralistic, with divisions along political and religious lines as well as separate centres for blue-collar and white-collar trade unions, and a few unitary trade unions which have joined neither of the two political centres.

The first attempt to bring the various individual unions into a confederation was undertaken by the free trade unions in 1906 and led to the formation of the Luxembourg Trade Union Cartel, a precursor of the Trade Union Council, established in 1918, and of the current Confédération Général du Travail du Luxembourg (CGT-L) which was established in 1927 at the initiative of the Luxembourg Mining and Metalworking industrial trade union (LAV) and the railway trade unions. Currently, the CGT, with 44,000 members, embraces the largest single union in Luxembourg, the Independent Trade Union Confederation of Luxembourg (OGB-L – *Onofhängege Gewerkschafts-Bond-Lëtzebuerg*), the FLTL (printworkers' union), and the FNCTTFEL (transport workers). The OGB-L itself was founded in 1979 in an attempt to overcome political divisions within the union movement. It has fourteen affiliated individual unions and some 33,000 members (1989). Two unions declined to join, the Luxembourg Confederation of Christian Trade Unions (LCGB – *Lëtzebuerger Chrëstleche Gewerkschafts-Bond*) and the largest white-collar union, the FEP/FITC. The LCGB was initially established in 1921 – a step which prompted other unions to come together in the CGT in 1927. It currently has some 15,000 members, of which one third are women. It consists of 11 individual trade unions in the steel

208

and engineering industries and the public sector. As well as organisations representing dependent employees, it also has affiliates for artisans and pensioners. Both main confederations, the OGB-L and the LCGB, are centrally organised, with regional, occupational and branch sections. Despite the protracted crisis in the steel industry, the trade union movement in Luxembourg has managed to sustain a high level of trade union density estimated at 66 per cent in 1989.

Workplace employee representation

Legislation dating from 1958 provides for representation at workplace level. In establishments with at least fifteen blue-collar (or twelve white-collar) employees, delegates are elected every four years by the entire workforce based on lists of candidates nominated by trade unions. Separate elections take place for blue- and white-collar employees in workplaces with a total workforce of a hundred or more. Delegates' tasks are mainly confined to social matters, but they do have rights to be informed on the state of the business.

Following a strike by the then largest trade union centre the LAV in November 1973 over the tardiness of the government in pursuing institutional reform, legislation was passed on employee codetermination in 1974. This guarantees employees consultative rights as already enjoyed by their representatives in the occupational chambers and in the Economic and Social Council. Where there are more than a hundred-and-fifty employees in an establishment so-called mixed works councils (*comité mixte d'entreprises*) are established consisting of representatives of all employee groups in proportion to their numbers together with the employer. The chair is appointed by the employer side. These bodies have extensive rights to codetermination on policies on recruitment, dismissal and transfer, on health and safety, on employee monitoring and appraisal, and on the company rule book. In public limited corporations with more than a thousand employees a third of the seats in the administrative board of the company are occupied by employee representatives. They have a right to participate in corporate decisions in economic, social and personal matters. In the iron and steel producing and fabricating industries, trade unions have a right to appoint three representatives to the employees side who must not necessarily work in the company concerned. Employee representatives also sit on the management bodies of public companies.

Although the new rights have led to improved information for workers and given employee representatives scope to express their opinions, strategic corporate decisions remain with managements.

National representation

One noteworthy feature of the pattern of employee representation in Luxembourg is the system of chambers which was established by legislation in 1924. This legislation provided for chambers of labour to parallel the chambers of commerce. Separate chambers were added for white-collar workers, for artisans, and, in 1964, for public sector white-collar workers and established civil servants.

The two chambers providing for statutory representation for employees are the workers' chambers and the chamber for private sector white-collar workers. These constitute a 'parliament of labour' and are subject to elections by all employees every five years. Those entitled to vote for the workers' chamber are all workers of Luxembourg nationality aged over eighteen and employed in a company in Luxembourg. In all twenty-one members are elected to represent two groups: the first, embracing seven seats, are reserved for employee representatives from large scale industry (primarily ARBED and MMR-A) with fourteen seats reserved for the representatives of workers from small and medium sized industry, commerce and public establishments.

Lists of candidates are proposed by trade unions and other groups. Since, as yet, only active trade union officials have been elected the workers' chamber is practically an extended arm of the trade unions, primarily the two confederations deemed representative for collective bargaining, the OGB-L and the LCGB, together with the Neutral Trade Union (NGL), an independent craft union.

As well as an executive and an administrative structure, the workers' chambers also embrace a plenary meeting which oversees the work of four commissions dealing with employment law, social security, the economy and public finance, and vocational training. The chamber is a legal entity registered under civil law and finances its activities through obligatory contributions levied on all employees and deducted from pay by the employer. At the same time it is also an institution under public law, which is entitled to play a consultative and initiating role in legislation. For example, the government is obliged to submit drafts for social and employment legislation and regulations to the workers' chamber to obtain its opinion. This also includes any declaration of the general applicability of collective agreements as well as the draft budget.

The individual areas covered by the chambers include preparing opinions on areas such as health and safety at work, minimum wages, family allowances, youth protection, social security, protection against dismissal, price policy and income tax and value added tax. A law passed by the Chamber of Deputies without prior examination by the workers' chamber remains in force. However, regulations issued by the Archduke or by ministers would not be valid under such circumstances.

Finally the workers' chamber can make legislative proposals to the government which must be submitted to members of parliament for consultation.

The workers' chamber is active in a consultative capacity in various public commissions such as the building commission and the price commission. Together with the corresponding employers' chamber it also has powers regulating the training of apprentices in all economic sectors. For example, it is represented on the joint commissions which supervise apprenticeship examinations and examinations for the status of *Meister*. It also appoints training advisers who are able to visit workplaces. Delegates from the workers' chambers, appointed by the Minister of Justice, are also active in industrial tribunals which conciliate and arbitrate in industrial disputes.

In 1966 a consultative Economic and Social Council (*Conseil Economique et Social* – CES) was established. This consists of thirty-five members in all, with fourteen from each employer and employee organisation, and seven independent members (of which three are nominated by government). In practice it functions as an umbrella organisation for the chambers and provides a forum for the discussion of issues which affect a number of occupational groups or the entire economy. The CES is required to discuss economic, financial and social questions and offer its opinion and advice. This becomes especially important if the chambers are unable to agree on a common view to be submitted to government. For its part, the government expects the CES to forge a compromise which will contribute to the maintenance of industrial and social peace. The fact that all the central employer, employee and trade organisations are represented on the CES lends weight to its reports both with government and business.

In November 1944 a national standing conference, the *Conférence Tripartite Générale*, was called into being with the aim of advising the government on the task of reconstruction. It was chaired by the Minister of Labour and consisted of equal representatives of workers, employers and the government. This organisation came into its own as the Tripartite Co-ordination Commitee (*Comité de Coordination Tripartite* – CCT) in 1977 when, after long discussion, an action plan for economic growth and full employment was passed. This gave rise to the so called 'Luxembourg model', a linking of labour market and social policy in which the social partners exercised joint regulation in the preparation of governmental measures in response to changes in the economic environment. In 1979 this form of concertation operated as the 'Steel Tripartite' *Conférence Tripartite Sidérurgie* during the rationalisation of the steel industry.

After the end of the war joint commissions were also established for regulating the labour market and for resolving social conflicts. For example, in October 1945 a national office of conciliation was established which was to intervene to conciliate in major industrial disputes on application from the social partners. The two sides of industry are also represented on the Economic Commitee *Comité de Conjoncture* which meets monthly to discuss developments on the labour market and make recommendations on the use of short time working and access to support funds.

Although Luxembourg has the smallest number of employees in the European Union, it is richly endowed with institutions for representing employee interests at both workplace, industry and national levels. However, despite the emphasis placed on public participation and the maintenance of social peace, serious industrial conflicts have by no means been wholly avoided. One important factor in this is the continuing rivalry within the politically divided trade union movement.

Netherlands

There are three main trade union confederations in the Netherlands: the politically pluralist Dutch Trade Union Confederation (FNV – *Federatie Nederlandse Vakbeweging*), created in 1981 through a merger of the socialist union centre and the Catholic confederation; the interdenominational Christian Trade Union Confederation (CNV – *Christelijk Nationaal Vakverbond*); and the Confederation of Senior and Higher Managerial Employees' Unions (MHP – *Vakcentrale voor Middelbaar en Hoger Personeel*). In addition, there are a number of smaller organisations not regarded as sufficiently large to be entitled to participate in national institutions.

Union density in the Netherlands has fallen since the 1970s, and in 1991 was put at 25 per cent, compared with 39 per cent in 1980. The FNV is by far the largest confederation, with just over 1 million members. The CNV has around 310,000 members and the MHP 130,000.

Organisational structure

The FNV consists of eighteen unions and occupational affiliates, together with a youth organisation spanning all its member unions. The largest affiliates, with a corresponding influence on FNV policy, are the public employees' union, the industrial workers' union and the building workers' union. The CNV has a similar structure, with its largest affiliates covering the public sector, industry and construction.

Within the FNV, individual unions are represented on the Confederal Council, which is the supreme decision-making body between congresses, by their Presidents. Voting strength of the affiliates in the congress is in accordance with the size of their memberships. The day-to-day running of the organisation is undertaken by a Confederal Board, which also oversees the FNV's district organisations linking the FNV's local sections with the national organisation.

Contact between the senior officials of the Confederations is maintained through their presence on the numerous public institutions on which they are represented, primarily the Social and Economic Council (see below).

There are no formal or organisational links between the union Confederations and political parties, and no political tendencies in the union movement. The parties do not have any distinct trade union wings; and the unions do not issue electoral recommendations. However, there is a degree of convergence between the policies of the FNV and of the Dutch Labour Party (PvdA – *Partei van de Arbeid*). Wim Kok, the former head of the FNV, leads the Labour Party and has a record of ministerial activity, including a spell as Prime Minister.

Workplace employee representation

Trade union representation at workplace level is primarily regulated by collective agreement, which makes provision for union facilities, including agreed protection for union representatives. There is no statutory right of representation for union workplace representatives. However, only trade unions are entitled to sign formal collective agreements.

The main form of employee representation at workplace and enterprise level is the statutory works council (*ondernemingsraad*), whose main rights embrace information disclosure and consultation. Legislation on works councils dates originally from 1950, when they were introduced as a corporatist institution, chaired by the employer, in enterprises with more than 100 employees. Amendments passed in 1971, 1979 and 1990 have enhanced their role as employee representative bodies. For example the 1979 change excluded the employer. Approximately 4,000 establishments are covered by the mandatory requirement to establish a works council under these provisions. Legislation introduced in 1981 extended the right of employees to elect a works council to smaller enterprises with fewer than 100 employees, embracing in all around 40,000 establishments, though with less stringent regulations on a number of issues compared with larger organisations.

Works councils are elected by the workforce, with the number of members varying between seven and twenty-five depending on the number of employees. Election is by slates of candidates submitted either by trade unions or non-unionised workers, provided they account for a third of the workforce and obtain a quorum of thirty signatures. Works council members remain in office for three years and are protected against all but the most pressing grounds for termination. They are entitled to paid time-off to attend meetings, or other necessary discussions related to their tasks, and have rights to further time-off for training; although they are not granted permanent time-off for their activities. Meetings must be held with management at least six times a year.

The rights of works councils are confined to regular disclosure of information and the right to consultation on decisions affecting working time, dismissals, recruitment, training, the organisation of the plant, major investments and changes in ownership. Managements are obliged to inform works councils before making large-scale investments or raising loans. Works councils can delay the implementation of decisions by up to a month, and appeal to the courts to have a decision rescinded. The assent of the works council is required should the employer want to change or introduce new provisions on pensions, profit-sharing or saving schemes, hours and holiday arrangements, pay and job evaluation, health and safety, apprenticeships and company regulations on recruitment, dismissal, appraisal and promotion, and employee grievances. Works councils can also demand that the provisions of any collective agreement are properly implemented. Finally, they can propose members for the supervisory board. Although the board can co-opt whom it chooses, works councils retain a right to object, with resort to the courts, if no agreement is possible.

Where one undertaking consists of a number of establishments, the individual works councils can establish a combine works council if they so wish. Joint commissions exist at branch level for resolving differences between works councils and managements, and to act as an arbitration body.

National structures of representation

The main public institutions on which trade unions are represented are the Labour Foundation, the Social and Economic Council, the Social Insurance Council and the Sickness Insurance Fund Board.

The Labour Foundation (*Stichting van der Arbeid*) was established in 1945 as a bipartite body for consultation and negotiation between the trade union confederations and employers' associations. The Foundation provides a forum for the discussion of general economic issues impinging on employment, primarily pay and working conditions. The original role of the Foundation was to act as an advisory body in the formulation of the highly centralised pay-setting machinery of the 1950s, when the government, through its Board of Mediators, effectively fixed the annual wage round after consultations with the main actors. In practice, the government took on any recommendation on pay agreed within the Foundation. After 1959 its role was confined to recommending pay guidelines, and from 1966 collective bargaining was carried out by the social partners either at industry level or within the larger undertakings.

In recent years the leaderships of the unions and employers' organisations have used the Foundation as an institution for agreeing on the bases of pay and employment policy before the annual pay round begins at industry or company level. The two sides have also chosen to use the

Foundation as the forum for settling specific questions, such as the introduction of educational leave, the timing of annual holidays, and for commissioning research into contentious topics, such as reductions in working time.

The Social and Economic Council (*Social-Economische Raad* – SER) was created by statute in 1950. It is a tripartite body with fifteen representatives of the union confederations, fifteen from the employers (including small firms, farmers and horticulturalists) and fifteen independent members nominated by the government. All forty-five members must be able to be act free of any institutional mandate. Ministerial officials enjoy only observer status, and meetings are held in public. The Council has three tasks: to advise the government on issues in economic and social policy; to exercise supervision over certain public bodies active in economic life (such as producer co-operatives which regulate the activity of certain branches, and which also have union representation); and to oversee directly the implementation of legislation on works councils, chambers of industry and commerce, and other aspects of company law.

The Social Insurance Council exercises a comparable role to the Social and Economic Council within its specific sphere. It is also a tripartite organisation, and includes representatives from the Ministry of Social Security. The Council is entrusted with the task of monitoring the operation of the social insurance system and advising the government on policy issues in this field.

The Sickness Insurance Fund Board operates within the health service. As well as employee and employer representatives, it includes equal numbers of representatives from the sickness funds, doctors and Ministry officials. The Board oversees the sickness funds, controls charges, and advises the government.

In 1983 legislation was introduced establishing a joint national council for safety at work (*Arbeidsomstandighedenraad*). This has the task of advising the Minister for Social Affairs on questions of health, safety and employee well-being at work, in association with works councils.

The trade unions also send representatives to the Council of the Social Insurance Bank, the General Unemployment Fund and around sixty ministerial advisory bodies.

Dutch workers are thus represented in a variety of public organisations and consultative bodies, where they receive information and can offer advice – in turn lending legitimacy to this network of institutions. They are also integrated into a structure directed at co-operation at company level. The pursuit of consensus does ensure a degree of employee influence on decisions, but without genuine rights of codetermination. Union density of around 24 per cent, in addition to general economic problems, regional disparities and relatively high unemployment, has militated against any form of struggle to extend codetermination in the 1980s. The dissolution of the two political and religious Confederations to establish the FNV gave only a temporary boost to union strength, much of which has subsequently been overwhelmed by economic conditions and other developments. And, as noted in Part I, although formally intact and unchallenged, institutions for co-operation and negotiation at national level have been increasingly bypassed by developments during the 1980s.

Portugal

During the long period of dictatorship in Portugal (1933–74) independent trade unionism was suppressed, although officially sanctioned unions did play an increasing role in collective bargaining which the government supported as a pillar of corporatism. The reorganisation of the movement independently of the state had already started during the phase of liberalisation following the assumption of power by Salazar in 1968. In 1970 these efforts led to the founding of the union confederation Intersindical. Following the revolution of the 25 April 1974, which, as in post-Franco Spain, triggered hopes for the establishment of a unified trade union movement, Intersindical and most of the individual trade unions were dominated by the Communist Party of Portugal (PCP). This was mainly the result of the Party's years of illegal organisation before the revolution which had created a well-trained cadre of activists. In contrast, the (social-democratic) Socialist Party (PS), founded in 1973 at a meeting held in Germany, had made few organisational preparations for activity or intervention in the emerging union movement.

The attempt by the Revolutionary Council to use the 1975 trade union law to grant Intersindical a monopoly of union representation and to require individual trade unions to join the confederation was short-lived. The law was repealed in 1976 following the adoption of a constitution guaranteeing freedom of association. Efforts to come to a settlement between the competing political tendencies within Intersindical, and differing expectations of the role of collective bargaining as a form of representation, finally foundered on the PCP unions' desire to retain power and the adoption by the socialist and social-democratic trade unions of the customary West European stance of separating themselves organisationally from communist-leaning organisations. As a consequence the non-Communist unions established an alternative centre, the UGT (*União Geral de Trabalhadores*) in 1978–79, leaving Intersindical (which renamed itself the CGTP-IN in 1977, *Confederacão Geral dos Trabalhadores Portugueses*) closely aligned with the Communist Party of

Portugal. Both confederations are now equally strong. There are besides a number of independent trade unions, mostly operating at regional level and representing specific occupations (see also Part I).

Organisational structure

Even after the removal of the Salazar-Caetano dictatorship no fundamental change was made to the occupational and status based structure of the trade unions, despite the declared aim of both confederations to establish industrial unionism. In fact, the number of occupational unions grew and attempts to integrate them into national federations has still only met with limited success.

Although the UGT has made efforts to limit fragmentation, its fifty-two affiliated unions include almost every model of organisation with federations representing entire branches co-existing with occupational unions. Unions may be either national organisations or unions whose geographical scope is confined either to one or several mainland regions or to the autonomous provinces of the Azores or Madeira.

In contrast, the unions affiliated to the CGTP-IN are overwhelmingly organised at local or district level. Most consist of occupational unions, some of which embrace one or several districts and some of which are grouped into national federations. There are also district unions which co-ordinate the activity of the individual unions in their areas.

The UGT's supreme decision-making body is its Congress which meets every four years with delegates from the affiliated unions represented in proportion to membership. The General Council, which supervises the activities of the union between congresses and implements the confederation's agreed political and trade union strategy, consists of 200 members drawn in part from the general councils of the member unions. There is also representation of the main political tendencies within the UGT, in accordance with their strength in the affiliated unions. The National Secretariat is the UGT's executive body, elected by secret ballot on lists of names. The UGT's President and General Secretary are also elected by the Congress.

The UGT and its nationally organised trade unions have been seeking to establish decentralised levels of organisation in the districts. Districts have their own general secretaries and are expected to strengthen co-ordination between member unions at regional level.

The basic organisational unit of the UGT is the workplace branch, which embraces all members of UGT-affiliated unions. Since, in general, unions are not organised on industrial lines, several unions are usually represented at a workplace. Union sections are represented by delegates elected by the members in accordance with union rules. At the same time, the delegates represent their respective trade unions and, where there are several UGT organisations at a workplace, will work together within the workplace trade union delegation (see below).

The CGTP-IN has the same bodies at national level as the UGT: a Congress, a General Council, a National Council, which is responsible for running the confederation, and an Executive Committee, which has twenty members nominated by the National Council.

Compared with the UGT, the individual trade unions in the CGTP-IN are more markedly differentiated along occupational lines. In order to achieve co-ordination, especially on collective bargaining, organisations exist at district level, maybe covering several districts, which bring together sectoral, branch or occupational trade unions. The CGTP-IN also has a relatively elaborate regional structure spanning all branches of the economy. The forty-two district unions (as of 1986) consist of representatives of workplace union delegations and individual trade unions.

Both confederations finance themselves through relatively modest contributions from their affiliated unions. In the case of the UGT this consists of 5 per cent, and for the CGTP-IN 7 per cent, of the total contributions from members in the individual affiliated unions. The efforts of the trade unions to introduce an automatic check-off system through national negotiations is one indicator of the financial difficulties faced by the individual trade unions. As well as the modest level of contributions from their affiliated unions, the power of the confederations is also limited by the fact that the individual unions are competent to bargain. Political differences within the organisations also hamper their effectiveness.

Membership

There are no entirely reliable figures on membership numbers and their distribution across sectors. Figures suggesting that each of the confederations represents around 900,000 employees, with a further 200,000 in unaffiliated unions, would seem to be too high by a considerable margin as this total would imply an overall union density of around 70 per cent. Following the abolition of compulsory union membership and automatic deduction of union dues, the Portuguese trade unions, which had around 1.4 million members by the end of the dictatorship through the operation of this system – even though unions were banned entirely in some industries – suffered a major loss of membership. Current estimates of union density vary between 30 and 40 per cent, and an unpublished Ministry of Labour survey in 1990-1 offered a figure of 42 per cent. According to this survey, the CGTP-IN accounted for 57 per cent of members, the UGT for 33 per cent, and autonomous unions for

10 per cent. Both confederations claim approximately equal membership, though with differing sectoral strengths. Whereas the UGT is more
strongly organised among white-collar employees, who took the initiative in breaking from Intersindical in 1977–8, the CGTP-IN remains
predominantly blue-collar.

Moreover, there are not only autonomous occupational organisations of a fairly marginal significance, but also well organised independent unions with a national presence representing specific industrial
interests (for example, the railworkers' union).

Workplace representation

As in a number of other European Union member states Portugal has
a dual structure of employee representation at workplace level, with
trade union delegations (usually termed *delegados sindicais*) functioning
alongside workers' committees or commissions (*commissões trabalhadores*).

Trade union representation at workplace level takes place through
trade union delegations elected according to union rules by trade union
members employed at the workplace. The dominance of occupational
unions means that one workplace will often have a large number of
unions belonging to one union confederation whose respective delegates
come together to form committees.

Trade union delegates function as the link between the trade union
membership, the leadership and management: their primary task is to
ensure compliance with collective agreements. They enjoy a degree of
protection from dismissal, and have some rights to limited time-off, and
also have enhanced protection against dismissal. Their most important
formal powers consist in their legally anchored right to conduct collective bargaining, although it is customary for this to be exercised by the
trade unions themselves with employers' organisations at industry level.
Company level bargaining with the aim of concluding a formal agreement is relatively undeveloped in the private sector, but negotiations
may produce an informal accord or be conducted between managements and workers' committees – strictly speaking in breach of the
unions' legally secured role in the workplace.

Workers' committees, which were set up by workers at grass-roots
level during and after the 1974 revolution, were given constitutional
recognition and guaranteed within an implementing legal framework in
1979. They are elected every two years by the entire workforce at a
workplace on the basis of slates, with no particular rights for unions to
submit proposals for candidates. Depending on the size of the establishment, committees have between three and eleven members, who enjoy
a degree of protection against dismissal and time-off to carry out their
tasks.

These committees, which function independently of the employer, have rights of information and consultation, and must meet management at least once a month. The right to receive information embraces details of the economic and financial situation of the establishment, production planning and labour requirements, pay and grading, and personnel policies. The employer must also present annual and quarterly balance sheets and the profit and loss account. Workers' committees have the right to give an opinion on issues related to the restructuring of production.

Consultation rights are primarily concerned with individual promotion and regrading, plans to shut down individual lines of production or the entire undertaking, and measures which change employment levels and working conditions, together with regulations which affect working time and holiday arrangements. In undertakings under state ownership, workers' committees also have a right of participation in the making of any changes to the articles of association and in the appointment of members of the management team.

Besides a largely nominal right to 'supervise' management in private sector firms, workers' committees have decision-making rights over the administration of company welfare funds. Tensions can arise between trade union delegations and workers' commissions, in particular in the sphere of collective bargaining where workers committees may informally negotiate on workplace provisions at the expense of formal workplace bargaining by union delegations.

Representation in national institutions

In 1984, the so-called Permanent Council for Social Consultation was established by decree. It is a tripartite consultative body of eighteen members, with equal representation from government, the two trade union confederations and employer organisations. Up until 1987, on the trade union side, only the UGT took part. However, the failure of the CGTP-IN's policy of militant defence of the achievements of the revolution and pursuit of a socialist society, accompanied by a general loss of influence, led it in 1987 to take up the three seats reserved for it.

Consultation on the Council has met with varying success. Recommendations have been issued on incomes policy, the regulation of minimum wages, national and sectoral programmes for restructuring and modernisation, the establishment of a wage guarantee fund, and unemployment insurance. The conclusion of an Economic and Social Agreement (*Acordo Económico e Social*) within the Council in 1990 has been seen as a major step forward towards the consolidation of national consultation and a broadening of the tripartite agenda to cover a wider range of issues, including labour law, health and safety, training, reducing working hours and the structure of industrial relations. However, the CGTP-IN declined to sign the Agreement because of the pay policy element, and the UGT subsequently encountered problems in retaining the loyalty of some of its affiliated unions on the issue. A further agreement was concluded for 1992, with provisions on pay: again, the CGTP-IN declined to sign. No agreement was reached for 1993 and 1994, although the council continues to meet. The European Trade Union Institute noted: 'The results of the work done by the permanent council are far from completely satisfactory, but much is being learned from the process of dialogue and mutual responsibility now underway' (ETUI, 'The trade union movement in Portugal' (ETUI Info 23), 1988).

At central government level, there are a number of other bodies with trade union representation, some of which were created in the years immediately following the revolution, with primarily consultative functions. These include the National Planning Council, the National Council for Health and Safety at the Workplace, the National Commission for Apprentice Training, and the Commission for Women's Equality on the Labour Market, as well as various institutes with a research and advisory role.

Spain

In the years immediately following the end of the Franco dictatorship (1938–75), a complex and pluralistic trade union movement emerged in Spain, once initial efforts to reform the labour organisations of the fallen regime had been abandoned as an unsustainable attempt to balance the search for stability against grass-roots strivings for democracy. The reform of trade union legislation in 1977, in which workforce pressure played an important role, provided for freedom of association and gave the trade union movement considerable scope for activity free of legal restriction. The subsequent development of union organisations either reasserted the traditions of the trade union movement from the period before 1939 or built on the illegal activities of the 1950s and 1960s.

By the early 1980s over 1,000 trade unions had registered themselves nationally with the authorities. Official regulation of this mounting number of trade union organisations through the setting of criteria for representativeness, ultimately entailed a link between union recognition and the placing of some limits on trade union pluralism. The final result of this controlled process of consolidation was the emergence of two main confederations at national level: the 'reformist' UGT (*Unión General de Trabajadores*), which is closely aligned to the Spanish Socialist Party (PSOE), and the more traditionally militant CC.OO (*Comisiones Obreras*), which is linked to the Spanish Communist Party (PCE). Attempts to develop unity of action between these two confederations in 1977–78 largely failed, initiating a long period of organisational rivalry only partly overcome in the jointly supported general strike against the Government in 1988. This national duopoly is complemented at regional level by a number of influential regional organisations, primarily the Basque ELA/STV and the INTG in Galicia, which do not enjoy representative status under trade union law. In the recent period, competing independent unions such as the CS/IDF have been able to defend the particular interests of civil servants in collective bargaining. In contrast, unions from the syndicalist tradition, such as the anarcho-syndicalist CNT, which had over 1 million members in the 1930s, and the Catholic USO, formed in the early 1960s, have generally lost influence (although the CNT has had some local successes in works council elections in recent years).

Organisational structure

Both the main confederations, the UGT and CC.OO, were able to build up national organisations within a few years of their formal establishment, helped initially by an enormous growth in membership. For the CC.OO, rapid early growth was favoured by its links with the workplace organisations in which it had been illegally and semi-legally active since the 1950s. The basic unit of organisation of both confederations consists of trade union cells or sections at workplace level; in the case of the CC.OO, individual workshop or departmental groups join to form plant level trade union sections.

Within the UGT, workplace trade union sections join one of fifteen financially and administratively autonomous affiliated industrial unions which have organisations at area and district level; above this there is a further tier of provincial and regional organisation. The confederation itself has parallel structures to the individual unions, with the exception of workplace sections. The UGT's executive and decision-making bodies (Congress, Federal Committee, Federal Executive, General Secretary, Finance Committee, Arbitration Committee and Audit Committee) include representation both from the industrial unions and the geographical units of the confederation. However, the scope for independent negotiation by the industrial unions has been curbed by the social accords concluded between the UGT, government and employers, which have tied bargaining to agreed guidelines and pay limits. Since the mid 1980s, however, as the process of modernisation undertaken by the Socialist Party has been pursued increasingly without any willingness to offer compensation for union participation, cracks have begun to open up in relations with the government. Moreover, the industrial unions, weakened by high unemployment and loss of membership, are unable to fill the bargaining vacuum left behind.

Aside from its greater emphasis on workplace level representation, the CC.OO has a similar organisational structure to the UGT though with a more important role for its organisations at provincial and district level. The CC.OO has its own independent industrial unions (twenty-two in all) with parallel structures for both the confederation and affiliated unions. Both are represented on the CC.OO's decision-making and executive bodies, the most important of which are the Federal Congress, Federal Committee, and Federal Executive Committee whose fifty members are elected by proportional representation from slates of candidates.

Membership

Although the UGT and CC.OO experienced a very rapid growth in membership in the period immediately following the fall of the Franco dictatorship, with both organisations growing from fewer than 10,000 to over 1 million members pushing union density to 40–50 per cent of the workforce, they were not able to retain them once initial high expectations had evaporated. Economic modernisation, linked with job losses and high unemployment as some sectors of the economy shrank, together with the inability of the unions to resist cuts in the value of real wages in the context of nationally agreed wage accords, all contributed to a drastic fall-off in membership, and a lowering of union density to around 10 per cent. Both confederations now have approximately the same membership, probably in the order of 500,000. And both organisations exhibit a similar pattern of much lower membership in the agrarian south compared with the industrialised north.

Because, as in France, membership figures are not an accurate indicator of the representativeness of each organisation, an important measure of their relative strength is their success in elections to works councils (*comités de empresas*) which are held every four years. The results of these elections determine which unions will be deemed to be representative for bargaining purposes. In order to obtain this status, which is associated not only with representation in collective bargaining but also with recognition as a national union and participation in public organisations, as well as entitlement to funds from the former Francoist unions, national trade unions must obtain at least 10 per cent of the votes cast and regional unions 15 per cent and at a total of at least 1,500 elected representatives. In the most recent elections, held in 1990, only the UGT, CC.OO and the regional ELA/STV were able to meet these criteria.

The following trends have emerged since the early 1980s.

— With a total of 80 per cent of elected delegates in 1990, the CC.OO and UGT have maintained and even enhanced their duopoly at national level, although there has been a shift favouring the UGT since the early 1980s. In 1982, for example, the UGT obtained 37 per cent of the vote and 44 per cent in 1990. In comparison, the CC.OO obtained 33 per cent in 1982 and 36 per cent in 1990.

— However, the CC.OO is dominant in large-scale enterprises with over 750 employees, and in public undertakings such as the railways, the airline Iberia, telecommunications, gas and electricity, the large banks, and also in the important industrial and commercial centres of Madrid and Barcelona.

— Basque regionalism has proved to be a stable component of trade union pluralism, with the ELA/STV winning the most votes relatively in its region, and obtaining 8 per cent overall.

— The share of the vote won by non-union candidates has fallen steadily since the early 1980s, with the UGT the main beneficiary.

As already noted, however, among civil servants there has has been a tendency towards greater union fragmentation based on particular employee categories, a development of which the Socialist Government has taken advantage to push through its pay policies. For example, *C.S. Independiente de Funcionarios*, which was formed in 1987, succeeded in winning 25 per cent of the vote in elections within the public sector compared with 23 per cent for the UGT and 24 per cent for CC.OO.

Loss of membership during the 1980s has placed Spanish trade unions in a crisis. Even while passing through their initial foundation period and into the the early 1980s, it was evident that membership dues were not sufficient to cover the costs of their organisations, with resources having to be shared out between the industrial unions, national federations, and the geographically based bodies. For example, in works council elections the UGT has been forced to rely on organisational and, in particular, on financial support from its European partners, which was provided primarily because of its rivalry with the Communist-aligned CC.OO.

A substantial portion of both unions' financial needs are met not only from membership dues but also from state-run funds, derived from the former Francoist unions, which are granted to trade unions deemed to be representative, as measured by works council election results.

Workplace representation

During the 1980s a dualist system of representation at workplace level was established. In addition to staff representatives, which represent employees in small enterprises with up to forty-nine employees, and works councils, which operate in larger undertakings and are elected by all permanent employees, trade union sections can also be established by any unions regarded as representative within a workplace.

The legal basis for staff representatives and works councils is the 1980 Workers' Statute which provides detailed regulation on employee representation (election procedures, rights and obligations), though also leaving scope for further elaboration by collective agreement (for example, the setting-up of representative bodies at corporate level, time-off provisions and so on).

There is no obligation on employers to set up works councils, although they must grant recognition once established. Elections for works councils are held every four years. All permanent employees are entitled to vote and voting takes place according to employee category (white-collar and blue-collar). Since the trade unions put up the most candidates for the elections these – in the absence of more precise membership figures – serve as a yardstick for assessing how representative the individual unions are.

Works councils are also significant for the trade unions as they have powers which to some extent compete and overlap with their bargaining and representational rights at workplace level. Furthermore, and more positively for the unions, works councils also have rights to office space and other facilities which can be used, where appropriate, for trade union work. They meet regularly, are independent of the employer, and have their own offices and means for disseminating information. They also have the right to call works assemblies, and their members enjoy special protection against dismissal. The time-off rights of members of works councils can be added together and transferred to enable some representatives complete time-off.

Both forms of representation have rights to information on the economic and financial situation of the undertaking, to scrutinise contracts of employment, and to information on the termination of contracts, disciplinary measures, and health and safety issues. They also have the right to express an opinion before the employer takes any action which affects the workforce, involves dismissals or short time, any reduction in working time, relocation of workplaces either in whole or in part, vocational training programmes and the introduction of, or changes to, systems of job evaluation. Works councils are further entrusted with the task of ensuring compliance with employment law, collective agreements at industry level and regulations on health and safety at work.

These rights to information and consultation are supplemented by bargaining rights – a factor of strategic significance in the overall industrial relations system since it enables works councils to sign collective agreements at company or undertaking level without any restriction on the range of issues subject to negotiation. Above plant level the right to conclude collective agreements rests solely with representative trade unions. The regulation of employment relations at workplace and corporate level is therefore open to resolution by local actors, as – in Spanish law – the right to strike is seen as a collectively exercised individual right open to works councils. In contrast to a number of other EU countries, no obligation to maintain industrial peace is imposed on statutory workplace representatives.

Trade union workplace representation

In part because works councils were beginning to reduce the scope for trade union activity at workplace level, new provisions regulating and strengthening rights of trade union representation were introduced by the 1985 Law on Trade Union Freedoms. Although trade union representatives were able to operate at workplace level prior to this legislation, under either collective or works agreements, the 1985 law gave trade unions with at least 10 per cent of the vote in elections to works councils, in workplaces with at least 250 employees, the right to establish trade union branches (this applies to workplaces of just 200 employees in the public sector). Branches function in accordance with the union's own rule book, and may appoint or elect trade union delegates who enjoy the same protection and rights to time-off as members of works councils. The number of recognised delegates varies depending on the size of the establishment's workforce.

As with works councils, trade union delegates also have the right to information from company or workplace management, the right to attend works council meetings, and time-off for union duties on full pay. In competition with works councils, trade union delegates have the right to conduct collective negotiations where the trade union branch represents the majority of the members of the works council or where negotiations are conducted only for members of their own trade union.

Trade union branches must be granted facilities for meeting at the workplace (though this must be outside working hours), as well as means of communicating with members (notice boards, etc.). Full-time union officials have a right of access to the workplace, and trade unions as organisations have a general right to operate both within and outside the undertaking. Since there are no limits on what trade unions may concern themselves with, this can also include political activity, provided that it is not directed at the immediate workplace. The 1985 law sought to reduce the competition between works councils and trade unions by strengthening trade union representation at the workplace and at the same time giving both equal rights in order to foster co-operation in representing employee interests.

Health and safety committees

In addition to works councils and workplace union representation, employees in establishments with more than 100 workers are also represented on workplace health and safety committees. Their legal basis rests on legislation originally introduced in 1971, although some revision is planned. Committee members are elected from the works council, or from the trade unions, where no works council exists. As well as employee representatives, the committees include management representatives, who chair meetings, a qualified health and safety technician and a medical specialist. The committees, which meet regularly, are responsible for monitoring compliance with safety regulations, and dealing with instances of occupational illness and accidents.

Employee codetermination at
enterprise level

In 1986 an agreement covering the public sector was concluded with the UGT which provided for the setting-up of supervisory boards with employee representation in state holding companies and other similar controlling organisations. Employee representatives must belong to a trade union represented in the undertaking. In individual state enterprises with more than 1,000 employees, the trade unions can choose between representation on the supervisory board or the appointment of two members of the management board (who do not have to be drawn from the workforce).

Representation on public bodies and
national representation

Spanish trade unions are represented on a variety of consultative bodies and other forums in important social institutions: these include the National Employment Institute (INEM) and the organisation which administers social insurance. From the late 1970s, the government and employers pursued a strategy of social concertation in which unions were involved in both tripartite and bipartite discussions on basic policy issues. Up until the mid 1980s this undoubtedly yielded a number of benefits for the unions, and in particular for the UGT. Trade union influence affected decisions on labour law, the regulation of collective bargaining, and employment policy, at least up until the PSOE's shift towards a more rigorous policy of modernisation. Formal tripartite accords petered out after 1986, and union disillusion with government policy hardened into a growing rift between the UGT and its nominal political ally, the PSOE. Growing pressure on the Spanish economy in the preparatory phase to European monetary and economic integration may have led to a revival of interest on the Government side in some rapprochement with the unions. In 1992, the Government finally moved to establish the long promised tripartite Economic and Social Council, in part as a quid pro quo for a number of austerity measures involving cuts in unemployment benefit and other social security expenditure. The council began its operations in February 1993. However, relations between the unions and government remained troubled as the economic situation deteriorated, and the government moved to introduce major changes to labour law to ease dimissal procedures and devolve greater responsibility on terms and conditions to the parties to collective bargaining.

A European Model of Employee Interest Representation

The marked differences in the organisational principles and strengths, forms of representation and political possibilities for and constraints on Europe's trade unions all serve to highlight the fact that these movements grew up within the context of the development of the nation-state, and are still subject above all to national traditions and cultures.

Differences and diversity can be observed in every sphere of trade union organisation. Pluralist systems, divided along political or confessional lines, contrast with those countries in which one union centre serves as the organisational focus. Industry unions, in which all the employees of a workplace will be organised by one trade union, create an entirely different union landscape to those situations dominated by large general unions co-existing with craft unions, with the corollary of multi-unionism at workplace level. In some countries, only trade unions are recognised as legitimate and lawful bargaining agents; in others, directly elected workplace systems of representation, such as works councils or staff delegates, also have extensive rights to conclude collective agreements. Negotiating rights and powers also vary within union movements: whilst some movements grant their central organisations extensive competences to bargain at national level, in others the central confederation serves at best as a co-ordinating forum or lobby organisation for general union interests. There are also substantial differences in the degree to which the state is prepared to intervene in collective bargaining and to participate in or initiate tripartite arrangements. No uniformity exists in the sphere of trade union rights and freedoms to organise, the regulation of industrial action – which in some countries is an individual right whereas in others it is lawfully solely the province of trade unions – or of the employer's right to resort to the weapon of the lock-out. Wide variations are found in systems of employee representation at workplace, company and national level, both in terms of formal employee rights (codetermination, consultation, information), and the organising rights of trade unions at workplace and corporate levels.

Despite these many differences, it is nonetheless still possible to postulate the existence of a distinctively European model of interest representation and codetermination. In general, throughout Europe trade unions are able to organise at workplace, and sometimes at company, level – albeit with widely varying powers and forms of legal protection – or are able to act indirectly as representatives of employees through their presence in established institutions, or are least able to exercise influence over decisions at workplace level by virtue of a high level of trade union membership. Scope for trade unions also exists where a dual system of employee interest representation has been established which formally separates the two spheres of workplace representation and formal collective bargaining.

All these varying modalities allow unions to influence, or directly shape through the medium of collective bargaining, decisions affecting terms and conditions of employment at workplace level. In contrast, the scope for formal influence or decision-making over business decisions at establishment level is severely limited. Where employee or trade union representatives are granted rights in this field, they are typically confined to an entitlement to be consulted or to information disclosure.

Rights at corporate level – where they exist at all or go beyond particular industry agremeents – providing for participation in decisions over strategy and linked with effective representation at board level are both weaker and less common. The system of codetermination in the German coal, iron and steel industries (*Montanbestimmung*) is notable by its rarity.

Scope for trade unions to influence governments and parliaments on social and economic policy issues depends on a variety of factors. In addition to the political approach of the trade union movement itself, these include the traditions of tripartite arrangements in the national setting, the ability of trade unions and employer organisations to represent and resolve their different interests independently of each other and the state, organisational (and individual) autonomy and interconnections, and the links between union movements and political parties, and not least the preparedness of governments to initiate or participate in and support bi- and tripartite institutions. With the exception of Great Britain since 1979, most European Union member states offer some form of institutionalised scope for trade unions to represent employee interests through tripartite arrangements, and not simply via collective bargaining. Such arrangements range from trade union involvement in central organisations which administer welfare and social and employment systems to participation in national consultative institutions which offer scope for unions to represent trade union positions and in some cases to exercise a veto over proposals.

The extent to which trade unions can exercise influence over decision-making processes, be it at workplace, company or national level, is not solely determined by formal statutory or otherwise secured rights. The absence of rights to effective participation or codetermination, especially in the economic sphere, may be counterbalanced in practice by rights to information or consultation which arise through the overlapping of different forms of representation, backed up by a high level of union membership, a corresponding capacity for effective mobilisation, and an individual right to resort to industrial action. The low level of juridification of employment relations, exemplified by Great Britain and the Republic of Ireland, may in turn open up avenues for trade union activity; at the same time, this has been bought at the cost of a form of representation which is heavily tilted towards the workplace and firm, and which is often only loosely integrated with higher levels of representation and organisation.

For the European Union as a whole it remains the case that, despite variations in form, levels and intensity, trade unions retain scope for exercising influence over decisions at a number of levels. The institutions and legal form through which this is effected are diverse, although there is a discernible trend towards the consolidation of dual forms through which employee interests can be articulated – trade unions on the one hand, statutory bodies for the entire workforce on the other. Abstracting from their specific forms, and setting aside the arguable prospects for a convergence of forms, the existing situation continues to offer scope for a co-ordination at European level of trade union policies and strategies.

PART III

The Co-ordinates of Trade Union Policy for Europe

FRITZ RATH

1 Europe as a challenge for the trade unions

The everyday experience of all trade unionists provides plentiful evidence of the need to co-ordinate trade union policies and activities at European level. For workers throughout Europe, the completion of the Single Market has become closely bound up with fears of closure and job losses, accusations of 'social dumping' and anxieties about the prospects for their own town or country as a viable economic location. For example, what is the virtue of a national system of effective employee co-determination or strong trade union representation if companies simply shift their business headquarters elsewhere? How much do local managements in multinationals really know about the European strategy being pursued by their corporate centres? And how effective is the international exchange of information between employee representatives?

The issue of competition between different national locations takes on a slightly altered complexion in the context of collective bargaining. Whereas demands for higher pay or shorter hours made by German workers are rejected by employers with the argument that Germany already has the highest costs in Europe, employers in Spain contend that their industrial prospects are at risk because of their low productivity. In fact, far from setting the European Union on the 'path of progress' almost unquestioningly assumed by the EEC's founders, the completion of the Single Market has initiated, or threatens, a downward spiral of worsening social standards and mutually antagonistic competition between countries compelled to undercut each other – in Euro-jargon, 'social dumping'. The furore caused by the decision of the domestic appliance manufacturer Hoover to shift production from its French plant in Dijon to Scotland, amidst accusations from the French trade unions that concessions had been negotiated in the UK which would not have been legally possible in France, illustrates how acute sensitivities are in this area. Similarly, advertisements placed in the German business press in 1992–93 by the UK government extolling low wage costs as a central competitive advantage for Britain were widely seen as reinforcing the trend towards a lowering of standards in Europe. Scarcely any national, sectoral or company bargaining round now takes place in Europe without reference to the pay or conditions prevailing in neighbouring countries.

And even where national sovereignty in theory continues to prevail, such as in the field of post and telecommunications (expressly excluded from the EEC treaties) or in media policy, the Single Market can insinuate itself through the back door opened by rules requiring free movement of goods and services. Moreover, any activity which holds out the prospect of a commercial profit can be transformed into a tradeable product within the meaning of the EEC treaty. Competition policy (regulations of monopolies, etc) and policies on external trade between member-states and the rest of the world are already determined in Brussels.

All these factors reinforce the arguments for a strong central trade union organisation in Brussels with the capacity to shape and influence these processes. The Single Market has made it impossible for the institutional arrangements of the past to continue. What remains at issue are the precise forms which the trade union response should take at a European level. For example, good arguments can be made against transferring powers from national trade union centres to the European Trade Union Confederation (ETUC) or European Industry Committees: the rights of employee representatives at company or plant level and scope for the exercise of employee co-determination are all rooted in national labour law and/or collective agreements concluded at national level. There is no European labour law offering employees comparable rights at European level, and as long as no such system of law exists no trade union can exchange the national bird in its hand for the mere prospect of something better in the European bush. The same applies in the case of multinational companies. Irrespective of how internationalised their operations might be, multinational companies are still subject to national company and tax law: in legal terms they are still national employers. Although laws to control them might be possible at European level, no such framework presently exists; and enforcing existing law through the European Court of Justice (ECJ) remains a complex and protracted affair.

Collective bargaining is a further area where national provision continues to hold sway. There are virtually no European level collective agreements. How such agreements might be enforced remains unclear, to say the least. For example, would a strike in support of European negotiating demands be lawful in all EU countries? And what effects would European level collective agreements have on existing national agreements? And should the trade unions seek to tackle certain questions primarily with the employers at European level? Again here, the trade unions find themselves in a difficult transitional stage as far as levels of influence and institutional arrangements are concerned. Although intervention at every level might be desirable, it would be impossible in practice. The trade union movement needs to engage in a discussion about the levels at which it is most important and appropriate to present a common European front and where it would be more desirable to be represented through separate national, regional or local channels. There is no simple answer to this question. This chapter sets out to explore some possible solutions, not merely from a theoretical standpoint but also by examining solutions which previous forms of co-operation between trade unions at European level might suggest. In order to do this, however, we need to look more closely at the pressures on them at each possible level of activity and co-operation.

This discussion of the position and perspectives of the trade unions in western Europe does not set out to outline the positions taken by the European Trade Union Congress or the Industry Committees, nor to judge the successes or failures of the national trade union confederations in their policies on Europe; rather, it seeks to illuminate the co-ordinates which define the current context for trade union policy at European level, and to provide ideas for future developments. Initially, this involves examining a number of policy dimensions.

First, the most important external determining factor in current trade union policy on Europe is the process of European integration itself. This is taking place at various speeds (via the EU, EFTA, the Council of Europe and the nature of East-West relations in general). Where the process of European integration, economic or political, results in a major shift of powers from the national to the European level, as is currently the case with the European Union, this represents a major challenge for the trade unions. In particular it highlights the question of how and to what extent the trade unions can exercise influence within a Single Market built on free market principles – a market which will also extend to embrace the EFTA countries with the creation of the European Economic Area (as well as by direct enlargement through the EU membership of countries such as Austria, Finland, Norway and Sweden).

Moreover, the movement towards European integration will itself be shaped by the choice of levels and instruments made by Europe's trade unions in their efforts to influence the process. The first challenge in the area of European policy for the trade unions, therefore, consists in understanding precisely how and in what spheres sovereign rights are being transferred from national states to European institutions, and in elaborating a strategy both to influence and, if appropriate, resist the process.

Second, given the extent of the Single Market, trade union policy at European level can no longer be conceived of as the foreign policy of national trade union confederations or individual unions. Equally, it can no longer be regarded as a sub-department of the international trade union confederations or trade secretariats. Trade union policy on Europe constitutes an independent level of trade union activity, the co-ordinates of which are derived from its own specific context. The trade union organisations which operate at this level, either the ETUC or European Industry Committees, currently serve as mediators between the powers and functions of the national and the international confederations. However, they are also now being increasingly obliged to assume powers for themselves in response to the fact that some developments can only be influenced at a European level. This problem represents the second challenge to the union movement's 'internal' system of co-ordinates: what tasks or powers ought best to be transferred to the European level? And how can an organisation be built which is fully competent to act at a European level?

Third, trade unions have members. As long as policy on Europe remained a kind of trade union foreign policy, most members knew little of the activities of the own confederations in Europe, aside perhaps from participation in an international visit or youth camp. However, the more that European development forces itself onto the domestic agenda of national trade unions, the more individual members will have direct experience of the powers and effectiveness of those European trade union organisations which represent their interests. As a result, the attractiveness and capacities of European trade union organisations will become a factor in judging the standing and strengths of the domestic organisations to which they belong. It is trade union members themselves who are making issues such as the creation of European Works Councils or cross-border interregional co-operation into priority areas for trade union policy. Thus the third challenge to European trade union policy is the need for the European trade union movement to develop new structures which match the development of the Single Market, and which enable trade union members at plant and at regional level to consider the European dimension to their union work and act accordingly. In other words the ETUC needs to develop into a trade union with a living connection to its members.

2 The political challenge of European integration – and the trade union response

2.1 The re-casting of Europe

For forty years the world was dominated by the two superpowers, the USA and the USSR – in theory, both federal political structures. However, in neither case has 'federalism' borne much resemblance to the project of advancing beyond the nation state as it emerged in the nineteenth century. The constituent states of the USA were not nation states when the United States' constitution was drafted; and as the ultimate break-up of the USSR has shown, the 'transcendence of the nation state' in the Soviet constitution can scarcely be regarded as entailing the voluntary surrender of sovereign rights. The integration of Western Europe therefore marks a unique model for this 'transcendence of the nation state'. The treaties which established and developed the European communities represent a body of international agreements containing far-reaching mechanisms for decision-making at a supranational level. The transfer of sovereign rights to the European Union by the nation states of Western Europe marks an unambiguous shift of powers away from national political decision-making centres.

What is unique in the process of European integration is that it has been accomplished on the basis of voluntary and democratic decisions. National political sovereignty has been transferred to a set of institutions, the European Community (from November 1993, the European Union), with powers to create its own body of legislation. Regulations are directly binding on all member states. Directives harmonise legal provisions and set common objectives which member states must fulfil. Community decisions have established common programmes. And Recommendations have been adopted in order to influence social and economic development in a variety of spheres. As the European Community has developed, spurred on by specific measures such as the Single European Act (1986), this body of legislation has come to embrace more and more spheres of social, economic and commercial iife. Grouped around the European Union – like an onion, according to Jacques Delors – are the European Free Trade Area (EFTA), the Council of Europe with its headquarters in Strasbourg, and developing East-West and North-South structures of co-operation (embodied, for example, in the Lomé Treaty). The creation of the European Economic Area (EC-EFTA), implemented from 1 January 1994, the EU membership from 1995 of Austria, Finland, Norway and Sweden, and Association Treaties with the Czech and Slovak Republics, Poland and Hungary might also mark the start of a 'Super European Union' raising new questions about how such a mammoth could or should function. Nevertheless, the nation state is not yet dead; and a European union is not yet entirely capable of independent life.

In general, Europe's trade unions have always supported the process of European integration on political grounds. This fundamental standpoint deserves emphasis, given the stern test set for trade union support by the recent focus on monetary issues and the Single Market. Political support for integration has always been seen by the trade unions as a contribution to securing peace in Europe – an approach summed up by G. Debunne, a past president of the ETUC, in the following terms: 'If Europe is to speak with one voice, then this Europe – the source of two world wars – must assume its responsibilities: responsibility for peace, for democracy, freedom, progress and justice. Building Europe – this must be the political aim of all those who defend the values of European society' (G. Debunne, in Hinterscheid (ed.), *Anders Leben – Anders Arbeiten in Europa* (Düsseldorf, 1986), p 142).

European integration has also always been viewed as a contribution to the safeguarding of democracy in Western Europe. The statutes of the ETUC, for example, require the organisations brought together in the ETUC to keep watch over the maintenance and strengthening of democracy in Europe. This is a mission taken seriously by the ETUC, and demonstrated in union mobilisation in October 1975 against the Franco dictatorship in Spain, and during the 1980s in support of the democratic trade union movement in Turkey. Such activities are either directly agreed in the ETUC or co-ordinated through it. However, this did not apply in the case of support by Western Europe's trade unions for free and democratic trade unionism in Eastern Europe. Although almost all the member confederations of the ETUC directly supported the Polish Solidarity movement, for example, the ETUC itself never went beyond a mutual exchange of information. Nonetheless, the ETUC's constitution does not confine itself to Western Europe, and the organisation is likely to play an active external role, especially with European Commission engagement in the provision of aid to Eastern Europe. The ETUC's new constitution, passed at its Luxembourg Congress in 1991, allows for membership and observer status for new unions in Eastern Europe.

2.2 Integration under democratic control?

The institutions of the European Union themselves also require greater democratic supervision. The legislative machinery of the EU turns the usual notion of the democratic separation of powers on its head. For example, the legislature is not the European Parliament but the Council of Ministers – that is, the directly represented governments of the member states. Formally the European Parliament cannot even submit its own draft legislation for formal consultation; the right to initiate legislation lies solely with the European Commission. In turn, it exercises

the executive tasks of implementing decisions and ensuring compliance
with Community law. Only since the Single European Act (SEA), passed
in 1987, has the European Parliament had a right to propose amendments to draft legislation via the 'co-operation procedure' (see p 246
below). These rights will be enhanced under certain circumstances by
the reforms made through the Maastricht Treaty, but, the choice of
procedure which determines the Parliament's influence still lies with
the European Commission. Over the years, the ETUC has repeatedly
complained about the democratic shortcomings of the Community and
called for changes which were not embodied in the Single European
Act:

> Democratisation of European institutions is indispensable in order to prevent
> them becoming bodies on which ministers, officials and diplomats have more
> power of decision than the democratically elected members of the European
> Parliament. Major reforms are needed to equip the European Parliament
> with true legislative powers in order to find a solution to the problems which
> are within the European competence and which can only be solved at that
> level. (Declaration of the ETUC on European Union, December 1984.)

However, the ETUC's strong support for the European Parliament in
its draft treaty for European Union was not followed up by a high level
of engagement in the subsequent preparation of the Single European
Act which reformed the Treaties of Rome.

Neither the call for more democratic control by the European Parliament, nor demands for a better correspondence between the economic and social development of the Community, were taken up in the
Single European Act. This dual failure may explain the closer alliance
which emerged between the ETUC and European Parliament in late
1989, following the Strasbourg summit and its, at that time, 'not-yet
solemn' declaration by heads of government on the Social Charter. The
ETUC continues to argue for greater democratisation and the anchor-
ing of social rights in the further development of the European Union.

3 Trade unions and the economic challenge
of the Single European Market

3.1 The imbalance between the Single Market and European social policy

The few indirect references to a political and social conception of the
European Community appear merely in the preamble to the Treaty of
Rome. The main aim of the founding treaties was almost certainly
economic in nature – the creation of a European Economic Community. The Treaty of Rome envisaged a process of economic unity based
on four principles: free movement of goods, of capital, of services and
of people. These four principles manifestly had their roots in a free

market philosophy. In contrast, the preceding treaty establishing the European Coal and Steel Community embraced a more explicit link between political, social and economic objectives. In other spheres, the treaties are based on the assumption that supportive financial measures, such as the European Social Fund, together with the harmonisation of a number of areas of policy otherwise liable to distort competition, would be sufficient to secure the functioning of the Common Market. The treaties did not provide for powers at Community level for harmonising policy in the economic and social spheres.

The reform of the Treaty of Rome through the 1986 Single European Act did not fundamentally change this situation: the Single Market was to be brought into being using the available instruments of the Community. In all, some 300 directives and regulations have been issued in order to realise the Single Market. The vast bulk of these are concerned with commercial and technical matters. As far as employee rights are concerned, the new instruments are either incomplete or wholly absent. The economic integration of the European Union, and its social consequences, have become one of the principal problems for trade union activity at a European level – both in terms of the appropriate level of intervention and the instruments available to effect it.

3.2 European Community institutions and the creation of the Single Market

Jacques Delors' controversial assertion that within a few years around 80 per cent of Europe's laws would be made in Brussels and not in Europe's national capitals may now seem somewhat far-fetched. However, Brussels has already been actively legislating in areas of direct concern to trade unionists. What decisions have already been taken, and how were they made? This section sets out the main instruments available to the European Union, and the procedures for co-operation with the European Parliament both under the Single European Act and the Maastricht Treaty.

There are three instruments which the Community can use to create legislation binding on the member states:

— Regulations are directly and generally applicable in all member states.
— Directives provide a framework: they are binding on the member states 'as to the result to be achieved' but leave the form and method of implementation to each national authority.
— Decisions are binding regulations directed at individuals or states.

In addition, the Commission can issue opinions and recommendations, as well as provide information, none of which are binding. The

Commission can also conclude international treaties and agreements, which bind the Union by international law. Legislation can be created on the basis of three different voting procedures; the original system was changed by the 1986 Single European Act, and was revised again under the Maastricht Treaty. (The procedures set out below are in the form laid down in Articles 189a-c of the Maastricht Treaty on European Union, which incorporates the Single Market procedures of the Single European Act, but supersedes and develops them in a number of respects.) Irrespective of the method of voting, it is the European Commission which proposes, at least formally, draft legislation, and the Council of Ministers, representing national governments directly, which decides whether a proposal becomes law ('is adopted') or not. The procedures are:

— Simple majority voting.
— Qualified majority voting: each state has a weighting reflecting the size of its population (the large countries have ten votes, others five, three or two): a majority of fifty-four out of a possible seventy-six is required to adopt a piece of legislation.
— Unanimity.

The main objective of the Single European Act was to accelerate legislation directed at completing the Single Market. As a result those legal instruments which the Commission viewed as necessary for the Single Market could be dealt with under qualified majority voting (QMV) rather than requiring unanimity (according to Article 100a, SEA, as amended by the Maastricht Treaty). Expressly excluded from this procedure were provisions on taxation, the free movement of individuals, and the 'rights and interests of employed persons': here unanimity was required. However, qualified majority voting was introduced in the case of measures intended to encourage 'improvements, especially in the working environment, as regards the health and safety of workers' (Article 118a, SEA). This provision has been used, for example, to introduce a Directive on Working Time, adopted in November 1993.

Under the Protocol on Social Policy ('the Social Chapter') agreed as part of the Maastricht Treaty in 1992, qualified majority voting under the SEM procedure was extended to cover, as well as health and safety, measures on 'working conditions, the information and consultation of workers', sex equality in the labour market and job opportunities, and the integration of people excluded from the labour market (see Appendix to this section for text of the 'Social Chapter'). The UK Government refused to accept these measures as part of the main treaty; so they form a separate element which the other eleven member-states will implement. In another example, the UK Government has thus far blocked progress on a Directive on European Works Councils through its veto on the Council of Ministers. However, under the qualified majority voting procedure of the Maastricht Treaty the other member states can proceed with the proposals (see below).

Where unanimity is required, the European Parliament is merely consulted. Where decision-making is according to qualified majority voting, Parliament can propose amendments to the Commission's legislative proposals. The following applies in the case of the *co-operation procedure* with the European Parliament (Article 189c, Maastricht Treaty):

1. The Commission proposes;
2. Parliament gives an opinion;
3. The Council adopts a common position with a qualified majority.

At this stage none of the institutions is under any time pressure.

4. This common position is communicated to the Parliament. Parliament then has three options:
a) Parliament either issues no opinion within three months or agrees. The proposal can then be adopted by the Council and becomes law.
b) Parliament rejects the proposal by an absolute majority. The Council can only now adopt the proposal by a unanimous vote.
c) Parliament proposes amendments to the Council's common position.

If this happens, the Commission re-examines the proposal together with the amendments.

5. Within one month the Commission must take one of two courses:
a) It may accept the changes made by Parliament. If this happens, the Council decides on the new proposal from the Commission by qualified majority. However, it can depart from the proposal made by the Commission only by unanimous vote.
b) The Commission can reject Parliament's amendments. In this case the Council can only adopt Parliament's amendments against the will of the Commission through unanimous vote.
6. If the Council cannot agree within three months then the whole proposal is not adopted.

The procedure then begins afresh either through a new proposal from the Commission or by disappearing back into the Commission's filing cabinet. Moreover, the Commission can change its proposal at any stage as long as the Council has not yet come to a decision.

Under the Maastricht Treaty, a new legislative procedure was introduced, termed *co-decision-making*, which enhanced the powers of Parliament beyond the procedure set out above. Where the Commission decides that this procedure should apply, Parliament may approve or not respond to a legislative proposal; in this case, the Council may proceed to adopt it by qualified majority voting. However, under the new arrangements, were Parliament to reject the common position, the Council of Ministers may convene a Conciliation Committee, consisting of an equal number of Council and Parliamentary representatives. Its task is to attempt to agree a joint text, with help from the Commission. Any agreed text is then submitted to the Council and Parliament, and both must agree within six weeks in order for the proposal to become law. Parliament may also propose amendments – with the same procedure for adoption by the council under qualified majority voting as above.

3.3 The Community's powers and the Single Market

In the course of the completion of the Single Market the Community has involved itself in an increasing number of areas which, directly or indirectly, have an effect on employees. These areas are set out in the overview in Appendix 4 (see p 282) which itemises the areas in which community law has already supplanted national competence through Single Market legislation. Although this list only offers a general overview, it highlights the widening scope of European-level regulation. The (approximately) 300 Directives identified as necessary to realise the Single Market, as well as the large number of individual programmes and legislative acts not directly related to the Single Market programme, pass through the full legislative process, beginning with the Commission's proposals, and then via consultations in the European Parliament and the Economic and Social Committee (ESC), which meets in parallel to the working group of the Council of Ministers. If a Directive or programme is decided upon, the application of the instrument is then monitored by a wide diversity of committees, usually including the representatives of national governments.

3.4 The scope for Europe's trade unions

According to the preamble to the ETUC's constitution, its affiliated unions have committed themselves 'to promote the social, economic and cultural interests of employees at European level in general and in all European institutions in particular'. The new constitution lacks any specific reference to European institutions; however, this remains the ETUC's most important task. In order to fulfil this role the ETUC's Secretariat must be able to influence the Community's complex legislative machine. At present, however, the ETUC's Secretariat, which in addition to a General Secretary and Deputy is staffed with four further political secretaries and six assistants, is hard-pressed to follow and influence Community policies. This also applies to the Industry

Committees, which usually only have one, or at most two, political secretaries. The main problems are as follows.

— The ETUC and Industry Committees need an adequate number of staff to be able to respond swiftly to legislative proposals, deal with them effectively, and isolate the most important problem areas for further political consultation.
— The ETUC and Industry Committees must be able to influence the legislative process at each stage of the procedure (see above) in the most effective and appropriate way. This implies a bigger presence in the committee discussions of the European Parliament and greater use of the potential for study groups within the Economic and Social Committee.
— The ETUC and Industry Committees must have adequate access to enable them to follow the discussions between government experts and responsible ministers, who are not usually keen to impart information.
— The Economic and Social Committee lacks weight within the overall institutional structure. In contrast, the directly elected Parliament has gained in importance. However, the Economic and Social Committee is vital if the trade unions wish to broaden the scope of consultations on EU legislative proposals, relieving the ETUC of some of the burden. At present both the ETUC and employee representatives on the ESC feel that each has abandoned the other to deal with the legislative process on its own. Consideration needs to be given to a reform of the Economic and Social Committee.
— The increasing involvement of the trade unions in the Community's consultative committees represents a success in the advancement of trade union influence. However, the growth of such consultative opportunities alongside the existing secretariat has led to the entire secretariat being overwhelmed by consultations which the ETUC cannot prepare for, or at least not entirely adequately (see again Appendix 4, p 282).
— The ETUC secretariat devotes about two-thirds of its organisational capacities to efforts to reach a common position among individual trade unions. This is absolutely necessary and has led to greater cohesion within the ETUC. But the effort involved can detract from an effective ETUC presence in the EU's institutions and the external need to work through the media and influence public opinion.
— The options for joint action by the ETUC secretariat, the Industry Committees and member confederations must be used more systematically. At the same time, any such joint lobbying to influence EU legislation must be agreed in order to prevent any individual member confederation introducing amendments through a national

member of the European Parliament which might either be incompatible with or lead to confusion about the ETUC's position.

Employees and trade union representatives need to mobilise their entire forces to oppose the thousands of specialists working for management ... who are, so to speak, constantly in motion over Europe. A mere change in international trade union structures (for example, employing ten times more trade union representatives in Brussels or Geneva) would at best only mitigate the problem but not really constitute an effective answer. (Franz Steinkühler, in *Handelsblatt*, 9 June 1989).

Even with an expansion on this scale, the trade union movement in Europe would be hard-pressed to advance its case when faced with the thousands of corporate lobbyists, the thousands of EU officials, the 567 Members of the European Parliament, government specialists, state secretaries and ministers. However, it would represent a first step and, in addition to influencing EU institutions, would create the preconditions for a second vital step. This is the development of joint powers to be exercised by the European trade unions in one of the classic fields of trade union activity – that is, the organisation of employees in multinational companies, bargaining with employers, and the wielding of forms of industrial action in order to advance the concerns of workers in Europe.

The next section is therefore concerned with the history and structure of the ETUC with the aim of setting out the current state of co-operation between West European trade unions and indicating the possibilities for expanding these fields of activity.

4 European trade union co-ordination

4.1 The history and structure of the European Trade Union Confederation

Before setting out the perspectives for the development of the trade union movement in Europe, it is important to look more closely at the present structure and history of the ETUC, and in particular the organisational response of the trade unions at European level to the process of European integration. In some respects the current situation is in essence still as described in a brochure prepared in 1979 by the French trade union centre, the CFDT: 'As it presently functions, the ETUC cannot be compared with a national trade union centre'. (CFDT, *Les syndicats dans le monde*, p114.) However, the structures of the ETUC do not intrinsically preclude the emergence of a strong trade union confederation at European level, with powers comparable with those of a national trade union centre. Some of the basic principles underlying the functioning of the ETUC could prove of great importance in the next few years, if the organisation is to be placed on a new structural and operational footing. Two key themes have shaped the ETUC since it emerged in the years 1973–74: developments in trade union policies in the post-war period, and the advance of European integration itself.

4.2 The post-war development of trade union policies

During the immediate post-war period the international trade union movement was increasingly shaped by the Cold War and the East-West conflict. For example, the majority of Christian trade unions did not join the Prague-based World Federation of Trade Unions (WFTU), founded in 1945, to which the majority of trade unions belonged. In 1949 the International Confederation of Free Trade Unions (ICFTU) was established. The result was a division of the international trade union movement into three blocs:

— The ICFTU, whose affiliates in Western Europe included socialist and social democratic trade unions as well as the large unitary trade union movements such as the British TUC and the Federal German DGB.
— The World Confederation of Labour (WCL), so named from 1968, which grew out of the International Confederation of Christian Trade Unions. Its affiliates in Western Europe include Christian trade unions in Belgium, France, the Netherlands, Luxembourg, and Switzerland.
— The World Federation of Trade Unions (WFTU) which, following the split in the West European movement, included the French CGT and the Italian CGIL.

Little movement occurred in this pattern for two decades until 1969, which proved to be a significant year for all three confederations. In 1969, following its refounding, the French CFDT began to become disenchanted with the WFTU: it finally left in 1979 and in 1989 joined the International Confederation of Free Trade Unions. 1969 also saw the beginnings of the process by which the Italian CGIL began to detach itself from the World Federation of Trade Unions. And in the same year, the United States confederation, the AFL-CIO, left the ICFTU. All three events, one year after the invasion of Czechoslovakia and parallel with the initial successes of Willy Brandt's *Ostpolitik*, created the preconditions for a restructuring of the West European trade union movement.

Following discussions between the organisations of the various blocs, one important step in this restructuring process took place with the founding of the European Trade Union Confederation (ETUC), at that time still confined to the seventeen affiliated confederations in the

ICTFU. In March 1974 further expansion took place with the admission of the several Christian trade union confederations, including the French CFTD. In the same year, the Irish Congress of Trade Unions, which had no international affiliation, the Finnish SAK and the Italian CGIL also joined. A number of other national trade union federations were admitted in subsequent years, including the GSEE (Greece) and DISK (Turkey). More recently, a number of confederations from smaller countries, and civil service and white-collar unions from larger ones, such as the German DAG, have also joined the ETUC. As a consequence, the ETUC has largely managed to overcome the political division of the union movement inherited from the Cold War.

Whether, and how rapidly, those confederations traditionally oriented to the Communist movement, such as Intersindical (Portugal) and the CGT (France), will be admitted to the ETUC is difficult to say. Whereas the Communist-led CC.OO (Spain) has now been admitted, the CGT is felt to have some way to travel with regard to both its position on trade union matters and its perspective on European integration. As long as the CGT continues to hold a view on European integration which is utterly at odds with that of the ETUC it is difficult to see how it could become a member. Current developments in Eastern Europe have been taken up by the ETUC through the establishment of a European trade union forum. With developments in Eastern Europe, the expansion of the Council of Europe requires a new perspective to be worked out by the ETUC.

4.3 European integration and the development of the ETUC

The second strand of development, which led to the ETUC in its current form, is represented by the two stages of West European integration: first, the establishment in the 1950s of the European Coal and Steel Community (ECSC), the EEC and the European Free Trade Area (EFTA); and second, the expansion of the Community in 1973 to include Great Britain, Ireland, and Denmark. Trade union support for a European solution to the reorganisation of the coal and steel industry was rewarded by considerable union influence within the emerging Coal and Steel Community. Trade union involvement was also motivated by a desire to hold back the emergence of an arms manufacturing sector by curbing the development of national coal and steel industries – a perspective shared by Jean Monnet. Accordingly, the trade unions obtained considerable influence within the ECSC authorities themselves.

However, when the EEC was established in 1957–58 it was evident that the trade unions would not enjoy this same degree of influence in the wider economic community. The establishment of the 'European Trade Union Secretariat' in Düsseldorf in 1958, consisting of ICFTU

members in the European community, constituted a direct response to
the Rome Treaties. ICFTU's regional organisations continued to operate alongside the new body. The integration of the unions within EFTA,
founded in 1959–60, was not as rapid as within the various stages of the
European Community. The EFTA trade unions were jealous of their
national influence and it was not until 1968 that they established their
own secretariat in Brussels, initially in parallel with the EC's union
structures. Although the renaming of the European Trade Union
Secretariat as the 'European Confederation of Free Trade Unions'
(ECFTU) in 1969 at first implied a somewhat greater degree of independence on the part of the West European trade union organisations
vis-à-vis the ICFTU, the latter's regional organisations nonetheless continued to function. As a result of the different political structures which
characterised the process of West European integration, there were
persistent organisational tensions between the EC and EFTA trade
unions within the ICFTU, and between these two sets of organisations
and the ICFTU itself. In addition, in 1965 the French CGT and Italian
CGIL had established a joint office in Brussels. In 1969 the 'newly'
founded World Federation of Labour (which had grown out of the
Christian trade union movement) also established a regional office in
Brussels. Western Europe's trade unions therefore now had five supra-
national organisations, all of which sought to influence European integration – a situation hardly designed to promote the efficiency of their
efforts at political representation.

It was the negotiations for the accession of Great Britain, Ireland
and Denmark to the EEC which finally triggered the restructuring of
the European trade union movement in 1973–74 with the foundation of
the European Trade Union Confederation. The European Commission
noted that: 'the existence of the ETUC, which unifies members of all
political persuasions, has been seen by many as a victory of regional
trade union organisation over the ideological differences which have
long divided the European trade union movement. In this connection,
the expansion of the European Communities proved to be an extremely
important driving force.' It should also be added that the phases of the
political integration of the EC and EFTA up until the establishment of
the ETUC produced constant tension between the necessity for new
political organisations able to influence the EC and EFTA and traditional organisational structures. The extension of the Community to
Southern Europe, with the accession of Spain, Greece, and Portugal,
was already anticipated by the organisational structure of the ETUC.
The ETUC had always called for closer relations between the EC and
EFTA, now realised in various forms with the creation of a European
Economic Area and the EU membership of several EFT countries, and
views these developments as entirely in accord with its interests.

4.4 *The structure of the ETUC*

Up until the fundamental revision of the ETUC's constitution at the May 1991 Luxembourg Congress, the organisation's structure had remained practically unchanged since its inception, with the exception of a few small additions passed at successive congresses. A number of factors were decisive in prompting the change.

— In view of the demands of the Single European Market and social dialogue, the ETUC needed a structure which would enable decisions to be taken more rapidly and flexibly. In particular, the negotiating mandate for participation in social dialogue and the ability to arrive at a conclusion had proved to be very unwieldy as the executive committee could only be asked to give its agreement to a negotiated text at a stage at which further amendments were virtually impossible.

— The formal description of the tasks of the Secretariat and Executive Committee no longer corresponded to the real situation as, in practice, the Secretariat and not the Executive Committee had taken on the task of representing the ETUC in European institutions. The Vice President's Committee – until 1991 termed the Finance and General Purposes Committee – had few clearly specified functions and in the main prepared disputed matters for resolution at meetings of the Executive Committee.

— The number and scope of the activities of the Industry Committees grew very considerably following the foundation of the ETUC. The form of their involvement in the ETUC's decision-making processes had, as a consequence, become increasingly unsatisfactory.

In contrast to the previous constitution, the new structure is built on the following basic principles.

First, the new ETUC constitution establishes a 'dual membership' in which both national confederations and Industry Committees have a seat and voting rights on all decision-making bodies. And although the national confederations continue to meet the ETUC's costs, they do not have voting rights on financial matters. The previous constitution had merely granted the Industry Committees a certain number of delegates at the ETUC's congress.

Second, under the new ETUC constitution the voting rights of the affiliated confederations are more closely in line with their membership. For example, under the old constitution the British TUC, with around 8 million members, had three votes and the two Maltese confederations two votes. Under the new constitution, each affiliated confederation has at least one vote, with 1–5 million members two votes, and more than 5 million members three votes, with an extra vote for each additional 1.5 million members. The Industry Committees send at least one representative, with two where they account for more than 4 million members. These have a vote, except on financial matters.

Third, the new constitution transforms the Executive Committee into a larger body representing the 'highest instance between congresses'. The Executive Committee meets four times a year – less than previously. The Presidium, which decides on 'urgent actions ... which must be undertaken in order to pursue the political strategy set out by the Executive Committee', has acquired new powers. It is entitled to 'enter into negotiations with the employers' organisations', with the Executive Committee determining the negotiating stance and 'evaluating' the results. Because the Presidium meets eight times a year, it has in practice acquired an important role. With nineteen members it remains relatively small. The Executive Committee must reserve three seats for the Industry Committees and one for the Women's Committee.

Fourth, the new constitution strengthens the role of the Secretariat. Its tasks give it the role of an executive committee. Whereas under the former constitution the General Secretary and a Deputy were elected by Congress, they did not have right to participate in the decision-making processes of the various committees. The new constitution gives the General Secretary and two Deputies a place and a vote on the Executive Committee and the Presidium. The President, directly elected by the Congress, also has a seat and a vote.

Fifth, women's representation was also enhanced at the 1991 Congress. Representatives of the Women's Committee sit in Congress (ten delegates), on the Executive Committee (three members), and on the Presidium (one representative); and previous limitations on their voting rights have been lifted. Moreover, Congress introduced a provision which requires all organisations to ensure that in selecting members for the Executive Committee, 'a balanced number of women and men exists in their delegations, reflecting the members which they represent'. In addition, at least one woman must be appointed to the Secretariat.

Sixth, a new provision was also introduced according to which national confederations and Industry Committees may have observer status without voting rights at Congress, primarily for Central and East European trade unions during the present transitional phase of democracy and market reform.

Seventh, the cross-border work of the Interregional Trade Union Councils has received some acknowledgement: each may now send an observer with speaking rights to the Congress. The same option was also granted to groups such as youth and pensioners.

Only time and use will indicate how effectively the new constitution works. Looked at overall, the duality of powers present in the former constitution continues. Although the confederations continue to domi-

nate the ETUC's bodies, the representatives of the Industry Committees can exert influence in two ways: through their relationship to the
confederations, and directly on decision-making bodies. The representatives of the Industry Committees can, as a result, experience a conflict
of loyalties when they have to advance a position of their European
committee which is opposed to that of the confederation to which they
belong. The Presidium and Secretariat have been strengthened under
the new constitution, with the Presidium receiving enhanced powers
vis-à-vis the Executive Committee. Although supervision of the Secretariat has been intensified through the bi-monthly meetings of the
Presidium, it is itself represented with three votes on both the Presidium and Executive Committee. It remains to be seen how the smaller
trade unions will respond if the Presidium takes major decisions, for
example in the context of 'social dialogue', which the Executive Committee can only examine after the event.

The restructuring of the ETUC's constitution lays down a precondition for tackling two problems. First, the Secretariat, with its current
size and organisational structure, is not yet in a position to exercise
effective influence over EU legislation. Although the Luxembourg Congress has established an additional Deputy General Secretary, there
continue to be four political secretaries, with a slight increase in the
overall numbers of staff. Second, the ETUC must become better known
as a relevant organisation to individual, national trade union members
and must become an effective medium for trade union activity at European level. The next section is devoted to this aspect of the ETUC's
work.

5 The new dimension: European level trade union activity

Midway between the 1789 French Revolution and the 1989 revolutions
in Central and Eastern Europe lies another important anniversary year.
1889 not only saw the foundation of many of Europe's trade unions but
also the decision by the International Congress of Labour to make 1
May into an international day of struggle (originally for the introduction of the eight-hour day). Fundamental social rights – such as trade
union freedoms and the right to strike – are achievements won mostly
by the trade unions at national level in Europe. However, unions have
always argued that these rights should be established internationally, as
they now are in the European Social Charter of the Council of the
Europe and in the international law set down by the conventions of the
International Labour Organisation.

Trade unions have profoundly influenced the social development of
Europe and left their impression on its politics, economy and the

development of the welfare state. However, the crucial measure of its influence has always been how comprehensively it represents the workforce and whether it has succeeded in mobilising collective action on the part of working people. The development of the Single Market has now posed this question at a European level. Under these circumstances, international solidarity becomes a very practical issue. The weaknesses of trade unions in one country have a direct effect on the strength of all. In turn, individual national trade unions now have a direct interest in fostering a capacity to take collective action internationally. This works both ways: a movement able to take action at European level will add to the attractiveness of individual national unions for potential members. In the following section, we aim to complement the many national discussions on the future of the trade unions with a distinctive European component.

5.1 Towards a membership-oriented European trade union policy

Any practical membership-oriented trade union policy at European level would include the following components, some of which are undoubtedly merely a minimum requirement.

— Representing employee interests at plant or company level in a European context. This would entail matching the international and European mobility of employers with a corresponding cross-border system of effective employee representation.
— Cross-border co-operation, discussed later in this chapter using the example of Inter-Regional Trade Union Councils.
— Recognising international employee mobility, with the Single Market viewed as a single *labour* market.
— Offering employees European opportunities for further training and career enhancement. The establishment of a European Trade Union College by the ETUC in 1990 marked a first step in this direction. For more than ten years the European Trade Union Institute (ETUI) has also been making a valuable contribution through research and the circulation of information.
— Developing a social dialogue with the employers in both an imaginative and an assertive way in the form of European collective agreements, scope for which has been enhanced in some respects under the Maastricht Treaty.
— Emphasising the international character of the trade union movement as a unique virtue compared with other types of organisation, offering additional benefits for national trade union activity.

In all these areas the issue is less one of transferring powers from national to European level, but rather enabling the European movement to develop its own range of capabilities which can directly serve the interests of individual trade union members and to build its own independent identity.

5.2 Trade union policy at company and plant level in the Single Market[1]

Across the world companies such as Philips, ABB, Daimler-Benz, Siemens and General Motors are currently engaged in a massive global restructuring of their operations. Mergers, co-operation agreements, acquisitions, drastic rationalisation and relocation to new sites are proceeding at an ever-increasing pace as companies plan and implement their strategies for the 1990s. The Single European Market has been an important factor in stimulating their endeavours.

Both production and the division of labour have become internationalised to an unprecedented degree. At the same time, the widespread application of micro-electronics has led to an enormous increase in corporate flexibility over the selection and implementation of both national and global strategies:

— Data-processing and information networks now extend across national borders and continents, collecting operational data at plant level and relaying information to corporate headquarters. The relevant data are made available to senior decision-makers on a 'just in time' basis, and can be immediately integrated into global strategic planning and locally implemented operations. This has brought about an enormous acceleration in the pace with which management decisions can be translated into practice.
— Corporate managements have themselves become subject to rationalisation ('delayering', 'flattening' of corporate hierarchies etc.) through the flexibility offered by information networks. Strategic decisions are made at corporate headquarters level, with management at local sites increasingly relegated to the administration of subsidiaries which are bound by instructions issued from above and with no power to negotiate freely with employee representatives.
— Corporate flexibility has increased enormously. The allocation of production to plants in several countries, combined with the technical scope for rapidly switching production between plants and a built-in excess capacity, has enabled entire products or individual components to be relocated rapidly from one site to another.

This new flexibility not only raises the potential power of companies in situations of acute industrial conflict, such as strikes, but also in everyday plant level negotiations over jobs and working conditions. The demand for cost-reduction programmes, weekend working, or the introduction of additional shift work, can now be more effectively backed up with threats of closure or relocation than was the case even a few years ago.

The growth in the power of the multinational employers sits alongside the increasing powerlessness of what are primarily national trade union strategies for the workplace. And national systems of employee representation are constantly subject to the threat of being played off against less regulated systems operating in other countries.

Trade unions are confronted on a daily basis with fresh examples of how companies are able to use a strategy of divide-and-rule to implement changes in work organisation. One major area of concern, especially for German trade unions, has been the employers' pursuit of new patterns of working time intended to extend the use of capacity. In the late 1980s, for example, General Motors succeeded in inducing workplace employee representatives at its plants in Saragossa (Spain), Antwerp (Belgium), Kaiserslautern and Bochum (Germany) to accept multi-shift working and regular weekend working by pointing to the readiness of workers at other sites to implement the proposals, rubbed in by the implication that the prospect of longer machine-running times would enhance the likelihood of future investment. In 1992, employee representatives of Robert Bosch, the German car components and electronics manufacturer, accepted three-shift working as a condition for new investment in Germany, rather than at sites elsewhere in Europe. Works councils, or immediate workplace employee representatives, have few weapons with which they can combat the threat of job losses or the withdrawal of investment. Detailed information about plant sites in other countries is difficult to collect and assess. Managements have an enormous advantage in the quality and availability of information – an advantage which they can, and do, readily transform into power.

The threat of a creeping erosion of employee rights in such multi-plant enterprises has long been acknowledged by both national legislatures and the European Commission. As yet, however, no measures to address the problem have passed into law. A series of proposals to improve information disclosure has been advanced by the European Community since the late 1970s.

— the 'Vredeling' Directive, originally proposed in 1980, envisaged mechanisms for information and consultation in multinational firms operating in the European Community and EEC-based firms operating in a single country with plants or subsidiaries employing at least 1,000 workers. The proposal has been stalled for several years, and has effectively been superseded by the draft Directive on European Works Councils (EWC).

— the proposal for a European Company Statute, resubmitted in 1989, would offer the possibility of incorporation at European-level, with some tax and legal advantages. In return, companies would be required to offer employee representatives scope to participate in the 'supervision and strategic development' of the enterprise through a number of possible institutional mechanisms for information disclosure and consultation. The most recent draft dates from 1991, and is currently under review.

— the draft Fifth Directive, the most recent draft of which dates from 1988, would require large companies with more than 1,000 employees scope for information and consultation at national level. The measure, largely related to proposals for the harmonisation of company law, is still under review but with little immediate prospect of realisation.

— the draft Directive on European Works Councils was originally issued in 1990 under the Action Programme established to implement the aims of the Social Charter. The proposal was blocked by the veto exercised by the UK government, as the measure required unanimity under the Single European Act. However, under the agreement on social policy agreed as part of the Maastricht Treaty (the 'Social Chapter'), measures intended to support 'information and consultation of workers' may be decided by qualified majority vote. Moreover, measures may also be introduced on employee codetermination, although these would require unanimity. Under the Protocol on Social Policy (also known as the 'opt out'), the UK government withdrew from any involvement in framing and passing legislation at European level under the Social Chapter. Nor would any legislation passed under its provisions, in theory, apply in the UK.

Under the draft Directive on 'European Committees', which can now be submitted through the new post-Maastricht procedures, undertakings with at least 1,000 employees in all member states and employing at least 100 workers in each of two or more member states would be required to allow employees to set up a European Committee, should they wish to. Under the UK's 'opt out', all UK operations could be excluded, although this interpretation may be open to legal challenge. These committees would have a right to annual meetings with the central management of the undertaking and would be entitled to 'timely' consultation over any management proposals 'likely to have a considerable effect on the interests of the employees'. In turn, committee members would be required to report back to employee representatives at subsidiary and establishment level.

The initial proposal, cautiously criticised by the ETUC as 'not entirely satisfactory' (in a motion of the Congress, 13–17 May 1991) was rejected by the employers' organisation UNICE, despite the fact that it provided little more than a bare framework. UNICE proposed instead that the Commission should issue a non-binding recommendation, although it has also promised that it would argue for the implementation of such a recommendation among its membership, and evaluate the situation after a few years.

The European Commission, UNICE and the ETUC in their various proposals all point to the autonomy of the social partners. The ETUC's attitude that it would accept even a less than totally satisfactory directive is due to a change of heart prompted by the disappointingly long period over which no legislative action has been taken. However, trade unions and works councils ought not simply to rest content with their justifiable criticisms of the tardiness of the European legislature. If the exercise of employee influence is not to vanish entirely as a factor which multinational employers must consider when shaping their strategies, it is essential to organise effective trade union power at an international level and to breathe new life into the idea of international solidarity. The information networks required for effective representation of employee interests must be established, and have the same speed and reliability as those used by managements. Employee representatives must also be able to exercise influence wherever decisions are actually made. At an international level this implies new powers vis-à-vis the corporate headquarters of multinational concerns. Finally, employee representatives must develop a unified, cross-border strategy towards corporate centres whose operations transcend national boundaries and sites. This task will require considerable effort: workplace representatives at different sites within a single national context already encounter difficulties in reaching agreement and co-ordinating their efforts. However, there is no alternative but to push ahead with this approach.

Establishing effective international trade union counter-power is unlikely to prove a swift or easy task. In the first instance, it is essential to make imaginative use of existing possibilities, by combining and developing them further. Information exchange and practical co-ordination, the substance of international solidarity, needs to be organised and renewed on an everyday basis.

A trade union information network (already born of necessity in a number of companies) would gather the scattered information relevant to representing employee interests, and would make it available via a uniform procedure. However, instead of a centralised trade union information exchange, which has to be planned and organised over the long term, greater use should be made of decentralised short-term information-sharing, established according to need and drawing on the expertise of as wide a group of specialists as can be found. 'Hotlines', offering direct dialogue with specialists, need to be established. Short-term co-ordination on specific questions is likely to prove immediately more effective than discussion of global themes.

Such a structure would allow an informed discussion on specialised subjects, such as weekly working time, quality circles or new technology, using detailed information and documentation, and encourage the collection of local information for compilation and distribution. At the same time, the greater ease with which information could be checked, and the scope for direct contact, would help to reduce mistrust and foster a more consistent approach.

Such an approach would encounter many practical problems: language, different legal systems and financial questions are perhaps the most significant. To some extent, national legal provisions might offer some assistance: in Germany and the Netherlands, for example, works councils are entitled to financial support from the employer for the consultation of experts. But even where this does not apply, it is vital to establish structures to carry out these tasks if the influence of the trade unions at workplace level is not to be further diminished.

As a consequence, trade unions must take steps to conclude agreements with individual companies on forms of employee representation at enterprise level across Europe. The trade unions within the European Trade Union Confederation are now agreed on this objective. At the ETUC congress in Stockholm in May 1988 there was an unambiguous call for the democratic representation of employee interests in all companies and a demand for the 'equal participation of employee representatives in all corporate decisions of significance for workers'. Employee representatives should be given the right in all undertakings active across Europe to be informed and consulted on European corporate planning, and to negotiate and represent their interests collectively at European level. The ETUC's Luxembourg Congress in 1991 emphatically supported these demands.

In July 1988 the European Metalworkers' Federation (EMF) proposed the establishment of European information and economic committees in enterprises active on a European scale. These would initially be established by collective agreement, but could later be validated by European legislation. According to the EMF resolution the committees should consist of workforce representatives 'who belong to representative trade union organisations at national level'. This therefore sanctions the necessity of co-operating with trade unions who are not members of the EMF. According to the EMF's proposal, agreements on European information and economic committees should contain the following provisions:

— The establishment of more closely defined rights of information disclosure and consultation.
— Procedures for delaying the implementation of 'measures extending over several countries which impinge on the concerns of employees' where there are differences of opinion.
— The allocation of seats in relation to workforce size in individual countries.
— The right of each committee member to be accompanied by a specialist who is not an employee of the company.
— The establishment of regular meetings and provision for additional meetings if required.
— The obligation on the part of the employer to bear all costs incurred.

Such committees should not affect the national rights of employee representatives in individual countries. Irrespective of the various national systems of employee workplace representation, European information and economic committees should be structured to allow international co-operation by employee representatives in undertakings and companies operating on a European scale, in order to lay the foundations for some counterbalance to the strategic dominance of the employer in a Europe without borders.

IG Metall developed this proposal in a position paper prepared in early 1989 to guide negotiations with companies headquartered in Germany. Talks and negotiations were started with a number of companies on the establishment of European information and economic committees. In some companies the first meetings of German works councillors took place with the workforce representatives of other European sites (Gillette, VW, CAS). In other companies such meetings already have a long tradition (Opel, Ford). Given the movement towards the Single Market, a formal agreement or legal guarantee for such structures are becoming of increasing importance.

Since the late 1980s, a number of examples of such voluntary initiatives in international consultation and employee representation have come into being, offering grounds for cautious optimism in some cases. In 1985, agreements were concluded with the French consumer electronics concern Thompson Grand Public on the establishment of a Liaison Committee with the European Metalworkers Federation (EMF) and a European Branch Committee. Each of these was responsible for ensuring that information is distributed to trade unions and employee representatives at European level on the economic, industrial and commercial situation of the undertaking in France, Germany, Italy and Spain. This TCE-EMF committee meets twice a year and the branch committee once a year. The latter consists of twenty-six employee representatives elected by works councils. The original agreement, which was signed for two years, was prolonged indefinitely in 1987. (The structure was reformed in 1992 with a single committee replacing the previous two bodies.) A similar model has existed in the French concern Bull since early 1988. It rests on an agreement with the French metal-working trade unions FGFMM-CFDT and FM-FO. This committee consists of twenty-three employee representatives from twelve countries. The appointment of employee representatives is agreed in each country between the management of each local company and the trade union or employee representatives. The French food concern BSN has had a European information committee since October 1986. It consists of fifteen delegates appointed by national trade unions. By late 1992, voluntary arrangements had been arrived at in some sixteen multi-national companies in Europe, with a substantial number of other companies having arrangements in the pipeline (for an assessment and overview, see *European Participation Monitor*, No. 62/1993). In addition to concluded agreements, or agreements under negotiation, the European Industry Committees have intensified their efforts to win information and consultation mechanisms in dozens more companies which had, as yet, turned the approaches down. The EICs have also stepped up their activities in the establishment of trade union committees for information exchange within multinationals. (See ETUI, *The European Industry Committees and Social Dialogue* Brussels, 1993.)

Compared with the original hopes of the EMF, such voluntary agreements still have many shortcomings. Aside from any questions of structure and operations of agreed arrangements, the sheer numbers involved illustrate the scale of the task. According to research, carried out by the Industrial Relations Research Unit at the University of Warwick, some 880 international companies would meet the criteria for the establishment of a European Works Council under the original draft Directive. Some 332 of these are headquartered in the UK, whose firms are absent from the lists of those with voluntary arrangements. However, as research has demonstrated, experience with existing arrangements has shown that 'enlightened' managements can benefit from information and consultation mechanisms internationally. For example, Thompson Grand Public, the first company to establish a European level national forum, had acquired a negative reputation as a 'job-killer' following its closure of Videocolour. Other companies have cited the benefits of effective communication with employees during major European restructuring operations.

In fact, the activities of companies as they develop and implement strategies for the Single Market have unleashed a torrent of social conflicts. Businesses are currently engaged in an intense phase of mergers and restructuring involving both the technical and personnel aspects of corporate organisation. And as noted above, trade unions are also confronted with pressures to intensify workplace-based activities aimed at developing cross-border co-operation within European scale undertakings. This alone will not be sufficient to ensure that the interests of employees are effectively represented within the Single Market. There is, therefore, still a need for the European legislature to take action.

The Maastricht Treaty, which redefines and removes the requirement for unanimity on measures relating to employee representation, has opened the way for new initiatives in this field, with fresh attempts to introduce legislation on employee rights to information, consultation and codetermination. The creation of new scope for negotiation and agreement under the Maastricht Treaty may also supplement, and in some areas replace, the legislative approach.

5.3 Cross-border co-operation through Inter-Regional Trade Union Councils

Trade union organisations located in frontier regions of the European Community member states have been engaged in co-operation via Inter-Regional Trade Union Councils for over a decade. The current list includes Saar-Lorraine-Luxembourg, Maas-Rhine, Weser/Ems-Noord-Nederland, Alsace-Basle-Südbaden, Rhine-Ijssel-Ems, Nord/Pas de Calais-Hainaut/West Vlaanderen, Lombardia-Ticino, Midi-Pyrénées (Barcelona-Toulouse-Montpelier), Galicia-Norte de Portugal (Santiago-Porto), Piemont-Val d'Aoste-Rhône-Alpes and Nordbaden-North Alsace-Pfalz. Others are expected to be established in the near future, and might involve the western coast of the Mediterranean and the regions between Turin and Lyons. According to the definition used by the European Commission, 48 million people live in frontier regions – 15 per cent of the total EU population. These areas are among the first to feel the impact of the Single Market and the absence of any truly European social policy. The Inter-Regional Trade Union Councils represent an area for European trade union activity which is simultaneously regional, national and European, and which is directed at the concrete problems, needs and interests of people living in frontier regions, in particular those of the employed workforce. The issues on which they are engaged include:

— Cross-border agency employment, as yet not regulated by EC law.
— The problems of double taxation and the jungle of social insurance regulations faced by frontier workers: tax issues remain unregulated, and social insurance is inadequately dealt with in Community law.
— The problems of sometimes contradictory policies for regional economic support and national planning regulations, with subsidies in one region creating problems in neighbouring areas.

— The problems of cross-border transport policies, especially for local public transport.
— The problems associated with cross-border employment policy.
— The difficulties connected with the completion of the Single Market itself which, as in the case of public tendering and the provision of services across national borders, can lead to problems of structural adjustment.

Inter-Regional Trade Union Councils are able to act autonomously in tackling these problems, strengthening the trade union movement at national level as well as the ETUC itself. Indeed, in 1990 the ETUC put the cross-border work of the Councils at the centre of its mobilisation campaign. As yet, however, the Councils are still struggling for recognition by national movements and, to some extent still, by the ETUC. The ETUC has now granted inter-regional representatives observer status with a right to speak at the ETUC's congress.

Frontier workers and employees who work on short-term assignments abroad, in some cases for employment agencies, often feel ignored by existing national trade unions. Although they ought properly to be in a trade union at their place of work, many of their broader problems arise in their country of residence. Trade union advice centres on both sides of the border and an effective cross-border representation of their interests could alert such people to the benefits of joining trade unions.

One important step towards European trade union membership was taken at the Luxembourg Congress. As from 1992 national confederations intend, 'to give employees who are members of a confederation affiliated to the ETUC the possibility of effective protection in all European countries'. While retaining the principle of trade union membership in the country in which work is performed, guidelines will be set out for 'mutual recognition of the rights and advantages of trade union members through the member confederations of the ETUC'. From 1993 all membership cards will bear the symbol of the ETUC according to a specific decision of the 7th congress of the ETUC (Luxembourg, May 1991). Determination to develop and implement this resolution could be crucial in demonstrating the attractions of trade union membership to the many employees in ETUC unions affected by the Single Market.

5.4 European trade union policy for internationally mobile workers

One side-effect of the political and social transformations taking place in Central and Eastern Europe has been a further fragmentation of the labour market within the European Union, as experience in the German construction industry has shown. The thesis, which continues to be advanced by the European Commission, that the mobility of skilled workers will increase within the Community but that the mobility of the unskilled will decline, may only apply to workers with a European Community passport. And even if this proves true, it is highly likely that precarious forms of employment will increase among those workers who work across national borders. This process is gaining ground as a result of the persistently inadequate protection of temporary workers under Community law, together with the broader advance of deregulation. On the other hand, the view that there is no labour market able to accept workers at dumping prices is confounded by the illegal or semi-legal activity of employees from the former Eastern Bloc. This migratory movement in turn prompts understandable concern on the part of employees from third countries (such as Turkey), including those associated with the EU through special treaties who work in EU countries but without the same right to free movement as European Union citizens themselves.

The ETUC is directly affected by these developments as trade unions from countries like Turkey, are themselves affiliated to the ETUC. The trade union forum with trade unions from Central and Eastern Europe, and their participation as observers under the new ETUC constitution, provides a further avenue by which the ETUC is involved. Delegates at the ETUC's Luxembourg Congress called for an approach to the problem based on integrating such workers. The right to free movement should be extended to all citizens from third countries who are legally resident in an EU member state. The right of asylum should be regulated at European level, with asylum seekers given the right to an independent appeals procedure. Furthermore, the ETUC calls for campaigns against discrimination and racism.

The ETUC will also almost certainly have to adapt to the fact that its own members – and especially those with high levels of skill – will increasingly be working across borders within the Single Market. For this group of workers co-operation between European trade unions will be of interest in three respects:

— First, in their capacity as organisations for representing interests which support genuine free movement for working people. In particular, there will be an increase in the number of skilled workers whose career path will embrace employment in several European countries. For such workers, the ability of Europe's trade unions to effect non-bureaucratic procedures for easing transfers between different national social insurance systems, and ensuring recognition of vocational qualifications will be an important factor in guaranteeing their security in old age, and safeguarding their rights within a cross-border labour market.

— Second, as a European organisation which can also offer services to members irrespective of which country they work in. Such a need is apparent in the case of frontier workers. In addition, it is also important for 'migrant workers', both within their country of residence and in the country in which they work, as well as in their original homeland, to maintain a link with the trade union movement. The various national European trade unions can certainly learn from each other in this field. The Italian trade unions, for example, have advice centres in several major cities in Northern Europe which support their members working abroad. The task of such advice centres may well change over time as the 'migrant workers' of the 1950s and 1960s become increasingly integrated into the social life of the countries in which they now live and work.

— Third, European trade unions could develop these initiatives by becoming the organisational focus for European exchange programmes. Such programmes, which the Commission already promotes for other groups of individuals, would have the attraction of preparing for a more mobile European labour market in which highly skilled employees, such as technicians and engineers, have opportunities for work and study visits.

Institutions such as the European Trade Union Institute and the European Trade Union College (established in 1990), might also have a role in such programmes. The ETUC secretariat has begun to intensify collaboration between trade unions and research centres on the scope for using EU programmes to persuade trade unions to participate in European programmes such as Comett.

However, material demands will also be placed on the trade unions. Setting aside the Council of Europe convention on *au pair* work, there is as yet no legal protection covering employees engaged in visits for cross-border work or education. The European trade union movement has access to a network which could facilitate co-operation across borders and offer points of contact which would enable those working abroad to feel at home, in trade union terms, in another country.

Such an approach shares nothing with the traditional 'immigrant policy' of the national trade unions of the North or the service offered to members working abroad by the trade unions of the South. Both must be transformed into a politics of European trade unionism aimed at safeguarding the interests of trade unionists whose work carries them across national frontiers and of other workers whose precarious status is directly reflected in exploitation and their uncertain status in casual labour markets.

Many 'migrant workers' have effectively grown up in two trade union cultures. Given the difficulties in establishing international understanding, and not only those rooted in language differences, the importance of bilingual members who understand the employment and trade union cultures of two countries should not be overlooked. Such individuals merit a special place within the European trade union movement and should not be lost when they move country to work elsewhere. An event for international solidarity organised by the Italian trade unions on 1 May 1988 coined the slogan: 'In my country there are no foreigners.' The growth of racial hatred and xenophobia, which has culminated in the representation of extreme right-wing parties in a number of national legislative assemblies and in the European Parliament itself, has confronted the European trade union movement with the task of ensuring that such a slogan is translated into practical action.

Trade union members who work outside their home country have often been active participants in national labour struggles. Their language skills and their trade union experience mean that they are urgently needed to help build more effective collaboration between Europe's trade unions. For the ETUC, the development of a network of organisations for safeguarding the interests of members and opening up cross-border information exchanges could represent an important independent area of work which would enhance the attractions of national trade unions.

5.5 The scope for European collective bargaining

In the light of the advances towards completion of the Single Market, and the associated strategies developed by employers, Europe's trade unions cannot rest content with an approach which merely seeks to influence political decision-making. If the employers in each member state set out to resist cuts in working time, to turn Sunday into a normal working day, and to push through workplace flexibility without the agreement of employee representatives, then there is only one logical trade union response – co-ordinated collective bargaining by Europe's trade unions to combat the European strategy pursued by the employers. What should such a strategy consist of, and how should it be co-ordinated? What are the possible subjects for negotiation, and with whom could unions bargain at European level?

Given the scope opened up by the Maastricht Treaty, and various initiatives at sectoral level, the situation remains fluid. For some time, the ETUC has been engaged in 'social dialogue' with the European Association for Public Enterprises (CEEP) and the private sector European Employers' Organisation (UNICE). The result so far has been a number of 'common positions' on such subjects as co-operative growth strategies within the Community; information and consultation, as well as education and training, during the introduction of new technologies;

vocational training and skills development; and perspectives on a European labour market.

How these various initiatives might evolve in the future remains unclear. In October 1991 the 'social partners' submitted a proposal to the inter-governmental conference at Maastricht for a new procedure for creating European social legislation. This was embodied in Articles 3 and 4 of the 'Agreement on Social Policy' (the 'Social Chapter') concluded between all member states of the Community with the exception of the United Kingdom. Under Article 3, before submitting proposals in the field of social policy, the European Commission must consult representatives of management and labour at European level. Any subsequent proposals made by the Commission should also be submitted for an opinion. Should management and labour decide that agreement rather than legislation offers a more appropriate route, they may initiate a new process, provided for under Article 4 of the Social Chapter. The initial consultations must normally be completed within nine months. Under Article 4, European level dialogue between the employers and employee representatives may lead to agreements between them: these may either be implemented in accordance with respective national practices or, at their joint request, by a decision of the Council of Ministers on a proposal from the Commission.

The 1991 joint proposal by the ETUC, UNICE and CEEP, and its embodiment in Community law, marked a further important step towards the creation of a structure for European collective bargaining. Although initially concerned with broad issues of employment conditions, further advance towards economic and currency union could directly turn on collective bargaining. Given this framework, the forms of joint pressure that could be exerted by the ETUC member confederations becomes an issue.

The October 1989 demonstration in Brussels organised by the ETUC provided one example of how the European trade union movement could express a common culture of contestation. Creating such a culture is vital for the trade unions, if only as means of inducing the most obdurate employers' organisations to come to the European bargaining table under the provisions of the Single European Act (Article 118b, EEC Treaty) and the Maastricht Treaty.

However, the real process of negotiation over the content and aims of social dialogue cannot be carried out properly at the level of national confederations, represented at European level by the ETUC. European level accords between management and labour will only be possible once European Works Councils have been established and have the power to conclude European workplace or company agreements. These will be complemented by branch level framework agreements on major issues related to industrial restructuring. At any event, collective bargaining at European level will represent an additional tier on top of current bargaining levels. This will involve extending the role of the national and branch trade unions – by means of the so-called European 'Industry Committees' – which, provided recognition is granted by the ETUC, will constitute a second vehicle for the influence of union memberships alongside the national trade union centres. Initially, when the ETUC was established, the prevalent view was that the role of the Industry Committees was to reinforce the ETUC and not develop into a parallel European organisation at branch level – a view advocated at that time by the British and Scandinavian trade unions. In 1991 sixteen committees met the criteria for recognition which are as follows:

— Their geographical scope should correspond with that of the ETUC: that is, it must not extend beyond the European Union.
— The committees must be formally independent of the international trade secretariats.
— Their political and ideological standpoint must correspond with the ETUC's.

Although all three criteria have led to repeated difficulties with committees seeking recognition, the Industry Committees have become an indispensable component in the search for consistency in the structures of European trade unionism. The transformation of relations between the EU and EFTA countries, which represents one of the main motors of European integration, means that trade unions need a broader European perspective than an exclusive concern with the European Union as such. At the same time, the rapid moves towards further integration within the European Union mean that a specific focus on Europe must be maintained, at least for the time being. Global issues, such as trade union recognition and the struggle for human rights, can be tackled through the engagement of the ETUC's Industry Committees with the International Trade Secretariats. Nor can the delicate issue of accepting important Communist-oriented confederations (such as the CGT in France, and Intersindical in Portugal) be tackled without a common underlying political perspective.

Such fundamental issues point to areas of European trade union policy which are likely to be of increasing significance in the future and therefore which must be addressed and resolved. In particular, they embrace the pressures at branch level, transmitted primarily by collective bargaining, for trade union integration. The trade union centres and the Industry Committees agree that, in addition to effective information exchange and well co-ordinated internal co-operation, the following areas of priority need to be tackled (with existing means and resources): the struggle against unemployment and for full employment;

cuts in working hours; new technologies; employee status; safety at work; and special provisions in the area of precarious employment relations.

Together with the increasingly important area of education and training, this list demarcates the main fields of potential conflict between the union movement and governments and employers. As well as the areas in which the ETUC has typically pursued a classic lobbying approach (already noted above), the Industry Committees naturally have an interest in the prospect of tackling these questions by developing the medium of European collective bargaining. All national experience shows that the political pressure exerted by trade unions is only stable and effective in the long term when it is firmly anchored in their capacity to conduct collective bargaining. However, the climate for European level collective bargaining remains unfavourable:

— There is no binding European-level legal provision for the conclusion and enforcement of collective bargaining agreements.
— There is no European law providing for and regulating industrial action.
— The employers continue to refuse to grant recognition of union organisations' right to bargain at European level.
— As yet, there have been no pan-European positive experiences of international solidarity strike action.

Although there are other difficulties – such as the differing national status of collective agreements, differing national legal frameworks, differing levels and intensities of regulation, and substantial differences in national trade union densities and structures – standing in the way of greater uniformity, these are not as great a problem as the four issues highlighted above because they are not an impediment *in principle*.

Different strategies are required to overcome each of the four main obstacles. The Maastricht Treaty's Agreement on Social Policy (see pp 288–93) integrates the possibility of European-level agreements into the EU's legislative machinery. However, there is great employer resistance to using this as a free-standing negotiating forum, separate from proposals eminating from the Commission.

However, the most important and most difficult task is one for the trade unions themselves: without the credible use of solidarity action, legal regulations and negotiating arrangements will remain a dead letter. Only by establishing European, and broader international, solidarity at workplace and company level will it be possible to develop a full capacity for collective bargaining which both represents a natural extension of unions' potential for national mobilisation and is able to match the international activity and capabilities of employers. The many difficulties that the trade unions face with this task correspond to the problems created by the differential economic situation and power of both countries and companies, and the varying importance of particular factors at different national locations. So the first steps towards European co-ordination should aim at concluding broad framework agreements, to be fine-tuned at national level, dealing with qualitative rather than quantitative matters, and with maximum scope for integrating intermediate organisations and reflecting their interests and concerns.

One key problem with the social dialogue promoted by Jacques Delors has consisted in finding employers able and willing to engage in negotiation. UNICE, the central association of industrial and general employers, has viewed its primary role as one of upholding the principles of free enterprise within the debate over the nature of the Single Market, and of resisting Community legislation in the social policy field. The structure of its working groups provides a clear illustration of its priorities. Since 1989 the Economic and Finance Committee has been primarily concerned with taxation policy within the Community, on which it has issued six opinions, and with the possibilities of increasing the commercial use of the Ecu. The Foreign Trade Committee has concentrated on GATT and the negotiating mandate given to the Commission regarding Eastern Europe. The Industry Commission is interested mainly in telecommunications policy and the framework programme for research, in EU transport policy and some environmental questions (e.g., the greenhouse effect and the transportation of dangerous goods). The Commission for Enterprise Affairs has focused on the question of intellectual property rights (issuing five opinions), the opening-up of markets, and proposals for environmental directives. The Commission for Social Affairs has worked on two opinions concerning the question of basic social rights.

UNICE's chief concern has, therefore, quite clearly been not general questions related to the political, social or economic development of the Community but rather very specific issues identified as being important in setting the framework for corporate activity. Social and employment policy has played only a comparatively minor role, largely subordinated to the overriding concern of maintaining business competitiveness. However, aided by the mediating efforts of Commission members and President Delors, the persistent efforts of the ETUC have gradually succeeded in raising the status and importance of social dialogue within UNICE. The Association of Public Enterprises (CEEP) took an independent line in this respect, and on 16 September 1990 signed the first European framework agreement with the ETUC on training in railway undertakings and in the energy sector. The change of heart on the part of the employers was indicated less by the substance of this agreement than by the fact that its opening page bore the (previously studiously avoided) term 'agreement'.

UNICE is also eager to supervise the conduct of social dialogue at sectoral level, and in particular to ensure that sectoral employer associations do not make any concessions which might be used as a benchmark by trade union Industry Committees in other sectors. The Western European Metal Trades Employers' Association (WEM), for example, had made it a precondition of participation in sectoral level social dialogue that there should be no negotiation and no conclusion of collective agreements.

Co-ordination between Western European trade unions on collective bargaining issues at national and industry level is, therefore, an important priority. Were it to succeed in a few key areas, such a demonstration of unity would generate more momentum for true social dialogue at European level than any number of formal meetings. In the field of training, for example, the social partners could commit themselves to the specific aim (already stated) of providing all young people with training in a skill. And in the field of further training, priority could be given to facilitating access to European training programmes and promoting training at company level. The range of relevant subjects extends from cross-border agency employment to the establishment of European Works Councils. What is important is not to create a form of bargaining superstructure at European level, but rather to ensure that the issues which make up the European social dimension, and which form the substance of the social dialogue, are seen as complementary to national bargaining.

This section began by asking the question as to where we should locate European trade union policy. Three strands have been outlined in the last two sections:

— Strengthening the means of influencing the process of European integration.
— Developing cross-border trade union work within companies.
— Developing the ETUC and Industry Committees in the area of co-ordination of joint activities directed at the needs of union memberships.

If the necessary steps to achieve these objectives are taken, then it will seem as normal and natural for trade union members to regard themselves as members of the European Metalworkers' Federation as of IG Metall, or the AEEU; not simply a member of the CGIL but also of the ETUC. This redefinition of trade union strategy has now become a necessity if the processes of directing European economic integration are to be matched by a strong European trade union movement.

Notes

1. Sections 5.2–5.4 were written by Michael Blank and Thomas Klebe, both full-time officials of the German metalworkers' union, IG Metall.

Appendix

1 European Trade Union Organisations

+ indicates that the code for international calls must be dialled: from the UK, for example, this is 010.

The European Trade Union Confederation (ETUC)
Rue Montagne aux Herbes Potagères 37, B-1000. Tel: +32 2 218 31 00; Fax: +32 2 218 35 66

European Trade Union Institute (ETUI)
The ETUI is the research, information and educational arm of the ETUC.
Boulevard Emil Jacqmain 155, B-1210 Brussels. Tel: +32 2 224 0470; Fax: +32 2 224 0502

Member organisations of the ETUC

Austria

Österreichischer Gewerkschaftsbund (ÖGB), Hohenstaufengasse 10-12, A-1011 Vienna. Tel: +43 222 53 444; Fax: +43 222 53 444 204

Belgium

Fédération Générale du Travail (FGTB), Rue Haute 42, B-1000 Brussels. Tel: +32 2 506 8211; Fax: +32 2 513 4721

Confédération des Syndicats Chrétiens (CSC), Rue de la Loi 121, B-1040 Brussels. Tel: +32 2 237 3111; Fax: +32 2 237 3300

Cyprus

Synomospondia ergaton kypron (SEK), Alkaios Str. 23, PO Box 5018, Engomia Nicosia, Cyprus. Tel: +357 214 1142; Fax: +357 476360

Kibris türk isci sendikalari federasyonu (TÜRK-SEN), 7–7A Sehit Mehmet, R. Hüsseyin, PO Bos 829, Lefkosa Kibris, Mersin 10, Turkey. Tel: +90 741 72 2444

Denmark

Landsorganisation i Danmark (LO), Rosenørns Allé 12, DK-1634 Copenhagen V. Tel: +45 35 353541; Fax: +45 35 373741

Funktionaerernes og Tjenestemaendenes Faellesraad (FTF), Niels Hemmingsens-
gade 12, PB 1169, DK-101 Copenhagen K. Tel: +45 3 315 3022; Fax: +45 3 391
3022

Finland

Suomen Ammattiliittojen Keskusjärjestö (SAK), Box 53161, SF-00531 Helsinki
53. Tel: +358 0 772 11; Fax: +358 0 772 1447

Toimihenkilö-ja Virkamiesjärjestöjen Keskuslitto (TVK), Asemamiehenkatu 4,
SF-00520 Helsinki 52. Tel: +358 0 155 2000; Fax: +358 0 14 30 58

France

Confédération Française Démocratique du Travail (CFDT), 4, Boulevard de la
Villette, F-75955 Paris Cedex 19. Tel: +33 1 42 03 8000; Fax: +33 1 42 03 81 44
or 55

Confédération Générale du Travail – Force ouvrière (CGT-FO), 198, Avenue du
Maine, F-75680 Paris Cedex 14. Tel: +33 1 45 39 2203; Fax: +33 1 45 45 5452

Confédération Française des Travailleurs Chrétiens, 13, Rue des Ecluses St.-
Martin, F-75483 Paris Cedex 10. Tel: +33 1 42 40 02 02; Fax: +33 1 42 00 44 04

Germany

Deutscher Gewerkschaftsbund (DGB), Hans-Böckler-Straße 39, Postfach 2601,
D-4000 Düsseldorf. Tel: +49 211 43010; Fax: +49 211 430 14 71

Deutsche Angestellten-Gewerkschaft (DAG), Karl-Muck-Platz 1, Postfach 30 12
30, D-2000 Hamburg 1. Tel: +49 40 349 1501; Fax: +49 40 349 15400

Great Britain

Trades Union Congress (TUC), Congress House, Great Russell Street, GB-Lon-
don WC1B 3LS. Tel: +44 71 636 4030; Fax: +44 71 636 0632

Greece

Geniki synomospondia ergaton ellados (GSEE), Patision and Pipinou 27, GR-
Athens. Tel: +30 1 883 4611; Fax: +30 1 822 9802

Iceland

Althyduasamband Islands (ASI), Grensasvegur, 16, Postholf 5076, ISL-108 Rey-
kjavik. Tel: +354 1 83 044; Fax: +354 1 68 0093

Bandalag Starfsmass Rikis of Beaja (BSRB), Grettisgötu 89, ISL-Reykjavik. Tel:
+354 1 26 688; Fax: +354 1 29 106

Irish Republic

Irish Congress of Trades Unions (ICTU), 19, Ragland Road, Ballsbridge, IRL-
Dublin 4. Tel: +353 1 680641; Fax: +353 1 609027

Italy

Confederazione Generale Italiana del Lavoro (CGIL), Corso d'Italia 25, I-00198 Rome. Tel: +39 6 84 761; Fax: +39 6 884 5683

Confederazione Italiana Sindacati Lavoratori (CISL), Via Po, 21, I-00198 Rome. Tel: +39 6 84 731; Fax: +39 6 844 4183

Unione Italiana del Lavoro (UIL), Via Lucullo, 6, I-00187 Rome. Tel: +39 6 49731; Fax: +39 6 497 3208

Luxembourg

Confédération Générale du Travail du Luxembourg (CGT-L), Case Postale 149, L-Esch Sur Alzette (Gd. Duché). Tel: +352 54 05 45; Fax: +352 54 16 20

Lëtzebuerger Chrëschtleche Gewerkschafts-Bond (LCGB), Boïte Postale 1208, L-Luxembourg (Gd. Duché). Tel: +352 48 97 97; Fax: +352 49 94 24

Malta

General Workers Union (GWU), Workers Memorial Building, M-Valletta. Tel: +356 62 43 00; Fax: +356 60 34 54

Confederation of Trades Unions, 13/3 South Street, PO Box 467, M-Valletta. Tel: +356 22 73 13; Fax: +356 23 05 20

The Netherlands

Federatie Nederlandse Vakbeweging (FNV), Naritaweg 10, Postbus 8456, NL-1005 AL Amsterdam. Tel: +31 20 581 6300; Fax: +31 20 84 45 41

Christelijk Nationaal Vakverbond (CNV), Ravellaan 1, Postbus 2475, NL-3500 Gl Utrecht. Tel: +31 30 91 39 11; Fax: +31 30 94 65 44

Norway

Landsorganisasjonen (LO), Youngs gate 11, N-0181 Oslo 1. Tel: +47 2 40 10 50; Fax: +47 2 40 17 43

Portugal

União Geral de Trabalhadores (UGT), Rua Buenos Aires 11, P-1200 Lisbon. Tel: +351 1 67 64 72; Fax: +351 1 32 70 54

Spain

Unión General de Trabajadores (UGT), Hortaleza, 88, E-28004 Madrid. Tel: +34 1 586 7694; Fax: +34 1 589 7603

Sindical Euzko Laguillen Alkartasuna-Solidaridad de Trabajadores Vascos (ELA-STV), Consulado, 8 – bajo, Apartado 971, E-20080 San Sebastian. Tel: +34 43 46 1688; Fax: +34 43 47 0858

Comisiones Obreras (CC.OO), Fernández de la Hoz, 28010 Madrid. Tel: +34 1 419 5454

Sweden

Landsorganisationen i Sverige (LO), Barnhusgatan 18, S-10553 Stockholm. Tel: +46 8 796 2500; Fax: (International Dept.) +46 8 796 2800

Tjänstermännens Centralorganisation (TCO), Linnégatan 14, Postbox 5252, S-10245 Stockholm. Tel: +46 8 782 9100; Fax: +46 8 662 3679

Switzerland

Schweizerischer Gewerkschaftsbund (SGB), Montbijoustrasse 61, Postfach 64, CH-Bern 23. Tel: +41 31 45 56 66; Fax: +41 31 45 08 37

Christlichnationaler Gewerkschaftsbund der Schweiz (CNG), Zentralsekretariat, Hopfenweg 21, CH-3007 Bern. Tel: +41 31 45 24 47; Fax: +41 31 45 79 41

Turkey

Turkiye devrimci isci sendikalari konfederasyonu (DISK), Cinnah CD 38-1, TR-Ankara. Tel: +90 4 140 77 74; Fax: +90 4 140 77 73

The *largest* confederations are:

DGB	(Germany)	11,015,000
TUC	(Great Britain)	8,190,000
CGIL	(Italy)	5,150,000

The *smallest* confederations are:

Turk-Sen	(Cyprus)	10,000
CMTU	(Malta)	11,000
LCBGB	(Luxembourg)	15,000

2 European Industry Committees

The following Industry Committes are members of the ETUC. Under the ETUC's 1991 constitution, Industry Committees have the same voting rights at the ETUC's Congress as delegates from affiliated organisations. The Industry Committees also have voting rights on the ETUC's Executive, with the exception of financial matters and applications for affiliation.

Industry Committees are financed by their affiliated unions. In addition to their role in discussions with employers associations at sectoral level ('social dialogue') they have been able to draw on Community funding to organise meetings and networks to enhance information and consultation of workers' representatives in multinational companies in Western Europe.

A review of their activities, including company level negotiations and discussions, can be found in: ETUI, *The European Industry Committees and Social Dialogue* (Brussels, 1993)

European Metalworkers' Federation (EMF)

Rue Fossé-aux-Loups 38/4, B-1000 Brussels, Belgium. Tel: +32 2 217 2747; Fax: +32 2 217 5963

Metalworking (electrical and mechanical engineering, electronics, automotive, shipbuilding, aerospace). No. of members: 6,000,000.

European Federation of Agricultural Workers Unions in the Community (EFA)

Rue Fossé-aux-Loups 38/4. Tel: +32 2 218 5308; Fax: +32 2 219 9926

Forestry, viticulture, horticulture, co-operatives and agricultural production. No. of members: 2,000,000

Postal, Telegraph and Telephone International-European Committee (PTTI-European Committee)

Avenue de Lignon 36, CH-1211 Le Lignon Geneva, Switzerland. Tel: +41 22 796 8311; Fax: +41 22 796 3975

All sectors of communications. No. of members: 1,900,000.

International Federation of Commercial, Clerical, Professional and Technical Employees (EURO-FIET)

15 Avenue de Balexert, 1219 Châtelaine-Geneva, Switzerland. Tel: +41 22 796 2733; Fax: +41 22 796 5321

Brussels office: Rue Joseph II, 3, B-1040 Brussels, Belgium. Tel: +32 2 230 7455; Fax: +32 2 230 7566

Commerce, financial services, white-collar employees in industry, property services, social insurance, health care and hairdressing. No. of members: 6,000,000.

Contact Office Inter Trade Union Commitee of Miners' and Metalworkers Free Trades Unions in the European Communities

Rue du Moniteur 18, B-1000 Brussels, Belgium. Tel: +32 2 218 3793

Coal and steel. No. of members: 400,000.

European Committee of Trades Unions in Arts, Mass Media and Entertainment (EGAKU)

International Press Centre, Blv. Charlemagne 1, B-1041 Brussels. Tel: +32 2 238 0808; Fax: +32 2 230 3633

Art, media and entertainment sector. No. of members: c. 100,000.

European Committee of Food, Catering and Allied Workers' Unions within the IUF (ECF-IUF)

Rue Fossé-aux-Loups 38/3, B-1000, Brussels. Tel: +32 2 218 7730; Fax: +32 2 219 9926

Food and hotel sector. No. of members: 1,400,000.

Miners European Federation

Avenue Emile de Béco 109, B-1050 Brussels. Tel: +32 2 646 2120; Fax: +32 2 648 4316

Mining and quarrying

Committee of Transport Workers Unions in the European Community

Rue de Pascale 22, B-1040 Brussels. Tel: +32 2 280 0238; Fax: +32 2 280 0817

Transport by rail, road, and sea, civil aviation, inland waterways, ports. docks and fisheries. No. of members: c. 2,500,000.

European Public Service Industry Committee

36 Aveneue de Tervuren (Bte. 18), B-1040 Brussels. Tel: +32 2 734 2095; Fax: +32 2 732 2079

All parts of the public sector. No. of members: 7,000,000.

European Trade Union Committee for Education (ETUCE)

Rue de Tréves, B-1040 Brussels. Tel: +32 2 230 6236; Fax: +32 2 230 6046

Education. No. of members: 2,800,000.

European Federation of Building and Woodworkers in the EEC (EFBWW)

Rue Fossé-aux-Loups 38/5, B-1000 Brussels. Tel: +32 2 218 1218; Fax: +32 2 217 5963

European Graphical Federation (EGF)

Rue des Fripiers 17, Galerie du Centre, bloc 2, B-1000 Brussels, Belgium. Tel: +32 2 223 0220; Fax: +32 2 223 1814

Paper (excl. production), print and media. No. of members: 700,000.

European Trade Union Committee: Textiles, Clothing and Leather (ETUC:TCL)

Rue Joseph Stevens 8, B-1000 Brussels. Tel: +32 2 511 5477; Fax: +32 2 511 0904

Textiles, clothing, leather and footwear. No. of members: 1,300,000.

European Federation of Chemical and General Workers Unions (EFCGU)

Avenue Emile de Béco 19, B-1050 Brussels. Tel: +32 2 648 2497; Fax: +32 2 648 4316

Chemicals, pharmaceuticals, rubber, plastics, glass, ceramics, cement, paper & pulp, energy and mineral oil industries. No. of members: c. 2,000,000.

European Group of Journalists (EGJ)

Boulevard Charlemagne 1/5, B-1040 Brussels. Tel: +32 2 238 0951; Fax: +32 2 230 3633

Journalists in print, audiovisual, press agencies and freelance journalists. No. of members: 180,000.

3 Standing Committees and Working Groups in the ETUC

— Women's Committee
— Trade Union Youth Committee
— Committee on Migrant Workers
— Committee on the Democratisation of the Economy and of Institutions
— Energy Coordinating Committee
— Economic Committee
— Collective Bargaining Committee
— Pensioner's Coordinating Committee
— Committee on Working Conditions
— Industrial Research and Development Committee
— Working Party on Vocational Training
— Working Party on Inter-Regional Trade Union Councils
— Working Party on Consumers
— Working Party on Regional Policy
— Working Party on the Environment and Living Standards
— Working Party on Safety and Health at Work
— Working Party on Agriculture
— Lomé Working Party
— Social Security Committee
— Working Party on the Trade Union Press
— Working Party on the Mass Media

4 European Union powers and trade union influence

Community powers and corresponding Advisory Committees with trade union

Subject	EU powers
Internal market: free movement of good, persons, capital and services (Art. 8a)	Relatively strong: qualified majority voting
Customs Union	Primary competence for external tariffs. Ban on tariffs and quantitative restrictions in the Single Market
Agriculture	Common Agricultural Policy, with considerable EU powers of intervention into the market
Economic policy	Co-ordination and policy development without regulatory powers on the principles of full employment, stable prices, balance of payments equilibrium and currency confidence. Unanimity required for common measures on macro-economic management. Greater powers in the implementation of monetary union under Maastricht Treaty.
Trade Policy (Art. 100ff)	EU competence in the field of external trade. On mandate from the Council, the Commission has authority to negotiate international treaties
Free movement of workers (Art. 48-51)	EU has powers to issue directives and regulations to secure free movement and ensure recognition of social entitlements in other countries
Vocational training (Art. 128, Art. 57)	Recognition of diplomas. Comparability of vocational training qualifications
Freedom of establishment (Art. 52ff)	EU powers to reduce barriers to establishment of subsidiaries etc.
Trade in services (majority voting)	EU competence, free trade for industrial, commercial, artisanal and professional services of all kinds
Movement of capital	EU competence, liberalisation of capital transactions. Aim of monetary union, removal of limits on establishment for banks and insurance companies

involvement or involvement of ETUC Working Groups.

Advisory committee (with TU participation)	ETUC committee or industry committee
	Dealt with by several committees
	Partly dealt with by the Economic Committee. Some industries with special concerns e.g. textiles through Multi fibre Agreement
Advisory Committees at Industry level	Working Party on Agriculture, joint discussion with industry unions and unions in food industry
Consultation on annual economic report	ETUC Economic Committee
Consultation, depending on the issue	Exceptionally may be dealt with by the Economic Committee; also by Industry Committees
Advisory Committee on Migrant Workers and the Social Security of Migrant Workers	Committee on Migrant Workers
Advisory Committee on Vocational Training and EU vocational training centre, CEDEFOP	ETUC coordination of worker members; also ETUC Trade Union Youth Committee
Consultation	ETUC Committee on the Democratisation of the Economy, industry unions and other ETUC Commitees: energy, media
	In part consultation in Economic Commitee, consultation with industry unions, especially Euro-FIET

4 **European Union powers and trade union influence** (cont.)

Subject	EU powers
Transport policy	Joint regulation of international transport. Approval of transport companies. No competition-distorting subsidies
Competition	Limited powers on competition control (e.g. mergers). Restrictions on public and monopolistic undertakings. Possible anti-dumping measures. Extensive powers over competition-distorting subsidies
Taxation	EU powers only where Council of Ministers is unanimous. Procedure for offsetting turnover tax and VAT
Social policy (Art. 117,118, 100a)	Vague EU powers on general social policy Recommendations on common objectives
Measures in the field of health, safety, environmental protection, consumer protection at a high level of protection (Art. 100a)	Unanimity required where measures affect the 'rights and interests of workers'. Unanimity on environmental protection
Working environment (Art. 118a)	Harmonisation of regulations combined with raising of standards: qualified majority voting
Labour market	Few EU powers
Social dialogue(Art. 118b). Management/labour consultation (Arts. 3 & 4, Social Chapter)	Possibility of agreements between ETUC and UNICE
Sex equality (Art. 119)	Direct effect of Treaty of Rome. EU can issue directives
Paid time-off	No direct EU powers

Advisory committee (with TU participation)	ETUC committee or industry committee
Joint committees	Little consultation with ETUC, mainly dealt with by industry committee for transport
	Economic Committee or Committee for the Democratisation of the Economy, depending on the issue. Industrial policy is dealt with by appropriate industry committee (e.g. shipbuilding, motor vehicles)
	Economic Committee, Working Party on Corporate Taxation
Ad-hoc consultation	No general social policy committee. Dealt with in various committees, including Ad Hoc Committee on the Social Charter, ETUC Committee on Social Security
Ad-hoc consultation in the field of health. *Environment*: consultation. *Consumers*: Advisory Consumers Committee	ETUC Committee on Social Security. ETUC Committee on the Environment. ETUC coordination of employee groups
Advisory Commitee on Safety and Hygiene. ETUC coordination of employee members. Dublin Foundation	Committee on Working Conditions. Working Party on Radiation Protection. European Trade Union Bureau for Health and Safety
Standing Committee on Employment	ETUC coordination
Steering Commitee and Working Party on Social Dialogue. Currently: labour market policy and education/vocational training	
Advisory Committee for Equal Opportunities (monitoring)	ETUC Women's Committee
Compliance with equivalence of regulations on paid time-off	Some consultation in ETUC Committee. Collective bargaining

4 **European Union powers and trade union influence** (cont.)

Subject	EU powers
European Social Fund (Art. 123)	Financing of measures for combating unemployment and for vocational training
European Regional Fund (Art. 130)	Attainment of economic cohesion for disadvantaged areas, areas in industrial decline and agricultural problem areas
Research and technology (Art. 130 f-q)	Co-ordination and running framework programmes; individual programmes in all major areas of science and technology
External relations	Lomé Agreement and association agreements with nearly all areas in the world
Mediterranean	

Advisory committee (with TU participation)	ETUC committee or industry committee
Social Fund Committee	Coordination and help in making applications
Consultation on Community framework for regional pro-grammes	ETUC Working Party on Regional Policy
Representation on IRDAC (Industrial Research and Depart-ment Advisory Committee) (1 representative)	ETUC Committee on Industrial Research and Technology
ACP Advisory Commitee	ETUC Lomé Working Party
	ETUC-ICFTU co-ordination ETUC Mediterranean Conferences

5 Member confederations of UNICE

Austria	Vereinigung österreischischer Industrielle	VöI
Belgium	Fédération des Enterprises Belgique	FEB
Cyprus	Omospondia Ergodoton ke Viomichanon	OEB
Denmark	Industriradet	IR
	Dansk Arbejsgiverforening	DA
Finland	Teollisuuden Keskusliitto	TKL
France	Conseil National du Patronat Français	CNPF
Germany	Bundesvereinigung der Deutschen Arbeitgeberverbände	BDA
	Bundesverband der Deutschen Industrie	BDI
Great Britain	Confederation of British Industry	CBI
Greece	Syndesmos Ellinikon Viomichanion	SEV
Iceland	Vinńuveitendasamband Islands	CII
	Félag Islenskra Idnrekenda	FII
Irish Republic	Irish Business and Employers Confederation	IBEC
Italy	Confederazione Generale dell'Industria Italiana	CONFINDUSTRIA
Luxembourg	Fédération des Industriels Luxembourgeois	FEDIL
Malta	Malta Federation of Industry	MFOI
The Netherlands	Verbond van Nederlandse Ondernemingen	VNO
	Nederlands Chriselijk Werkgeversverbond	NCW
Norway	Næringslivets Hovedorganisajon	NHO
Portugal	Associção Industrial Portuguesa	AIP
	Confederação da Indústria Portuguesa	CIP
San Marino	Associazione Nazionale dell'Industria Sammarinese	ANIS
Spain	Confederación Española de Organizaciones Empresariales	CEOE
Sweden	Industriförbundet Svenska Arbetgiverföreningen	SAF
Switzerland,	Zentral verband Schweizerischer Arbeitgeber-Organisationen	ZSAO
	Vorort des Schweizerischen Handels- und Industrie-Vereins	VORORT
Turkey	Türkiye Isveren Sendilarai Konfederasyonu	TISK
	Türk Sanayicileri Ve Isadamlari Dernegi	TUSIAD

6 Agreement on social policy (the 'social chapter')

Concluded between the member states of the European Community with the exception of the United Kingdom

Article 1

The Community and the Member States shall have as their objectives the promotion of employment, improved living and working conditions, proper social protection, dialogue between management and labour, the development of human resources with a view to lasting high employment and the combating of exclusion. To this end the Community and Member States shall implement measures which take account of the diverse forms of national practices, in particular the in field of contractual relations, and the need to maintain the competitiveness of the Community economy.

Article 2

1. With a view to achieving the objectives of Article 1, the Community shall support and complement the activities of the Member States in the following fields:

— improvement in particular of the working environment to protect workers' health and safety;
— working conditions;
— the information and consultation of workers;
— equality between men and women with regard to labour market opportunities and treatment at work;
— the integration of persons excluded from the labour market without prejudice to Article 127 of the Treaty establishing the European Community (hereinafter referred to as 'the Treaty').[1]

2. To this end, the Council may adopt, by means of directives, minimum requirements for gradual implementation, having regard to the conditions and technical rules obtaining in each of the Member States. Such directives shall avoid imposing administrative, financial and legal constraints in a way which would hold back the creation and development of small and medium-sized undertakings.

The Council shall act in accordance with the procedure referred to in Article 189c of the Treaty after consulting the Economic and Social Committee.[2]

3. However, the Council shall act unanimously on a proposal from the Commission, after consulting the European Parliament and the Economic and Social Committee, in the following areas:

— social security and social protection of workers;
— protection of workers where their employment contract is terminated;
— representation and collective defence of the interests of workers and employers, including co-determination, subject to paragraph 6;
— conditions of employment for third-country nationals legally residing in Community territory;
— financial contributions for promotion of employment and job-creation, without prejudice to the provisions relating to the Social Fund.

4. A Member State may entrust management and labour, at their joint request, with the implementation of directives adopted pursuant to paragraphs 2 and 3.

In this case, it shall ensure that, no later than the date on which a directive must be transposed in accordance with Article 189[3], management and labour have introduced the necessary measures by agreement, the Member State concerned being required to take any necessary measure enabling it at any time to be in a position to guarantee the results imposed by that directive.

5. The provisions adopted pursuant to this Article shall not prevent any Member State from maintaining or introducing more stringent protective measures compatible with the Treaty.

6. The provisions of this Article shall not apply to pay, the right of association, the right to strike or the right to impose lock-outs.

Article 3

1. The Commission shall have the task of promoting the consultation of management and labour at Community level and shall take any relevant measure to facilitate their dialogue by ensuring balanced support for the parties.

2. To this end, before submitting proposals in the social policy field, the Commission shall consult management and labour on the possible direction of Community action.

3. If, after such consultation, the Commission considers Community action advisable, it shall consult management and labour on the content of the envisaged proposal. Management and labour shall forward to the Commission an opinion or, where appropriate, a recommendation.

4. On the occasion of such consultation, management and labour may inform the Commission of their wish to initiate the process provided for in Article 4. The duration of the procedure shall not exceed nine months, unless the management and labour concerned and the Commission decide jointly to extend it.

Article 4

1. Should management and labour so desire, the dialogue between them at Community level may lead to contractual relations, including agreements.

2. Agreements concluded at Community level shall be implemented either in accordance with the procedures and practices specific to management and labour and the Member States or, in matters covered by Article 2, at the joint request of the signatory parties, by a Council decision on a proposal from the Commission.

The Council shall act by qualified majority, except where the agreement in question contains one or more provisions relating to one of the areas referred to in Article 2(3), in which case it shall act unanimously.

Article 5

With a view to achieving the objectives of Article 1 and without prejudice to the other provisions of the Treaty, the Commission shall encourage co-operation between the Member States and facilitate the co-ordination of their action in all social policy fields under this Agreement.

Article 6

1. Each Member State shall ensure that the principle of equal pay for male and female workers for equal work is applied.

2. For the purpose of this Article, 'pay' means the ordinary basic or minimum wage or salary and any other consideration, whether in cash or in kind, which the worker receives directly or indirectly, in respect of his employment, from his employer.
Equal pay without discrimination based on sex means:

(a) that pay for the same work at piece rates shall be calculated on the basis of the same unit of measurement.
(b) that pay for work at time rates shall be the same for the same job.

3. This article shall not prevent any Member State from maintaining or adopting measures providing for specific advantages in order to make it easier for women to pursue a vocational activity or to prevent or compensate for disadvantages in their professional careers.

Article 7

The Commission shall draw up a report each year on progress in achieving the objective of Article 1, including the demographic situation in the Community. It shall forward the report to the European Parliament, the Council and the Economic and Social Committee.

The European Parliament may invite the Commission to draw up reports on particular problems concerning the social situation.

Declarations

1. Declaration on Article 2(2)

The eleven High Contracting Parties[1] note that in the discussion of Article 2(2) of the Agreement it was agreed that the Community does not intend, in laying down minimum requirements for the protection of the safety and health of employees, to discriminate in a manner unjustified by the circumstances against employees in small and medium-sized undertakings.

2. Declaration on Article 4(2)

The eleven High Contracting Parties declare that the first of the arrangements for application of the agreements between management and labour at Community level – referred to in Article 4(2) – will consist in developing, by collective bargaining according to the rules of each Member State, the content of the agreements, and that consequently this arrangement implies no obligation on the Member States to apply the agreements directly or to work out rules for their transposition, or any obligation to amend national legislation in force to facilitate their implementation.

7 Protocol on social policy (The UK 'opt out')

The High Contracting Parties[5], noting that eleven Member States, that is to say the Kingdom of Belgium, the Kingdom of Denmark and Federal Republic of Germany, the Hellenic Republic, the Kingdom of Spain, the French Republic, Ireland, the Italian Republic, the Grand Duchy of Luxembourg, the Kingdom of the Netherlands and the Portuguese Republic, wish to continue along the path laid down in the 1989 Social Charter; that they have adopted among themselves an Agreement to this end (reproduced above); that this Protocol and the said Agreement are without prejudice to the provisions of this Treaty, particularly those relating to social policy which constitute an integral part of the 'a quis communautaire';

1. Agree to authorise those eleven Member States to have recourse to the institutions, procedures and mechanisms of the Treaty for the purposes of taking among themselves and applying as far as they are concerned the acts and decisions required for giving effect to the abovementioned Agreement.
2. The United Kingdom of Great Britain and Northern Ireland shall not take part in the deliberations and the adoption by the Council of Commission proposals made in the basis of the Protocol and the abovementioned Agreement.

By way of derogation from Article 148(2) of the Treaty,[6] acts of the Council which are made pursuant to this Protocol and which must be adopted by a qualified majority shall be deemed to be so adopted if they have received at least forty-four votes in favour. The unanimity of the members of the Council, with the exception of the United Kingdom of Great Britain and Northern Ireland, shall be necessary for acts of the Council which must be adopted unanimously and for those amending the Commission proposal.

Acts adopted by the Council and any financial consequences other than administrative costs entailed for the institutions shall not be applicable to the United Kingdom of Great Britain and Northern Ireland.

Notes

1. i.e. the Treaty of Rome. Article 127 regulates the operation of the European Social Fund
2. That is by qualified majority voting and in conjunction with the European Parliament.
3. Article 189 states: ' ... A directive shall be binding, as to the result to be achieved, upon each Member State to which it is addressed, but shall leave to the national authorities the choice of form and methods.' 'Transposition' is the EU term for the application of a piece of EU legislation to a national jurisdiction.
4. That is, the 12 Member States less the United Kingdom..
5. That is, all 12 Member States.
6. This Article regulates the requirements for achieving a qualified majority on the Council of Ministers. Under normal circumstances, a proposal must obtain 54 votes out of a possible 76. Each country has between two and ten votes on the Council, depending on population (Germany, France, Italy and the UK each have 10; Spain 8; Belgium, Greece, and the Netherlands 5; Denmark and Ireland 3; and Luxembourg 2.

Select Bibliography
and Sources

General Sources

British Journal of Industrial Relations, *The Single European Market and Industrial Relations*, Volume 30, Number 4 (December, 1992).

Anthony Ferner and Richard Hyman (eds), *Industrial Relations in the New Europe*, (Oxford, Cambridge, Mass., 1992). Individual country chapters and extensive national bibliographies.

Paul Teague and John Grahl, *Industrial Relations and European Integration* (London, 1992).

European Foundation, *P+ European Participation Monitor*, No. 6 'Participation in European Multinationals' (Dublin, 1993).

Incomes Data Services, *European Report*, various issues.

IDS/IPM, *Industrial Relations* (London, 1991).

Industrial Relations Services, *European Industrial Relations Review*, various issues.

Labour Research Department, *Labour Research*, various issues.

Ulrich Zachert (ed), *Die Wirkung des Tarifvertrages in der Krise* (Baden Baden, 1991).

Belgium

European Trade Union Institute, *The Trade Union Movement in Belgium*, ETUI Info 18 (Brussels, 1987).

Denmark

ETUI, *The Trade Union Movement in Denmark*, ETUI Info 22 (Brussels, 1987).

France

Jeff Bridgford, 'French trade unions: crisis in the 1980s', *Industrial Relations Journal*, Vol. 21, No. 2 (Summer, 1990).

ETUI, *The Trade Union Movement in France*, ETUI Info 20, 2nd edition (Brussels, 1990).

Germany

Volker Berghahn and Detlev Karsten, *Industrial Relations in West Germany*, (Oxford, New York, Hamburg 1987).

Reinhard Bispinck, 'Collective bargaining in East Germany: between economic constraints and political regulation', *Cambridge Journal of Economics*, 17 (1993).

ETUI, *The Trade Union Movement in Germany: the DGB*, ETUI Info 9 (Brussels, 1984).

Michael Kittner (ed), *Gewerkschatsjahrbuch*, various years.

Great Britain

Arthur Marsh, *The Trade Union Handbook* (Aldershot, 1991).

David Marsh, *The New Politics of British Trade Unionism* (London, 1992)

Kenneth Miller and Mairi Steele, 'Employment legislation: Thatcher and after', *Industrial Relations Journal*, Vol.24, No. 3 (September, 1993).

Neil Millward *et al*, *Workplace Industrial Relations in Transition*, (Aldershot, 1992).

Michael Rose, 'Trade Unions – Ruin, Retreat, or Rally', Review Article, *Work, Employment & Society*, Vol. 7, No. 2 (June, 1993).

Trades Union Congress, *TUC Directory*.

Greece

ETUI, *The Trade Union Movement in Greece*, ETUI Info 8 (Brussels, 1984).

Irish Republic

Industrial Relations in Ireland, 2nd edn. (Dublin, 1990).

Industrial Relations News (Dublin), various issues.

Italy

Guido Baglioni, 'An Italian mosaic: collective bargaining patterns in the 1980s', *International Labour Review*, Vol. 130, No. 1 (1991).

ETUI, *The Trade Union Movement in Italy*, ETUI Info 11 (Brussels, 1985).

Michael Terry, 'Workplace unions and workplace industrial relations: the Italian experience', *Industrial Relations Journal*, Vol. 24, No. 2 (June, 1993).

Luxembourg

ETUI, *The Trade Union Movement in Luxembourg*, ETUI Info 28 (Brussels, 1989).

Gary Tunsch, 'Luxembourg: an island of stability' in Ferner and Hyman, *Industrial Relations in the New Europe, op. cit.*

Netherlands

ETUI, *The Trade Union Movement in the Netherlands*, ETUI Info 35 (Brussels, 1992).

Portugal

ETUI, *The Trade Union Movement in Portugal*, ETUI Info 23 (Brussels, 1987).

Spain

ETUI, *The Trade Union Movement in Spain*, ETUI Info 17 (Brussels, 1987).

European Trade Union Confederation

ETUI, *The European Trade Union Confederation: Its History, Structure and Policy*, ETUI Info 29, 2nd edition (Brussels, 1991).
ETUI, *The European Industry Committees and Social Dialogue* (Brussels, 1993).
ETUI, *The European Dimensions of Collective Bargaining after Maastricht: Working Papers* (Brussels, 1992).

The Social Dimension

ETUI, *The Social Dimension of the Internal Market*. Four Volumes: i) Employment (1988), ii) Workers' Rights in European Companies (1988), iii) Worker Representation in the Workplace in Western Europe (1990), iv) European Works Councils (1990).
Michael Gold (ed), *The Social Dimension* (London, 1993).
Michael Gold and Mark Hall, *European-Level Information and Consultation in Multinational Companies: An Evaluation of Practice* (Dublin, 1992).

Main Works Used in the German Edition

F.J. Harper, *Trade Unions of the World* (London, 1987).
H.O. Hemmer and K.Th. Schmitz (eds), *Geschichte der Gewerkschaften in der Bundesrepublik Deutschland* (Cologne, 1990).
O. Jacobi, 'Vom heißen Herbst zur socialen Kooperation. Zur Neuorientierung der italienischen Gewerkschaften', in W. Müller-Jensch (ed), *Zukunft der Gewerkschaften. Ein internationaler Vergleich* (Frankfurt/Main, 1988).
A. Jeammaud and M. Le Friant, 'Gewerkschaftsrechte im Betrieb nach französichem Recht', *Arbeitsrecht im Betrieb*, Vol. 10, No. 12 (1989).
H. Koch, 'Die Luxemburger Arbeiterklasse und ihre Gewerkschaften', in *Hémecht*, Vol. 30, No. 4 (1978).
M. Kreile, 'Die italienischen Gewerkschaften zwischen Defensive und Neuorienteierung', *WSI-Mitteilugen*, 1986, No. 9.
W. Lecher, 'Deregulierung der Arbeitsbeziehungen', *Soziale Welt*, No. 2 (1987).
L. Mariucci, 'Gewerkschaftsrechte im Betrieb nach italienischem Recht', *Arbeitsrecht im Betrieb*, Vol. 10, No. 12 (1989).
S. Mielke (ed), *Internationales Gewerkschaftsjahrbuch* (Opladen, 1983).
H.-U. Niedenhoff and W. Page, *Gewerkschaftshandbuch*, (Cologne, 1987).
A. Ojeda Aviles and M. Perez, 'Gewerkschaftsrechte im Betrieb nach spanischem Recht', *Arbeitsrecht im Betrieb*, Vol. 10, No. 12 (1989).

St.C. Papagiannopoulos and C. Schnabel, 'Chaotische Strukturen. Entwicklung der Gewerkschaftsbewegung in Grechenland', in *Gewerkschaftsreport*, Vol. 3 (1989)

P. Roos, 'Workers' participation and personnel policy in Denmark', *International Labour Review*, Vol. 125, No. 6 (1986).

H. Slomp and T. van Mierlo, *Arbeitsverhoudingen in Belgie* (Utrecht, 1984).

H. Rühle and H.-J. Veen, *Gewerkschaften in dem Demokratien Westeuropas*, (Paderborn, 1983).

T. Treu and S. Negrelli, 'Workers' participation and personnel management policies in Italy', *International Labour Review*, Vol. 126, No. 1 (1987).

C.V. van Vuuren and P.L. Koopman, 'Medezeggenschap door de ondernemings-raad nieuwe stijl', *Tjidschrift voor Arbeidsvragen*, Vol. 3 (1987/2).

M. Wilke, *Die Funktionäre. Apparat und Demokratie im Deutschen Gwerkschaftsbund* (Munich, 1979).

J.P. Windmuller and C. de Galen, *Arbeitsverhoudingen in Nederland* (Utrecht, 1983).

G. Wölke, 'Rebellion der Mitte. Zur Situation der Gewerkschaften in Italien', *Gewerkschaftsreport*, No. 2 (1989).

G. Wölke, 'Zur Situation der französchen Gewerkschaften', *Gewerkschaftsreport*, No. 1 (1989).

C. Wurm, 'Die Gewerkschaften in der französchen Politik', *Politische Viertel-jahresschrift*, Vol. 25, No. 2 (1984).